THE COMPLETE IDIOT'S GUIDE® TO

Jokes

by Larry Getlen

ALPHA

A member of Penguin Group (USA) Inc.

ALPHA BOOKS

Published by the Penguin Group

Penguin Group (USA) Inc., 375 Hudson Street, New York, New York 10014, U.S.A.

Penguin Group (Canada), 10 Alcorn Avenue, Toronto, Ontario, Canada M4V 3B2 (a division of Pearson Penguin Canada Inc.)

Penguin Books Ltd, 80 Strand, London WC2R 0RL, England

Penguin Ireland, 25 St Stephen's Green, Dublin 2, Ireland (a division of Penguin Books Ltd)

Penguin Group (Australia), 250 Camberwell Road, Camberwell, Victoria 3124, Australia (a division of Pearson Australia Group Pty Ltd)

Penguin Books India Pvt Ltd, 11 Community Centre, Panchsheel Park, New Delhi—10 017, India

Penguin Group (NZ), cnr Airborne and Rosedale Roads, Albany, Auckland 1310, New Zealand (a division of Pearson New Zealand Ltd)

Penguin Books (South Africa) (Pty) Ltd, 24 Sturdee Avenue, Rosebank, Johannesburg 2196, South Africa

Penguin Books Ltd, Registered Offices: 80 Strand, London WC2R 0RL, England

Copyright © 2006 by Larry Getlen

All rights reserved. No part of this book shall be reproduced, stored in a retrieval system, or transmitted by any means, electronic, mechanical, photocopying, recording, or otherwise, without written permission from the publisher. No patent liability is assumed with respect to the use of the information contained herein. Although every precaution has been taken in the preparation of this book, the publisher and author assume no responsibility for errors or omissions. Neither is any liability assumed for damages resulting from the use of information contained herein. For information, address Alpha Books, 800 East 96th Street, Indianapolis, IN 46240.

THE COMPLETE IDIOT'S GUIDE TO and Design are registered trademarks of Penguin Group (USA) Inc.

International Standard Book Number: 978-1-59257-538-1
Library of Congress Catalog Card Number: 2006924212

09 08 07   8 7 6 5 4 3

Interpretation of the printing code: The rightmost number of the first series of numbers is the year of the book's printing; the rightmost number of the second series of numbers is the number of the book's printing. For example, a printing code of 06-1 shows that the first printing occurred in 2006.

Printed in the United States of America

Note: This publication contains the opinions and ideas of its author. It is intended to provide helpful and informative material on the subject matter covered. It is sold with the understanding that the author and publisher are not engaged in rendering professional services in the book. If the reader requires personal assistance or advice, a competent professional should be consulted.

The author and publisher specifically disclaim any responsibility for any liability, loss, or risk, personal or otherwise, which is incurred as a consequence, directly or indirectly, of the use and application of any of the contents of this book.

Most Alpha books are available at special quantity discounts for bulk purchases for sales promotions, premiums, fund-raising, or educational use. Special books, or book excerpts, can also be created to fit specific needs.

For details, write: Special Markets, Alpha Books, 375 Hudson Street, New York, NY 10014.

Publisher: *Marie Butler-Knight*
Editorial Director: *Mike Sanders*
Managing Editor: *Billy Fields*
Acquisitions Editor: *Michele Wells*
Senior Production Editor: *Janette Lynn*
Copy Editor: *Jan Zoya*
Cartoonist: *Shannon Wheeler*
Cover Designer: *Becky Harmon*
Book Designer: *Bill Thomas*
Indexer: *Angie Bess*
Layout: *Ayanna Lacey*
Proofreader: *Aaron Black*

Contents at a Glance

* Thank you, Cheech and Chong.

**Once again, ladies and gentlemen—George Carlin.

Foreword

Hi, I'm Gilbert Gottfried. A few days ago, the downstairs buzzer rang at my house, unforgivably waking me up at 3 in the afternoon. It was a delivery man with a package. The package contained an early draft of *The Complete Idiot's Guide to Jokes*. It had a note that said, "Dear Gilbert, We would like you to read this book, and if you enjoy it as much as we know you will, we would love for you to write the foreword. Thank you, the Publishers." I cheerfully picked up the early draft, went through it, and enjoyed it, as the publishers knew I would. I then cheerfully picked up a pen and started to write the foreword. Then it hit me.

I called the publishers. I said, "Wait a minute. This is a book on comedians and comedy, and all the funniest things they've ever said. How come I'm not in it?"

"Well, Gilbert," the publishers responded. "If you had said anything funny in your entire life, it definitely would have been in this book."

I cheerfully thanked them, hung up, picked up my pen, and started to write the foreword again. Then it hit me. I picked up the phone again—this time, angrily—and said, "Wait a second. If you don't think I'm funny, then why did you ask me, Gilbert Gottfried, to write the foreword to *The Complete Idiot's Guide to Jokes?*"

"Well, Gilbert," they explained. "We never said you were funny, but we all agree here that you're a complete idiot." I thanked them again, hung up, picked up the pen, and started to write the foreword. Then it hit me again.

This time I picked up the phone, well beyond angrily. "Wait a second," I told them. "You didn't include me in the book because you didn't think I was funny, but now I'm at the front of the book—the first comic you read. So *now* who's the idiot?"

The publisher's silence answered that one. I hung up, proceeded to write the foreword, and then I called back the publisher. I said, "Hello?" And they said, "All right, all right, dammit! We'll put you in the book! I'm sure if we look hard enough, you may have said something funny in your entire career." I was totally flattered by this. So now, please enjoy *The Complete Idiot's Guide to Jokes*.

Gilbert Gottfried

Introduction

The ability to be funny is one of the greatest things about being human. It's what makes life worth living, what distinguishes us from other animal life forms, and what often imbues one with the charisma needed to become a great leader. After all, where would North Korean leader Kim Jong Il be today without his rapier wit and his deft way around a punch line?

Well … that may be a bad example.

But we all know both genders list "sense of humor" as one of the sexiest traits (although a great body and/or a BMW don't hurt), and we've all worked with at least one complete doofus who—despite a complete lack of skills, intelligence, or proper hygiene—has used his expert telling of jokes, stories, and subtle put-downs to elevate himself far beyond his natural abilities, right into a cushy job in the House of Representatives.

The point I'm trying to make, people, is that jokes are, as Martha Stewart would say, a good thing.

And this book has some of the goodest.

The Complete Idiot's Guide to Jokes is meant to serve three purposes. First and foremost, it is meant to make you laugh. Filled with more than 1,500 of the funniest lines and bits in comedy, the best use of this book is to pick it up, turn to any random page, read, and commence laughing.

But this book is also more than that. These fine jokes haven't just been randomly tossed on the page like some C-list wrestler slammed to the mat after an unsurprisingly crushing loss to The Rock. No, my good friends, this book is a virtual *encyclopedia* of humor. Arranged by category and indexed by reference and subject, this book will not only make you laugh, but will allow you to laugh at whatever you want to laugh about at any given moment. Kids driving you batty? Turn to the "Parents and Parenthood" section for the hysterical empathy of some of the funniest comedic minds working today. And speaking of work, if that's what's got you down, there's a "Work" chapter, giving you lots of loving, soothing jokes to share with your equally frustrated co-workers as you all bond in one united cause—to spread shaving cream on the boss's keyboard. (Not that I'm endorsing that, of course. After all, most bosses have lawyers.)

As if that's not enough, I'll not only make you laugh, but also share valuable tips on how *you* can make *others* laugh as well. In addition to the funniest jokes on the circuit, I've included tips from some of the world's finest comedians and humorists on how you, too, can be funny, right in the privacy of your own home! (Well, that is, if there are other people in your home with you. If not, you really should get out more. And if you are just sitting home alone telling jokes out loud, you don't really need advice for that. Except to maybe cut out the "out loud" part. Just sit there, read to yourself, and try not to move your lips.)

So there you have it, folks. Welcome to the book. Now open the pages, dive in, and start laughing, keeping in mind that each time you do, you elevate yourself one step above the rest of the animal kingdom—or, for that matter, that humorless simp Kim Jong Il.

Enjoy.

Extras

This book is divided into two parts—the jokes and the nonjokes. In the first chapter, I give you information on the status of jokes today. In the rest of the chapters, you get the good stuff—more than 1,500 jokes and bits divided by category.

In addition, this book contains extras designed to heighten both its usefulness and its enjoyment. To this end, there are four types of sidebars you'll find throughout the book. Two are designed to give you information on how you, too, can tell jokes in a funny way. The other two are strictly for your enjoyment. Here's what to look for:

HA HA HA Make 'Em Laugh

These sidebars contain tips from some of the funniest comedians and humorists around today on how to really drive a joke home.

Who Made the Funny?

These boxes contain trivia and biographical information about some of your favorite comedians.

Blatant Lies

The items in these boxes are distinguished by the fact that they are blatantly untrue. In other words, they aren't really "facts" at all. I made them up—solely for your enjoyment.

Hackity Hack

These are additional tips, but these tell you what *not* to do—in other words, how to avoid being a total hack.

Acknowledgments

There are many people to thank for their help in the creation of this book, but two especially—my agent, Marilyn Allen, who has either the world's best memory or the world's best filing system or both, for remembering enough about me after a long period of time to realize that I would be right for this project; and Michele Wells at Alpha Books, who believed in my vision of this book from day one, was forever encouraging, and went to bat for me when needed to ensure that the book stayed true to that vision.

Thanks also go to Gina Anderson at Penguin for her help in navigating confusing waters, and everyone else there (including several folks I'm probably not even aware of) who put their time and energy into bringing this book to print.

Special thanks as well to all the funny and gracious people who shared their wisdom about how to make people laugh, including Gilbert Gottfried, Dave Barry, Tony Hendra, Wendy Liebman, Penn Jillette, Jonathan Ames, Mark Katz, Patton Oswalt, Leo Allen, Eugene Mirman, Jesse Joyce, Mitch Fatel, Kerri Louise, Christian Finnegan, Brian Kiley, D. C. Benny, Mike Daisey, Gene Perret, Brian McKim at *Shecky Magazine*, Tim Cavanagh, John Marshall, Lisa Lampanelli, David Lee Roth, Steve Hofstetter, Jim Florentine, Ted Alexandro, and Phil Proctor, plus all the publicists and managers who helped make these interviews happen.

On a personal note, special thanks go to my mom, Ann, for bringing me up in a house where laughter and entertainment were not only prized and appreciated, but encouraged; and my sister Sharon, who, where laughter was concerned, was my first real audience.

Finally, special thanks to all the comedians whose jokes appear in these pages, for dedicating so much of yourselves to making people laugh, for putting in the time to figure out what makes people laugh, and for having the guts to get up there onstage and give it your all.

Trademarks

All terms mentioned in this book that are known to be or are suspected of being trademarks or service marks have been appropriately capitalized. Alpha Books and Penguin Group (USA) Inc. cannot attest to the accuracy of this information. Use of a term in this book should not be regarded as affecting the validity of any trademark or service mark.

Crazy Little Things Called Jokes

In This Chapter

- Is the joke dead?
- Is yesterday's joke funny today?
- What makes a joke funny?

> *Deborah Solomon:* I just read somewhere that jokes are less popular than they used to be.
>
> *Stephen Colbert:* You mean like, "Two guys walk into a bar?" I think you are right. I get e-mailed jokes a lot—by friends who are not in the business. Jokes live on in e-mail. E-mail has become a museum of jokes.— *The New York Times Magazine,* 9/25/05
>
> "Seriously, the Joke Is Dead"—Headline from *The New York Times,* 5/22/05

Can that be right? Is the joke dead? Has the joke become an artifact of another time, appropriate only for museums or telling to people who've spent the last decade or two stranded on a desert island?

The answer, my friends, is yes—and no.

How the Joke Has Changed

The truth is that the joke, like any other form of entertainment, changes over time. What was popular 50 years ago is considered quaint or cheesy today, and what's cutting edge today will be old and moldy to our grandkids to come—but what the heck will they know, right? Whippersnappers.

The "joke" referred to in the *Times* article and by *Daily Show* correspondent and *Colbert Report* host Stephen Colbert is the standard setup/punch line, priest-and-a-rabbi-go-into-a-bar type of joke, which has been replaced, very slowly over the past 30 years or so, by observational comedy, conversational comedy, surreal one-liners, irony, and its most recent incarnation, snark.

To some of you—like, anyone who watches VH1, E!, or Comedy Central—this is *very* old news. To others, it may come as a bit of a shock, because you received an e-mail just last week with a very funny joke about Bill Gates, Paris Hilton, and a llama.

Jokes will never die, but they will change, and these changes presented a challenge in planning and compiling this book.

> **HA HA HA** **Make 'Em Laugh**
>
> You know what really grinds my gears? No one's come up with a new priest-and-a-rabbi joke in, like, 30 years. Okay. "A priest and a rabbi go into a supermarket, and the priest wants to buy a ham. And the rabbi says, 'Oh, I can't eat it. It's forbidden. Can't eat it. Not allowed.' Pigs are, like, superheroes to them." Is it perfect? No. But I don't see *you* coming up with anything.—Peter Griffin, from *The Family Guy Presents Stewie Griffin: The Untold Story*

An Avalanche of Jokes

With the advent of the Internet and e-mail, jokes have become so ever-present, featured on hundreds of joke-collection websites and forwarded in millions of e-mails every day, that the idea of paying for a joke book has become the equivalent of "why buy the cow when you can get the milk for free?" Jokes are so pervasive in our inboxes that many of us spend half our days deleting them. They are a completely and constantly free item. So the concept of paying for jokes seems almost as silly at this point as the concept of paying for water.

Hmmmm ... bad example.

Or is it? I don't know about you, but I spend way more money than any human being should on a substance that comes out of my tap for free—and, judging by the health of the bottled water industry, so do you. And why do we do this? Because somehow, the bottled water industry has convinced us that their water is better.

Whether it really is better is a discussion for another day. But while thinking about this, my challenge for this book became clear—to create a book of jokes that is clearly "better" than any collection of jokes you'll have forwarded to you by your friends, your uncle, or your company accountant.

Which brought me back around to the central question—is the joke dead?

The Status of "The Joke"

The joke will never die. There, I've said it.

Mankind has brightened its day with jokes since the beginning of time, and mankind has been grateful for it just as long. The day Adam first appeared on the earth and said, "God, this place is great, but I'm starving. What's for dinner?" and God replied, "Ribs," jokes were there.

The day Noah turned to his wife and said, "The funny thing? I don't even *like* animals," jokes were there.

The day Joseph turned to Mary and said, "Okay, so his name is God … and he did *what?!?*" jokes were there.

But jokes *cannot* remain the same over time, because jokes are a reflection of the society from which they emerge. People in England "get" certain jokes that we here in the United States do not. Telling a joke in a foreign language to a native speaker of that language comes with

HA HA HA Make 'Em Laugh

There's nothing wrong with a culture where everybody has a different idea of what's humorous. The last time I can remember an entire nation being on the same page, it was Germany in the late thirties, and it didn't really turn out that funny.—Dennis Miller

a whole new set of barriers for someone from a different culture. Men and women often find different things funny (for proof, try watching *The Three Stooges* with your wife), and teenagers find many things funny that baby boomers do not.

But that's all part of what makes comedy and humor such a joy—the mystery of it. No matter what you think you know about people, there's no telling what makes some people laugh. Some comedy crosses geographical, gender, and age barriers to bring laughter to a diverse audience, and then there are jokes that even identical twins disagree on. Some trends in humor hold steady, and others phase out with time.

Let's take a look, for example, at Henny Youngman's classic, "Take my wife—please." It's a classic because when the joke was new, audiences howled. And why not? It's a very well-constructed joke—only four words long, fueled by a classic misdirection, and reflective of the society of the time, when a husband expressing frustration at his silly little wife was impetus for laughter.

Try saying this out of the blue (or especially onstage) to someone now, and the person would probably look at you like you were insane. For one thing, some people will perceive it as sexist. More important from a comedy standpoint, the joke is so old and oft-told that there's no misdirection, no surprise. It's just an old, hackneyed line. We can respect it as a product of its time, but there's nothing left of it to laugh at.

And so it goes with so much old-style humor. Which is not to say that anything old is unfunny—not at all.

Who Made the Funny?

It's been reported that "Take my wife—please" happened by accident. As the story goes, Youngman was with his wife at an event and said that line to an usher as a genuine request—asking the usher to escort his wife to her seat. The usher, seeing the funnyman, thought he was making a joke and started laughing. Youngman saw the reaction and brought the line onstage, where it killed. If this story is true, then while Youngman said the line, the joke was really created by the usher.

The Key to Laughter

What makes a joke funny, whether it's old or new, is its ability to surprise us. "Take my wife—please" hasn't worked in decades because the
surprise is long gone, and it's the same with many older jokes and joke
forms—like the "Two men walk into a bar" structure Stephen Colbert
spoke of as a museum piece in *The New York Times Magazine*.

As the Internet has become the world's most popular joke-distribution
tool, jokes that were already withering with age became virtually mass-
produced, and what little humor they had left in them was drained
away through fiber-optic cables and radio waves (or whatever it is the
Internet passes through—there's a reason I'm writing about comedy,
not technology). It's rare today to receive a joke through the Internet
that surprises you, because most of what you receive has been passed
around before in one version or another.

So in approaching this book, the prevailing thought was, *Where do
today's funny jokes come from?* The answer was immediate and obvious.
They come from comedians.

Hackity Hack

"Invest in stocks, not jokes," says Mark Katz, who spent eight years
writing jokes for President Bill Clinton. "There are two ways to deliver
a joke. One, as an inquiry. A joke that implicitly asks 'do you guys think
this is funny?' The second way is as a statement, which reads, 'I think this
is funny—and I'm not especially concerned what you think.' I recommend
the latter. Jokes delivered in a 'please God, please let them laugh' tone
will only earn the un-heartfelt laugh of the kind-hearted. The rest of your
audience will find their entertainment much like the Romans once did in
those public match-ups of Christians and lions."

Comedians Don't Tell "Jokes"

Wanna piss off a stand-up comic? When you meet him and find out
he's a comedian, make this the first thing out of your mouth:

"You're a comedian? Great! Tell me a joke."

Watch closely. If you stare at his mouth, you can actually see his teeth start to grind. That's because—to the shock of millions who still haven't picked up on this—*comedians don't tell jokes*. That may sound bizarre to some, but virtually every comic you meet, if you ask them to tell you a joke, will respond as such. And that creates an awkward moment, because if you're asking a comic to tell you a joke, then you already don't get this concept.

I've had this happen to me many times. So has just about every comedian I know. Someone learns you're a comedian and asks you to tell a joke, and you respond that you don't know any—because you genuinely don't. Then the person who asked gets that look in his eyes that a dog gets when you fake-throw a ball—he looks like he just saw the sun set at noon. You can practically read the thought process on his face.

But ... but ... he's a comedian! What does he mean he doesn't know any jokes? That's what he does—he tells jokes! Is he messing with me? Why? What did I do to him? I've heard that comics were bitter ... boy, was that right!

Well, hold on now ... let's all take a deep breath. In saying that comedians don't tell jokes, what I mean is that comedians don't tell the standard setup/punch line type of joke, and when people say "Tell me a joke," that's usually what they're asking for.

Comedians in the modern era "talk." They converse with audiences (albeit in a one-sided conversation). They share thoughts and observations. They deliver one-liners, quips, stories, and whatever they can use to convey a piece of their comedic selves without losing that essential tool of comedy, misdirection—or, as it may be easier to think of it, surprise.

> **HA HA HA** **Make 'Em Laugh**
>
> Every joke is a one-liner, if you type it small enough.—Geoff Holtzman

The Ever-Changing Meaning of *Joke*

Here's where the word *joke* becomes confusing, even in the comedy world. Comedians themselves are conflicted about the word. When someone we meet says "Tell me a joke," we all know what he means—the old-fashioned, setup/punch line kind. And we recoil.

But when comedians talk amongst themselves about their own material, the word *joke* still applies. "What did you do last night?" "Stayed in, worked on some jokes." Do they mean "Two men walked into a bar"? Never. They mean whatever it is that comes out of their mouth that will (hopefully) be funny onstage.

The concept of the joke is, frankly, too great to let slide, too joyful to give up on, and too all-encompassing to be phased into the woodwork. And besides, the meaning of words often changes with time. When I was a kid, *thongs* were what we wore to the beach on our feet. Now, those are called *flip flops*, and anyone wearing a *thong* on their feet would be carted away. (Especially if it left what the thong is now supposed to cover exposed.)

Joke is like that. It's flexible, malleable. Henny Youngman told jokes. So did Woody Allen. So does Jon Stewart. Andy Kaufman didn't. But Bill Hicks? Even though he was a comic philosopher as far from the cheesy old school as it gets, he also had punch lines that were rock solid. Those are jokes. Many comic performers are more story-oriented now. They tell funny stories about their lives and our world. But oftentimes, within those stories, there are punch lines of some kind. These are "jokes."

In fact, to preserve the honor of the word *joke*, comedians have come up with another term for the old-fashioned, hackneyed kind of joke. That sort of joke is now called a "joke-joke," or "jokey-joke."

HA HA HA Make 'Em Laugh

I write jokes for a living. I sit in my hotel at night and think of something that's funny and then I go get a pen and write it down. Or, if the pen's too far away, I have to convince myself that what I thought of ain't funny.—Mitch Hedberg

Surprise Is the Key

Whatever you call it, the bottom line is that the key to comedy is surprise. If someone says to you, "Two men/priests/rabbis/giraffes walk into a bar," that sense of surprise is already lost.

So in assembling this book, I looked for jokes that surprise, lines and bits and quips and routines that fool your brain into thinking they're going one way, when in fact they are headed in a completely different, creative, thought- and laughter-provoking direction. You'll see lots of great jokes here from comedians you know and some from comedians you don't. Some of the jokes might even be familiar to you—but I'm betting that most won't be.

In compiling this book, I've aimed for jokes from different eras and for varying sensibilities. Some are older, but most are not. Some are cosmopolitan and worldly, and some are as down-home as it gets. Some have been told on TV, and some have only been told in clubs and bars—so far. But whatever your sensibility, I believe there will be plenty here to surprise you, to delight you, and to inspire you to share the laughter with your co-workers, your friends, and your loved ones.

This book not only contains more than 1,500 of the funniest "jokes," but also comedy trivia; snarky, wiseass comments about the jokes and comics themselves; information about comedians you may be unfamiliar with but who just might become your new favorites; and lots of advice from top comedians and humorists on what you, too, should keep in mind when telling a joke—whichever type of joke you choose to tell. So not only is this book funny, but it just might make *you* funnier as well.

> **HA HA HA Make 'Em Laugh**
>
> My all-time favorite joke, handed down in my family since time immemorial: "Two Irishmen walk out of a bar." It's a great example of a metajoke.—Author/humorist Mike Daisey

In the end, a "joke" is what you make of it. Whatever you think is funny, if you tell it in such a way that it makes others laugh as well, that's a joke. Tell it; enjoy it; and whatever I or *The New York Times* or anyone else tells you, never believe that the joke is dead. Or putting it a bit differently, the joke *is* dead—long live the joke. And if this book can help keep it alive, all the better.

The Least You Need to Know

- What people find funny changes with time.
- *Never* ask a comedian to "tell you a joke."
- The key to good comedy is misdirection, or surprise.

America and the World Around Us

Our Country 'Tis of Thee—Sweet Land of Travesty

I was in Las Vegas, and I was at the New York, New York casino, and while I was there, I started wondering—do you think on September 11, the people who worked at the New York, New York casino felt it a little deeper?—David Cross

The art of exotic dancing is catching on all over the world. In Iran now they're having wet veil contests.—Bill Maher

Who Made the Funny?

David Cross is everywhere. Not only can he be seen on some of TV's funniest shows such as *Arrested Development* and *Mr. Show,* but you can even enjoy him in the privacy of your own Xbox. Cross provided the voice for Zero in *Grand Theft Auto, San Andreas* and also had a cameo as a Marine in *Halo 2.*

Iraq awarded its first nationwide mobile telephone licenses to three Middle Eastern companies on Monday, saying service could begin by the end of the month. This means Iraqis will soon be able to talk anywhere, at any time ... about how they have no water, electricity, or food.—Jimmy Fallon

In an effort to appeal to Arab customers, McDonald's has a new sandwich called the McArabia. In a related story, they also cut off the Hamburglar's hands for stealing.—Conan O'Brien

I think we should take Iraq and Iran and combine them into one country and call it Irate. All the pissed off people live in one place and get it over with.—Denis Leary

I visited Africa, and you know what they say: "Whatever happens in the former republic of Congo, stays in the former republic of Congo." I mean, we got crazy. We were raising the roof on that thatched roof hut. No, seriously, we were raising the roof. It caved it. It was monsoon season. —Rosie Tran

I was in Florida last week. Lot of strip clubs in Florida. Florida has so many strip clubs they need to change their state flag to a brass pole.—Wanda Sykes

Who Made the Funny?

Lewis Black is known as a brilliant, politically astute stand-up comic who makes TV audiences howl on *The Daily Show*, but his primary creative endeavor has been playwriting. A graduate of the Yale School of Drama, Black has written more than 40 plays and ran his own underground theater throughout the 1980s.

There are people who've never left this country who talk about how we're the greatest country on Earth. How dumb is that? Because, you don't know. There are countries that may be giving shit away every day. Canada's one of those countries. You know what they give away? *Health insurance!* —Lewis Black

When voters in California went to the polls Tuesday for the gubernatorial recall race, they found the names of the 135 contenders on a ballot 6 pages long—thus making it the longest thing most Californians have ever read.—Tina Fey

I was dating this woman from Cuba who was trying to teach me Cuban. It's very close to Spanish, except there are fewer words for luxury items.—Emo Philips

China has a population of a billion people. One billion. That means even if you're a one-in-a-million kind of guy, there are still a thousand others exactly like you.
—A. Whitney Brown

America is like a giant, retarded trust-fund kid with nuclear weapons. "This country's nice, can we have Disney World here?" "Well, this is Paris ..." "*Disney World!*"—Patton Oswalt

When the Germans found out that America was mistreating people in a prison, they were *this close* to suing for copyright infringement.—Richard Jeni

In China, if you get caught driving drunk, they put you in jail for 6 months. Not because you're guilty, but because that's how long it takes to recite the alphabet backward.
—Craig Sharf

They call New Jersey the Garden State. Yeah, if you're growing asbestos.—Rich Vos

Blatant Lies

Unbeknownst to Mr. Vos, asbestos is actually New Jersey's second-largest export—right behind *Sopranos* cast members.

I grew up in a part of Brooklyn that had only two types of people—Italians and Jews. If you wanna know what that was like, imagine Woody Allen and Pauly Walnuts fighting for turf.—Larry Getlen

Las Vegas is loaded with all kinds of gambling devices— dice tables, slot machines, and wedding chapels.—Joey Adams

This country has a kick-ass military, and really good bull- shit marketing people. If this country was a person, it would be a used-car salesman with a flame-thrower.
—Richard Jeni

The post office has come out with a new stamp that incorrectly labeled the Grand Canyon as part of Colorado. The error got through because nobody wanted to tell the postal workers they'd made a mistake.—Conan O'Brien

If you don't believe that America is anti-intellectual, then why is it that on *Gilligan's Island*, the character who had the worst billing was the professor?—Bill Maher

I know people don't like America, 'cause we're arrogant. I tell you how arrogant I am—I refer to people in their own country as foreigners. When I'm visiting you, I act like you're visiting me. "When are you foreigners gonna learn how to cook a steak? What is this language you speak here in Japan?"—Patrice O'Neal

HA HA HA **Make 'Em Laugh**

There's a key theory in comedy called the law of opposites. In a nutshell, it states that contrast produces laughter. If you're a loud, brash fellow and you tell raunchy jokes, you'll get laughs. But if you're a shy, retiring female and you tell that same joke? Jackpot. The same goes for where and when you're telling the joke and even the joke itself. Is the punch line the opposite of what people expected, told by the opposite of the person you'd expect to tell that joke? That's comedy gold. "Tell some talking animal joke or whatever, which seems benign, then hit them with a nice morbid punch line," says comedian D. C. Benny. "The key is to contrast the environment, the teller's persona, and the subject matter. Nothing is funnier than what you are not supposed to laugh at, told in a place that you're not supposed to laugh in, by a guy you didn't know was funny."

I was in a record store in Seattle and they had those *Sound of Rain* CDs. Who the hell in Seattle is going to pay money to hear that? *Sound of Rain* is a local band there.—Moody McCarthy

Chicago is known as the Windy City, and Montana is called the Big Sky State, so I think that we should somehow combine the two to create the ultimate kite-flying experience.—Mitch Hedberg

Hollywood's a terrible place. When you meet a guy there, the first question you ask yourself is, "I don't know. Is this the man I want my children to spend their weekends with?"—Rita Rudner

I did a show for victims of the earthquake, including my sister, who continues to live here in California, in spite of all the risks. She always says the same thing to me, that "you can get killed crossing the street." Which is true—but what if the street is also crossing the street?—Jonathan Katz

When I first saw *French Women Don't Get Fat*, I was insulted on behalf of American women. But then I thought, well, all they're really saying is that French women have a different lifestyle, and maybe we could get thinner by adopting their habits. So I thought about it, and I think I figured it out—shaving your pits must make you fat. —Jennifer Dziura

The Chinese can rewrite history. They have a different calendar. It's a rat one year and a cow the next. According to their calendar, they won World War II.—Tim Allen

Who Made the Funny?

Tim Allen's real name is Timothy Alan Dick. The reason he changed it for show biz is … oh, you can figure that out.

Ireland doesn't use pounds or kilograms. They use the stone, which equals 14 pounds. That's the least amount you can weigh anything in Ireland—14 pounds. That's why there are no Irish drug dealers—'cause unless you need a 14-pound bag of heroin, you have to be very familiar with calculus. You can't even weigh a baby there till it's 6 months old. "This child weighs nothing! Get him a sandwich, for Christ's sake!"—Jesse Joyce

I was in Chinatown, and everybody's speaking Chinese. What a beautiful language that is, the rhythm, the cadence. I think to myself, I don't speak Chinese, but if I try, I gotta be saying something, right? So I'm like, "Hong-tiiiii! Dong-diiiiiiii! Yack-daaaaaaaaa!" Some little kid ran up, gave me an egg salad sandwich.—Harland Williams

A band instructor at a Texas high school is taking heat for having the band put on a halftime show that had Nazi flags. The interesting thing is that the French class surrendered to the band.—Craig Kilborn

It's fine when people from other countries come to America to live, but the least they can do is learn to speak Spanish.—Linda Sweig

I grew up in Europe. Where the history comes from. —Eddie Izzard

I live in Brooklyn, and none of my Manhattan friends will come out to play. Getting Manhattan people to Brooklyn is like getting Dick Cheney into assless chaps for the Gay Pride Parade.—Larry Getlen

The median IQ in this country is 100. That means half the population has double-digit IQs. And we still rule the planet? That's like the special ed kids ruling the high school.—Patton Oswalt

Who Made the Funny?

Charlie Callas is known for rubber-faced, flailing-limbed mania, but he wasn't just a manic madman on the comic stage. Callas was an accomplished jazz drummer who played with the likes of the Tommy Dorsey Orchestra.

In France, Jerry Lewis is hailed as a genius. That's the same country that burned Joan of Arc.—Charlie Callas

I visited China and discovered an amazing fact: in a country of 1 billion Chinese people— no Chinatown.—Craig Sharf

I love New York so, because this city is always surprising. Today I went out to a deli. Pastrami sandwich, $13.75. Walked back out on the street. Genuine Rolex watch, 6 bucks.—Richard Jeni

I'd rather be in Las Vegas in 104 degrees than New York in 90 degrees. You know why? Legalized prostitution. In any weather, that takes the edge off.—Ray Romano

I got into a big hassle—I got caught smuggling books into Kentucky. I got off on a technicality. No one could prove they were books. —Barry Crimmins

What a wonderful thing to be conscious. I wonder what the people in New Jersey do?—Woody Allen

I don't like being in the South. I don't like being anywhere that "mosey" is a speed. —Alonzo Bodden

Blatant Lies

Alonzo wrote this joke after getting a speeding ticket in Alabama—while on foot. He was caught doing 2 in a 1.

I don't think I could raise kids in L.A. There's choppers searching for fugitives, like, once a month. What do you tell a kid? "Daddy, what makes that noise at night?" "Oh, Timmy, that's the sound of poorly planned escape routes and the fear of being sodomized."—Paul Gilmartin

L.A. annoys me, because everybody thinks they're in show-biz. I went to the gas station, and the gas station attendant told me he was a former porno movie star. I think he was serious, because halfway through filling the tank he pulled out and sprayed it all over the car.—Greg Fitzsimmons

I'm arguing with a French Canadian and he says, "You don't understand our European culture." What? You live 5 hours from Buffalo. I don't remember Hitler leveling Quebec.—Rich Vos

The American family is more unstable than a hostage situation being negotiated by Crispin Glover. My clan was so dysfunctional, MCI had an administrator on call 24 hours a day just to update our "Friends and Family" package.
—Dennis Miller

Hackity Hack

Trust me when I say that comedian D.C. Benny speaks for all comedians when he says, "*Please* don't tell comics any jokes; we've heard them all a million times, and we're going to be forced to fake laugh, which is going to act as fodder for you to think, *Hey, maybe I can do this for a living,* and then you're going to leave your job and family and ruin your life chasing a dream whose foundation is built on the fumes of our little white lie because we didn't say, 'I don't wanna hear your sh*tty little joke about a Jew, an Italian, and the pope on a desert island,' but instead we laugh because we don't want to hurt your feelings by saying 'Scram kid, you bother me.'"

We had the druids, and they built Stonehenge, one of the biggest henges in the world. No one's built a henge like that ever since. No one knows what a henge is. Before Stonehenge, there was Woodhenge and Strawhenge, but a big bad wolf came and blew 'em down, and three little piggies were relocated to the projects.—Eddie Izzard

New York was so patriotic after 9/11. A hooker offered me oral sex for $50—but said she was giving $35 to the Red Cross.—Larry Getlen

My Italian neighborhood in Brooklyn has some interesting "businesses." There is a bakery, which, I don't want to say is a "front," but all they ever have is three cookies and a donut. I asked for a seeded rye, sliced. They gave me an envelope full of cash.—Eric Deskin

Appearance and Fashion

Your Face and My Dog's Rear End– Separated at Birth?

Where lipstick is concerned, the important thing is not color, but to accept God's final word on where your lips end.—Jerry Seinfeld

This one guy said, "Look at that girl. She's got a nice butt." I said, "Yeah, I bet she can sit down excellently!"—Mitch Hedberg

Make 'Em Laugh

Some people have the ability to make a long story fascinating—but most don't. So if you're going to tell a joke, "chop it down as much as possible," advises Brian Kiley, longtime staff writer for *Late Night with Conan O'Brien*. "People think, *I'll weave this long tale, and I'll add this stuff*, and whatever. But brevity is the soul of wit. If you can get to the punch line quicker, you have a much better chance of making a joke work."

Life is a little easier for attractive people. Think about it— if a stranger smiles at you and they're attractive, you think, oh, they're nice. But if the stranger's ugly, you're like, what do they want? Get away from me, weirdo.—Jim Gaffigan

The only thing you gotta remember about boxers is, don't wear flannel with corduroy. Because if you start running, you will burn something up.—Alonzo Bodden

This is a huge deal in West Hollywood. They're now calling for a ban on plastic surgery performed on pets. The controversy all started when a poodle got a chin lift, but the poodle turned out to be Joan Rivers.—Craig Ferguson

> **Who Made the Funny?**
>
> Joan Rivers is one of the many famous alumni of Chicago's Second City improv troupe.

You know how you can tell whether a woman's had her face lifted? Every time she crosses her legs, her mouth snaps open.—Joan Rivers

When you get a tattoo, you have to think about two things—what to get, and where to put it. That's why if I ever got a tattoo, I'd get a beautiful woman, and I'd put it right over my girlfriend.—Geoff Holtzman

I asked this woman, "Why did you get fake breasts?" She said, "Guys like fake breasts." Who cares? That's not your responsibility. Guys like beer, too—why not have a tap put in? You get a tap put in, you're not gonna need big breasts. You're gonna need a bouncer and a cut-off time.—Nick Griffin

I do have a tattoo. I won't say where, but it says, "Inflate here."—Bruce Cherry

Society's idea of beautiful has much too much to do with thin. My feeling is that when you can actually see a woman digesting, then she's too thin.—Jonathan Katz

If something about the human body disgusts you, complain to the manufacturer.—Lenny Bruce

I was watching TV with my fat friend the other day, and Brad Pitt's on TV with his shirt off. My friend's like, "Oh man, if I had his money, I could look like that." No you wouldn't. If you had his money, you'd just buy more expensive food.—Jim Florentine

I don't know when to wear my robe. People are like, "What are you talking about? Just put it on after you take a shower." And I'm like, "So you take a shower, dry off, put your robe on, then you take your robe off and put your clothes on?" I feel bad for my robe. It's in my closet, and every day I'm like, "Sorry bro, not today."—Greg Behrendt

Who Made the Funny?

In addition to a successful stand-up comedy career, Greg Behrendt spent several years as a consultant for *Sex and the City* and then collaborated with one of his fellow *Sex and the City* writers on a little book called *He's Just Not That Into You* (Simon & Schuster, 2004), which became a phenomenon, and a number one *New York Times* best-seller. Since then, Greg has hit that chart again with *It's Called a Break-Up Because It's Broken* (Broadway, 2005), which he wrote with his wife, Amiira.

People call me statuesque because I'm tall, and I often stand still in the park with no clothes on.—Jessica Delfino

They say the clothes make the man. But I think it's the man that makes the clothes; especially if he's a tailor, or an Indonesian child.—Myq Kaplan

I like body piercings, but I call them by their original name—stab wounds.—Larry Getlen

I like to wear a hair net to bed at night, but sometimes I'm disappointed when I wake up because I haven't caught anything.—Molly Anderson

The world's upside down. Rich people are skinny, poor people are fat; women have muscles, men have highlights; priests are having sex, I'm not. It's no fair.—Nick Griffin

The leading cause of death among fashion models is falling through street grates.—Dave Barry

I have the classic Italian male body—the thighs of a 270-pound man and the chest of a small Romanian gymnast. —Jeff Cesario

I wish I had a twin, so I could know what I'd look like without plastic surgery.—Joan Rivers

I saw a guy at a party wearing a leather jacket and I thought, that is cool. But then I saw another guy wearing a leather vest, and I thought, that is not cool. Then I figured it out: it's all about leather sleeves.—Demitri Martin

Blatant Lies

Blue Collar comedian Ron White often lifts up girls in bikinis just to hear the sound of the ocean. He also watches porn for the dialogue.

They have bikinis now made out of seashells. If you're ever walking down the beach, and you see a girl dressed in a bikini made out of seashells, and you pick her up, and you hold her to your ear, you can hear her scream. I thought I'd hear the ocean, but not over that woman.—Ron White

I like to wear black. It reflects my level of joy.—Greg Banks

My photographs don't do me justice—they just look like me.—Phyllis Diller

Last week, I went out and bought myself a camouflage shirt. Put it in the closet, and I can't find it nowhere.—John Fox

Tattoos are cool because they don't belong on your body, but you put them there to say something about yourself.

Much like my rolls of fat. That does not belong on a human body. And I put it there to say something about me: I don't like fruit.—Dave Attell

The man with the world's most tattoos probably has at least a couple he regrets. But the guy with the world's second-most tattoos regrets them all.—Geoff Holtzman

I was 5-foot-6 in the fourth grade. Yet, I still had all my baby teeth. When I smiled I looked a lot like a killer whale.—Margot B. Leitman

There's so much Botox around now that you can't tell when a Jewish girl is angry.—Mort Sahl

According to a new survey, women say they feel more comfortable undressing in front of men than they do undressing in front of other women. They say that women are too judgmental, where, of course, men are just grateful.—Jay Leno

Charity bracelets have become very popular. I wear one myself. It's to fight the use of child labor overseas. They appreciate the support. I know they do. They made the bracelet.—Shane Lou

I don't talk about my hair anymore, because I realize that looks aren't important. It's what kind of hair you have inside.—Garry Shandling

I bought this shirt the other day and it was cut all weird. A friend explained that the shirts are all cut like that now because we're supposed to be layering—that shirt goes over another shirt. That is the biggest scam ever! Layering is the "lather-rinse-repeat" of our generation.—Jennifer Dziura

Hackity Hack

The phrase "but seriously, folks," went out with the horse and buggy. When your joke is done, move on.

Used to be that in L.A., you just had to be skinny. Now, you gotta have muscle tone. Pretty soon, it's gonna be almost impossible. You're gonna have to be morbidly obese, while maintaining tiny little tweety-bird ankles and a wandering eye.—Maria Bamford

I look just like the girl next door—if you happen to live next door to an amusement park.—Dolly Parton

My friend says I'm superficial, but I think she just doesn't like it when I call her ugly.—Danny Hirsh

I bought some Rogaine, and my friend goes, "If you're gonna use Rogaine, put it somewhere you're gonna remember to use it everyday." So I put it next to my Prozac. But it feels pathetic using both these products at the same time, 'cause if either one works, I don't really need the other one.—Greg Fitzsimmons

I don't like when women wear running sneakers with their dresses—who started that? It's gotta stop. Women are like, "Oh, it's more comfortable." Who gives a crap? Please—do you think I like carrying around these balls?—Mitch Fatel

I dress as well as I can. My underwear always matches my outfit. In case you're wondering, that's why my shirt has urine stains.—Bruce Cherry

I have an addiction to the tanning salon. My friends say, "Do you know how bad it is for you to go tanning?" I said, "Yes, but do you know how good it is for me to look Haitian?"—Margot B. Leitman

I have no boobs whatsoever. On my wedding night my husband said, "Let me help you with those buttons," and I told him, "I'm completely naked."—Joan Rivers

I'll never be able to understand how a woman can take boiling hot wax, pour it on her upper thighs, rip the hair out by the root, and still be afraid of a spider.—Jerry Seinfeld

Celebrities

America's Self-Imposed Royalty

Planet Hollywood has shrunk from 75 locations around the world to just over 35 over the past 2 years. No new Planet Hollywoods are opening, which in turn has caused a 100 percent decline in opportunities for Bruce Willis to play the harmonica.—Jon Stewart

A lot of people say Pam Anderson wouldn't be anyone without her tits. That's not true. She'd be Paris Hilton. —Sarah Silverman

Who Made the Funny? _____

Jon Stewart is not only one of our more intelligent comics, but one of our more romantic ones as well. To propose to his wife, Tracey, Jon hired a professional crossword-puzzle maker to produce a puzzle specifically for her and proposed within the puzzle.

P. Diddy went on *The Today Show* and told the world he was "Diddy" because "the P. was getting between me and my fans." R Kelly had the same problem.—Steve Hofstetter

On September 21, 2006, Stephen King celebrated his 59th birthday. Every year, he asks for the same present—Prozac.—Ben Schwartz

You've got to wonder if people would be as intimidated by Mr. T if they knew that the T stands for "tickle."—Chad Lehrman

Tom Cruise and Nicole Kidman say their split is amicable, and they want everyone to know that after the divorce is final, their two adopted children will be returned to the prop department at Universal Studios.—Tina Fey

Carol Dennis, a former backup singer for Bob Dylan, said this week that from 1986 to 1992, she and Dylan were secretly married. Dylan, however, insists that the marriage was not a secret. It's just that whenever he told people about it they couldn't understand a word he said.—Jimmy Fallon

Michael Jackson met with his priest today. Not for spiritual advice. They went on a double date.—Jay Leno

Who Made the Funny?

While Jay rules the roost on *The Tonight Show,* his wife, Mavis, spends her time in her own worthwhile endeavor—trying to change the world. She was one of our country's highest-profile critics of the Taliban's treatment of women in Afghanistan and the chairperson of the Feminist Majority Foundation's Campaign to Stop Gender Apartheid in Afghanistan, which was nominated for the Nobel Peace Prize in 2002.

I got kicked out of the Ashley Simpson fan club for stalking her. They let me back in because I was the only one in it. —Schizo Bill

Mick Jagger made an appearance as a cartoon character on a recent episode of *The Simpsons.* The strange thing is that both Lisa and Marge are pregnant.—Craig Kilborn

Sources say that Michael Jackson is so deep in debt that he had to borrow $70 million from friends this week. Which is difficult, because most of Michael's friends make money selling lemonade.—Conan O'Brien

Today is Fat Tuesday—or, to Kirstie Alley, just Tuesday. —Craig Ferguson

They're talking about banning cigarette smoking now in any place that's used by 10 or more people in a week— which, I guess, means that Madonna can't even smoke in bed.—Bill Maher

Two Long Island teenagers were arrested after trying to steal a 9-foot-tall inflatable SpongeBob SquarePants from the top of a Burger King restaurant. The teenagers explained that Star Jones asked them to steal SpongeBob so she can have a contraceptive that fits properly.—Ben Schwartz

Martin Scorsese got married. After they exchanged vows, the priest said, "You may whack the bride."—David Letterman

Prince Phillip, he's a card! Has a habit of saying things like, "You're all bastards!" then, "Was that wrong? Oh, I'm sorry ..." —Eddie Izzard

Courtney Love is like the girl next door—if you happen to live next door to a methadone clinic.—Jeffrey Ross

Who Made the Funny? _____

According to *Entertainment Weekly*, Jeffrey Ross came *this close* to being the "Weekend Update" anchor for *Saturday Night Live*. When Lorne Michaels held auditions for the available "Update" slot in 2000, he narrowed it down to two contenders—the team of Tina Fey and Jimmy Fallon, and Ross. Michaels gave it to Fey and Fallon but described it as a difficult decision.

Val Kilmer is playing the role of Moses in a Broadway musical. The musical opens up with the words, "Thou shall not listen to thy agent again."—Craig Kilborn

Those little Mary Kate and Ashley outfits are super cute and cheap ... when you consider they come with gonorrhea.—Joanna Parson

Don't you hate hairy women? Madonna—you talk about hair. I saw her at a party. She raised her arm, I thought she had Tina Turner under there. What do you say to her? "Your hair looks great—who does your knees?"—Joan Rivers

Here's some sad news. Harrison Ford and Calista Flockhart have broken up. They were engaged, and this must be final, because Calista took the engagement ring off her waist. —David Letterman

Hackity Hack

If you must use an accent in a joke, be sure the accent doesn't wander. "If a character in a joke has an accent at the beginning, they should have the *same* accent at the end of the joke," say Jesse Joyce and Kevin Miller, saving you from certain embarrassment.

Famous radio personality Dr. Laura Schlessinger apologized for the nude photos of her that have popped up on the Internet. Apparently, the photos reveal why Dr. Laura is on the radio.—Conan O'Brien

Pam Anderson says she got hepatitis from Tommy Lee. I'm sure that's the least of what she got from Tommy Lee. I saw Tommy Lee at an awards show. I got crabs from looking at him.—Kathy Griffin

Cindy Crawford said that it is not easy being a model while breast-feeding because during photo shoots she leaks sometimes. It sounds like the greatest "Got Milk" ad ever. —Conan O'Brien

In an interview this month, Matthew McConaughey said that he wants to die the same way his father did, right after having sex. McConaughey's mother has said, "Absolutely not."—Tina Fey

So there I was, in Donald Trump's car. There's a warning— "The objects in the mirror may be *the largest objects in the wooooorld*."—Joanna Parson

I had some stalkers. I just said screw it, didn't bother me. I just bought them all cameras, and now I pretend they're paparazzi.—Ant

I was walking down the halls here at CBS, and I ran into Dr. Phil. So I see him, and I ask him, "Hello, how are you doing, Dr. Phil?" And he says to me, "Dave, don't ask unless you're prepared to hear the tough answers."—David Letterman

Actors Harrison Ford and Kevin Spacey have each given $100,000 to the Screen Actors Guild to assist out-of-work actors. In a related story, actor Arsenio Hall would like to thank Harrison Ford and Kevin Spacey.—Jimmy Fallon

Congratulations to Britney Spears. She had a boy. Mother and son are doing fine. The father is still not doing anything.—Jay Leno

I was in Vegas last week, first time ever. It's kinda neat to see your name on the big signs for the first time. I turned the corner at the Riviera Hotel, and there my name is on the signs, in 2-foot letters, "Ron White." And right above that in 3-foot letters, "Prime Rib Dinner, $3.99."—Ron White

Blatant Lies

One of the most popular new words in this year's *Oxford English Dictionary* is *Federlineage*, which means "any child born of the union between a parent with no discernable talent who has somehow tricked the world into bestowing fame upon them, and Kevin Federline."

A new spin-off series will be starring Jeff Garlin on HBO. It's called *Curb Your Appetite*.—Adam Ferrara

Star Jones married Al Reynolds. If you would like to send a gift, they are registered at McDonald's.—Ben Schwartz

A lot of people say Andy Dick is gay. But I can tell you he's definitely straight. He just asked out Katie Holmes.—Sarah Silverman

Who Made the Funny? _____

Red Buttons's real name was Aaron Chwatt. Due to his red hair, he was given his showbiz name by a renowned bandleader with a distinctive name of his own —Dinty Moore.

Elizabeth Taylor has a big heart. She recently built a halfway house for girls who don't want to go all the way. —Red Buttons

There was so much I wanted to say about Princess Diana, but when I saw Steven Seagal speak so eloquently on CNN, I said, "What do *you* have to contribute to this moment?" When Tom Cruise described how many times *he* had driven through that same tunnel, it gave me the chills.—Sandra Bernhard

Madonna said today that we should pull all of our troops out of Iraq. Donald Rumsfeld said, "No, I think we'd better wait and hear what Britney Spears has to say about it first."—Jay Leno

Michael Jackson broke his wrist and had to be taken to the hospital. When Jackson got to the hospital, his only request was that his doctor be Doogie Howser.—Conan O'Brien

For years and years, people have been guessing who the father of Melissa Etheridge's children were. It's David Crosby. It works out great. She gets the kids, and he gets two potential liver donors.—David Letterman

Cher had a commercial; she said, "I call my perfume 'Uninhibited' because there are so many people in me." Yeah, and they're all under 18.—Joy Behar

I have performer's paranoia. I worry that Jay Leno's phone is more tapped than mine. —Dennis Miller

Blatant Lies

Actually, Cher has one group of men inside her who just celebrated their twenty-second anniversary in their current location. Congratulations, guys! Well done!

Tommy Lee's d*ck is so big it has an elbow.—Jeffrey Ross

In an effort to improve her image, Shannen Doherty has signed on to produce and act in a new sitcom about a young woman with a reputation for being difficult and mean, but who is really kind at heart. Doherty will play that woman's bitchy friend.—Tina Fey

Michael Jackson interviewer Martin Bashir told the pop star that his relationship to children was so spectacular, "it almost makes me weep." When asked for comment, every parent in America said that, "When it comes to Jackson's relationship to children, we have the exact same reaction."—Larry Getlen

"Frankly, my dear, I don't give a damn" was named best quote from a U.S. movie. Second place went to "Paris, make sure there is enough battery to tape this."—Ben Schwartz

Yesterday, 66-year-old Larry King and his 40-year-old wife gave birth to their second child. The mother is doing fine, but she says she's still a little grossed out by having sex with Larry King.—Conan O'Brien

Zsa Zsa Gabor has been married so many times she has rice marks on her face.—Henny Youngman

HA HA HA Make 'Em Laugh

When you do get a laugh, milk it. Don't "step on" (talk over) the laugh. Wait for it to die down, almost gone, before you start talking again. That helps ensure you have your audience's attention again once they're ready to listen.

Dino de Laurentis is 80 years old. Or as Anna Nicole Smith calls him—fresh meat.—Steve Martin

I feel like Zsa Zsa Gabor's sixth husband. I know what I'm supposed to do, but I don't know how to make it interesting.—Milton Berle

I love staying at the Hilton. It's the only hotel where the porn is homemade.—Steve Hofstetter

A celebrity birthday today—Elvis turned 67 today. Elvis spent the day celebrating quietly at home with family and friends.—David Letterman

Mick Jagger and Jerry Hall want to see a marriage counselor. They realized divorce can lead to bitterness, financial ruin, and disgrace, since at least one of them would end up dating Rod Stewart.—Bill Maher

John Travolta said he wants to make some improvements to *Battlefield Earth* before it is released on video. The changes are in the title—the movie will now be called *Blank Tape*.
—Conan O'Brien

Donald Trump just proposed to his girlfriend. I can just hear the vows now: "Do you promise to love, cherish, and never turn 30?"—Craig Kilborn

In an interview, Steven Seagal said his Buddhist spiritual adviser told him to stop making movies because it would bring bad karma. Interestingly, the spiritual adviser's name is Roger Ebert.—Craig Kilborn

Who Made the Funny? _____

At 6'5", it's no surprise that Craig Kilborn played basketball. He attended Montana State University on a basketball scholarship and even received an offer to play professionally—in Luxembourg.

Donna Hanover, the estranged wife of New York Mayor Rudy Giuliani, made her debut in the play *The Vagina Monologues* this week, in which she talked about orgasms and lesbian sex. In response, the mayor has already made plans to have Hanover torn down and replaced with a Disney store.—Tina Fey

It's a bad day today for the defense in the Michael Jackson case. The judge asked Michael what kind of laptop he had, and Michael said, "His name is Timmy."—Craig Ferguson

There are people who pay $25,000 to have Paris Hilton at their parties. I don't have that kind of money, but if I threw a party, I *would* pay security guards $12.50 an hour to keep her out.—Larry Getlen

The New York Post says that Chelsea Clinton got so drunk the other night at a New York bar, she had to be helped outside by the bouncer. Afterward, Chelsea said, "I'm sorry, I'm really competitive with the Bush twins."—Conan O'Brien

I'm on the Hollywood Walk of Fame, and I stumble across Tony Danza's star. And I urinated on it, just yelling out, "Who's the boss now?"—Zach Galifianakis

Cher is thinking about adopting a baby girl. The adoption agency is leery about letting Cher have a kid. They believe she might use the kid for spare parts.—Craig Kilborn

Who Made the Funny?

Sometimes it really is all in a name. Johnny Carson's first three wives were Joan, Joanne, and Joanna—and he wound up divorced from all of them. He finally caught on in 1987, when he married Alexis Mass. The couple remained married for the rest of Johnny's life.

If life was fair, Elvis would be alive and all the impersonators would be dead.—Johnny Carson

In a recent interview, Celine Dion vehemently denied that she's anorexic. However, Celine did admit that her music is one of the leading causes of bulimia.—Conan O'Brien

Tommy Lee is 38 today. Hey, don't believe me—get out a ruler!—Craig Kilborn

There was a fire at a wax museum. Only the Joan Rivers model survived.—Craig Sharf

You can tell it's the holidays. Authorities raided the Neverland Ranch today and found Michael Jackson in bed with the little drummer boy.—Jay Leno

Sometimes I like to go clothes shopping with Calista Flockhart. Whenever she comes out of the changing room with an outfit, she goes, "Does this dress make my spinal cord look big?"—Gilbert Gottfried

Paris Hilton has reportedly trademarked the phrase, "That's hot." In a related story, her doctors have trademarked the phrase, "That's contagious."—Conan O'Brien

A new study came out saying that monkeys suffer from depression. Even *they* can't believe Paris Hilton's famous. —Larry Getlen

How is it possible that Courtney Love looks worse than Kurt Cobain?—Jeffrey Ross

Who Made the Funny?

Ross actually told this joke in front of Love at Comedy Central's Roast of Pamela Anderson, but as cruel as it seems, he wasn't far off the mark. That night, Love slammed her head into a photographer's lens and continually lifted her skirt toward the crowd. Within the week she was (re)admitted to drug rehab.

The Source Hip-Hop Awards were held last night in Miami. The show went fine, except there was a strange moment when both P. Diddy and Old Dirty Bastard both showed up wearing the same bullet-proof vest.—Craig Kilborn

Traffic here in L.A. was bad today. It was so bad that it took Billy Joel 2 hours to flip his car over.—Craig Kilborn

Today is Earth Day. Michael Jackson said even though Earth has its problems, he's still glad he moved here.—Jay Leno

Madonna has agreed to star as a kinky, leather-clad dominatrix in Britney Spears's new music video. This should be really hot—for anyone who finds sad desperation hot. —Jimmy Fallon

Michael Jackson is putting together a new charity song with many celebrity guests. Per Michael's request, the background vocals will be sung by the Harlem Naked Boy's Choir.—Ben Schwartz

It's a confusing world. I just found out Jamie Kennedy and Seth Green are two different people. Who knew?—Larry Getlen

Blatant Lies

Kennedy and Green actually capitalize on the confusion surrounding who's who, with each one pretending to be the other to get girls, depending on who's got the hottest buzz that particular week.

I'm glad that O. J. Simpson has custody of the kids. I think O. J. will make a great father. When O. J. tells you to do your homework, you do it! The average parent says, "Do your homework," and the kid says, "I'll do it after I get done watching TV." O. J. says "Do your homework," it's like, "YES! I'M DOING IT RIGHT NOW! AND I'M DOING NEXT YEAR'S HOMEWORK ALSO!" —Gilbert Gottfried

Britney Spears gave birth yesterday. The child has already lip-synced his first words.—Ben Schwartz

Kiefer Sutherland said he had to sleep in his car for a year. Yeah, I'm sure it was tough tossing and turning in a Mercedes 560 parked outside your father's mansion. He says his father didn't help him with his career. Yeah, and Tori Spelling is an orphan.—Nick DiPaolo

Tom Cruise told a German tabloid that he believes space aliens really exist. Cruise said that after all these years, he's tired of trying to convince the world that he's straight, and just decided to tell a more believable story.—Larry Getlen

Halle Berry has a black father and a white mother. So according to Jewish law, she's white.—Julia Gorin

Bono sued his former stylist, saying she stole a Stetson cowboy hat, green sweatshirt, black pants, and a pair of metal hoop earrings. The stylist refused to return the items, because she said it was always her dream to dress like Shania Twain.—Larry Getlen

Authorities have tested Michael Jackson's DNA and made an astonishing discovery … they now think Michael Jackson may be a black man in his 40s.—Jay Leno

Everyone knows that on the cover of *Abbey Road*, Paul isn't wearing shoes. But nobody mentions that John isn't wearing mittens.—Geoff Holtzman

 Blatant Lies _____

Also unmentioned—when writing that joke, Geoff wasn't wearing pants.

Despite mixed reviews, Roberto Benigni's film *Pinocchio* broke Italian box office records its first weekend, making over $7 million. Viewers especially loved the ending, where, against all odds, Benigni was somehow transformed into a real actor.—Larry Getlen

Childhood and Adolescence

The Reason You're Like This

I was so naïve as a kid I used to sneak behind the barn and do nothing.—Johnny Carson

When I was kidnapped, my parents snapped into action. They rented out my room.—Woody Allen

My friend has a baby. I'm writing down all the noises he makes so later I can ask him what he meant.—Steven Wright

I'm a film nut. I broke into a studio called Pinewood Studios near London when I was 15, and I crept around, hoping that some guy with a big cigar would go, "Hey, a creeping kid! For my film, *The Creeping Kid!* You're in." —Eddie Izzard

I'm the youngest in my family. I was always getting beaten up by the two oldest—Mom and Dad.—Tom Cotter

I always remember the last words of my grandfather, who said, "A truck!"—Emo Philips

When I was a kid, I had a friend who worked in a radio station. Whenever we walked under a bridge, you couldn't understand what he said.—Steven Wright

What a childhood I had. My whole family were drunks. When I went missing, they put my picture on a bottle of scotch.—Rodney Dangerfield

> **Who Made the Funny?**
>
> Sarah Silverman's not the only funny one in her family. Her sister Laura is a stand-up comedian, actress, and comedy writer who has appeared in *Half Baked, State and Main,* and HBO's *The Comeback.* Laura also voiced the receptionist Laura in the animated series *Dr. Katz, Professional Therapist.*

When I was 14, I went out with my father's best friend. It was embarrassing—my father having a 14-year-old best friend.—Sarah Silverman

I remember being about 3 and standing on the front seat of the car with my dad. What was I doing *standing* on the *front seat* of the *car?* Back in those days, kids weren't too good to go through the windshield with the rest of the family.
—Jeff Foxworthy

People say you should never strike a child. Put him in time out. Why, so they can plan other evil sh*t to do?—Steve McGrew

Why is it when David Copperfield brings a little 4-year-old girl up on stage, then asks her if she has a boyfriend, it's really cute. But when I do it … creepy.—Deric Harrington

There was this one time I was lost, and I asked a policeman to help me find my parents. I said, "Do you think we'll ever find them?" He said, "I don't know, kid. There are so many places they can hide."—Rodney Dangerfield

I was born by C-section. That was the last time I had my mother's complete attention.
  —Richard Jeni

Who Made the Funny?

Rodney Dangerfield was a struggling comedian for years—performing under the name Jack Roy—who gave up on comedy in his 30s to sell aluminum siding. He didn't return and find success under his new name, Rodney Dangerfield, until his early 40s.

I saw my father naked once. But it was okay. Because I was sooo young—and sooo drunk.—Sarah Silverman

When my mom got mad, she would say, "Your butt is my meat," and I always wondered, what wine goes with that?
—Paula Poundstone

I had the "plastic furniture you couldn't sit on" house. It's like living in a museum—towels you could never touch, china that no one's ever gonna use. Everything in my mother's house is for a special occasion that hasn't happened yet. The pope may show up. The pope, Tony Danza, and Chachi. That's the chain.—Ray Romano

My 6-year-old niece says that when she grows up, she wants to be a surrealistic artist. So I bought her a Paint-by-Irrational Numbers set.—Tim Cavanagh

My mother used to feed us Count Chocula for breakfast, and when that ran out, we had Franken Berry or Boo Berry. Very healthy. We had the four main food groups covered—chocolate, strawberry, blueberry, and Fruity Pebbles.
—Larry Getlen

It was a simpler time back then. We were so easily entertained. We would watch anything. We'd watch a flying nun; we'd watch a talking horse. We are so much more sophisticated now, watching people eat bugs and marry strangers for money.—Ellen DeGeneres

My nickname as a kid was Mister Baseball—because of the stitches in my face.—Emo Philips

When I was 16 years old, the morning of my birthday, my parents tried to surprise me with a car—but they missed. —Tom Cotter

HA HA HA   **Make 'Em Laugh**

Simplicity is a virtue in all things, but in few things more so than in a joke. "Some comics and storytellers diminish the effect of a good joke by slowing it down with jokes that get in the way," says Gene Perret, former head writer for Bob Hope. Perret has heard people throw a joke in the middle of another joke and muddle it completely. "Many times the added joke simply slows down the pace of the main joke, or it destroys the natural rhythm of the original joke." Perret uses a Henny Youngman example. "Imagine it delivered this way: 'Take my wife, who is not a very good cook. She can burn Jell-O. So take her—please.'" Not good. Avoid this.

A child develops individuality long before he develops taste. I have seen my child straggle into the kitchen in the morning with outfits that need only one accessory—an empty gin bottle.—Erma Bombeck

I grew up in the suburbs in a neighborhood that was not very tough at all. Even our school bully was only passively aggressive. He wouldn't take your lunch, he'd just go, "You're gonna eat all that?"—Brian Kiley

My mom was a ventriloquist, and she was always throwing her voice. For 10 years I thought the dog was telling me to kill my father.—Wendy Liebman

At my lemonade stand I used to give the first glass away free and charge $5 for the second glass. The refill contained the antidote.—Emo Philips

When I was a kid, we had a quicksand box in the backyard. I was an only child … eventually.—Steven Wright

When I was a kid, I had two imaginary friends. They would only play with each other. —Rita Rudner

I didn't go to my prom. I tried to. I bet a friend of mine I could get a date—then got shot down 27 times. My friend just kept rubbing it in. "Loser. I can't believe you couldn't get a date. You're such a loser." But I got even, because a couple of years later … he drowned.—Pat O'Shea

I was 5'7" in fifth grade. My two best friends were 4'9". We used to run around at the gymnasium having the time of our lives, taking the place over. A woman walked up to me and said "Lady, can't you control your children?" I said, "I'm 12 years old." She looked up at me and said, "Slut!" —Margot B. Leitman

Science says that some babies as young as 8 months old can suffer from depression. Some babies are optimistic, though, and see the diaper as half full.—Craig Kilborn

We never talked to each other in my family. We communicated by putting Ann Landers articles on the refrigerator. —Judy Gold

I asked my old man if I could go ice-skating on the lake. He told me, "Wait 'til it gets warmer."—Rodney Dangerfield

HA HA HA **Make 'Em Laugh**

Love your joke so much that you feel like laughing along with the crowd afterward? Go right ahead, says science-fiction legend Isaac Asimov, a joke raconteur who wrote two joke books. As he wrote in *Asimov Laughs Again*, "There is nothing wrong with laughing at your own joke after you have told it."

Babies don't need a vacation, but I still see them at the beach. It pisses me off. I'll go over to a little baby and say, "What are you doing here? You haven't worked a day in your life."—Steven Wright

Children are smarter than any of us. You know how I know that? I don't know one child with a full-time job and children.—Bill Hicks

Little kids buy cereal the same way grown men buy lingerie. They will buy stuff they care nothing about just to get the prize inside.—Jeff Foxworthy

I'm the oldest of 14 children. My mom worked on a commission basis for the pope.—Joe Bolster

My mother never saw the irony of calling me a son-of-a-bitch.—Richard Jeni

Adults are always asking little kids what they want to be when they grow up—because they're looking for ideas. —Paula Poundstone

I was born by Caesarian section. Now, when I leave a house, I go out through the window.—Steven Wright

I remember being 9 years old, my parents bought me a wood-burning kit. A sharp metal stick that heated up to 5,000 degrees. Our dogs and cats didn't have a tag around their neck, but everybody in the neighborhood knew who they belonged to.—Jeff Foxworthy

I saw a 7-year-old girl wearing pants with the word "Juicy" written across the ass. Any father who allows his daughter to wear pants like that should be put in jail for child endangerment, and his jumpsuit should have the word "Juicy" written across the ass.—Veronica Mosey

I got lost tonight driving here. I see a sign that says, "Caution. Small children playing." I slow down. But then it occurs to me—I'm not afraid of small children.—Jonathan Katz

HA HA HA   ## Make 'Em Laugh

When telling jokes, people sometimes get louder without realizing it. Generally, this is bad. But if you find yourself in a public-speaking situation that involves a microphone, it becomes deadly. "A microphone is a device that amplifies sound. THERE IS NO NEED TO YELL INTO IT," say Jesse Joyce and Kevin Miller from Jokevision. "Make sure you enunciate and speak clearly, and hold the microphone still and in front of your face." No need to blow out eardrums—blow them away with laughter instead.

My mom is very superstitious. I didn't have my Bar Mitzvah until I was 14.—Craig Sharf

I've got two wonderful children. And two out of five isn't bad.—Henny Youngman

I'd like to have kids one day. I want to be called "mommy" by someone other than Spanish guys on the street.—Carol Leifer

The scariest part of watching your dad scratch his backside is when he gets that look in his eyes like he found something new.—John Fox

Kids seem so much older today, with the way they act, the way they talk, the way they kiss … it's forceful, almost causing your tongue to get caught in their braces.—Bri Cowan

I'm a Big Brother, but I'm a little nervous. His name is Cain.—Craig Sharf

Where did this veneration of childbirth come from? "Oh, childbirth is such a miracle." Wrong. A miracle is raising a kid who doesn't talk at a movie theater.—Bill Hicks

I hate telling people my problems because they always say, "How bad can it be? You're so young!" Is there an age minimum for life to suck? Your life can suck at 2 months. It's called being a crack baby.—Rosie Tran

Who Made the Funny?

Rita Rudner has appeared on Broadway—but not as a comedian. Rudner began her career as a dancer, appearing in Broadway chorus lines as young as 15. By 25, she was playing Lily St. Regis in the Broadway production of *Annie* but soon tired of the lifestyle and made the switch to stand-up.

I wouldn't want a kid who was like me, because I was boring. Whenever we played doctor, the other children always made me the anesthesiologist.—Rita Rudner

I wasn't abused as a child. My parents wouldn't, because in order to abuse a child, you've got to spend time with them.—Greg Banks

I was so nerdy as a kid, the only thing that would have made beating me more attractive is if I'd been filled with candy.—Larry Getlen

When I was a little kid, I thought I wanted to be a fireman. I didn't really want to be a fireman. I just wanted to spray sh*t with a hose.—Dane Cook

I can remember the first time I had to go to sleep. Mom said, "Steven, time to go to sleep." I said, "But I don't know how." She said, "It's real easy. Just go down to the end of tired and hang a left." So I went down to the end of tired, and just out of curiosity I hung a right. My mother was there, and she said, "I thought I told you to go to sleep." —Steven Wright

My nephew is 6 years old, very precocious kid. I asked him if he knew about the birds and the bees. He said, "I can only assume they f*ck like people do."—Jonathan Katz

The Trench Coat Mafia was upset 'cause they didn't have any friends. "We were the outcasts." There was six of the motherf*ckers! I didn't have six friends in high school! I don't got six friends now! And everybody's like, what were they listening to? Who cares what they were listening to? What was Hitler listening to? What was in his CD case? —Chris Rock

Do you think Spanish kids play a card game called *ONE?* —Tony Liberati

I have one brother, five sisters. I had to wear a tampon just to fit in.—Dane Cook

Summer brings back memories of hot afternoons spent in the backyard playing Catch-22 with my father. He would say, "How do you get a job?" I would respond, "With experience." "How do you get experience?" "By having a job." We could go for hours like that.—Craig Sharf

Who Made the Funny?

Dane Cook's 2005 CD *Retaliation* debuted on the Billboard Top 200 at number four and quickly became the best-selling comedy album in 28 years—since Steve Martin's *Let's Get Small*.

I don't care what your hobby is before puberty hits, because as soon as it does, nature assigns you a new hobby. Let's just say when I was 14, I was treated for tennis elbow and I didn't even own a racquet.—Dennis Miller

I got picked on a lot as a kid, but now I'm a big guy, so I can get revenge. Only problem is, all those kids who beat me up—I don't know where they are now. So what I do is, I go to local public schools, and I beat up kids who *look* like them. "Not so tough now, huh, Amber?"—Larry Getlen

When I was a kid, the best present I ever got my father was suspenders. They hurt much less than a belt.—Craig Sharf

I could tell that my parents hated me. My bath toys were a toaster and a radio.—Rodney Dangerfield

Giving candy to a baby is easier than taking candy from a baby.—Myq Kaplan

I feel sorry for those who grew up the youngest in their house, the baby, because they got pushed down a lot and kicked for no reason. I don't care how big you turned out, if you grew up the baby in your house, you're really flinchy. If you wanna see if someone grew up the youngest, just make a quick motion at 'em, see if they freak out. "Sorry, I thought you were gonna give me a noogie." "Why would I give you a noogie? I'm your boss. Here's your check, you freak."—John Heffron

Blatant Lies

Red Buttons learned this lesson the hard way. Unfortunately for Red, his kids were almost grown by the time it sank in.

Kids today grow up so fast. One day they're being tried as juveniles, the next as adults. —Craig Sharf

Never raise your hands to kids. It leaves your groin unprotected.—Red Buttons

When things are bulletproof, bullets bounce off them. But when things are childproof, that's not how it works.—Myq Kaplan

I had a traumatic childhood. When I was 6, I was thrown from a moving experience.—Geoff Holtzman

Nothing good is about to happen when one kid says to the other, "Hey, let's build a ramp."—John Heffron

I remember the time I was kidnapped, and they sent a piece of my finger to my father. He said he wanted more proof.—Rodney Dangerfield

I spent all of my teenage years doing musical theater. I don't really remember how I got into it. All I know is that when I was 13, I contracted a severe case of jazz hands.—Bri Cowan

I figure if the children are alive when he gets home, I've done my job.—Roseanne

When I was in the Boy Scouts, I tripped on the ice and hurt my ankle. A little old lady had to help me across the street. —Steven Wright

Kids even have play dates. Playing is now done by appointment. What ever happened to, "You show me your wee-wee, and I'll show you mine?"—George Carlin

Who Made the Funny?

Spaced-out comedian Steven Wright is actually an Oscar winner. He won the 1989 Academy Award for Best Live Action Short Film for *The Appointments of Dennis Jennings,* which he co-wrote and starred in.

I hated having asthma as a child. I couldn't run around and play with the other kids at school. But it was great for show 'n' tell. I would get up in front of the class and jog in place until I had an asthma attack. Then I would show everyone how the inhaler is used.—Debbie Shea

My parents tried to buy us safe toys, but that didn't work. Any kid could turn any toy into a weapon. Once, my mom bought us a Nerf football and said, "Why don't you guys play with this? It's just a sponge football, so I shouldn't hear any crying." Really, Ma? I'll consider that a challenge. Let's see what happens when I soak this in water for a week, then freeze it. Now we have a game.—John Heffron

My friend Winnie is a procrastinator. He didn't get his birth mark 'til he was 8 years old.—Steven Wright

I like those new invisible leashes they make for kids ... called Ritalin.—Debbie Shea

My friend has to hide his violent video games from his kids in his collection of *Playboy*s. He got home one day and the kids had found the porn box. They were playing the video games. The *Playboy*s—untouched. Kids today see a *Playboy* and go, "Do they do anything?" "No, you just stare at them." "What? They don't move? That's dumb."—John Heffron

I was real little when I was a kid and my dad, trying to exploit me, wanted me to be a jockey. Only we lived in New York City and didn't have a horse, so he'd make me stand in front of the house holding a lantern.—Eric Deskin

Human beings are the only creatures who allow their children to come back home.—Bill Cosby

6 Crime

Stick 'Em Up–Your *Funny Bones*, That Is!

Capital punishment turns the state into a murderer. But imprisonment turns the state into a gay dungeon master.
—Emo Philips

Mayor Giuliani's crime-fighting plan is to get rid of all the squeegee guys so that everyone's car looks so crappy no one will want to steal it.—Bill Maher

The FBI will install high-tech scrambling devices to prevent people from picking up the closed-circuit broadcast of Timothy McVeigh's execution. Which means that on May 16th, some young man who thinks he's watching scrambled porn may actually be masturbating to a lethal injection.—Tina Fey

My husband gave me a necklace for our anniversary. It's fake. I requested fake. Maybe I'm paranoid, but in this day and age, I just don't want anything around my neck that's worth more than my head.—Rita Rudner

HA HA HA   **Make 'Em Laugh**
Professional comedians spend years rehearsing to master their craft—so why shouldn't you? "It's just like anything else—you need to practice," says comedian Leo Allen, "whether it's telling joke-book-style jokes, or your own jokes in front of an audience. Or even just making quips or japes in your everyday life." So for example, if you're hoping to impress a certain someone with wit and charm, why not practice in a scenario where there's less at stake and see what works and what doesn't? Plus, if you're paying attention, you may learn ways of being funny you hadn't thought of. "You need to notice what (and if) people laugh at about you when you are not trying to be funny," says Allen.

There was a blizzard where you couldn't see right in front of you, that's how hard it was snowing, and this dude stuck me up. But he was an albino. I couldn't even see him. All I heard was, "Gimme your wallet!" I was like, "The snow is robbing me. I gotta quit smoking."—Deon Cole

Over the weekend a hijacker got away with an armored truck with more than 2.1 million dollars in it. The hijacker reportedly spent all the 2.1 million dollars on gas for the truck.—Conan O'Brien

I actually gave money to a guy in the street today, which I don't always do. But it was such a sh*tty day, and he had a gun. It's time to think of others.—Brian Kiley

I was watching a documentary about serial killers that said there are three things all serial killers had in common when they were little kids—fascination with fire, bed wetting, and torturing small animals. Don't all little kids like fire and wet the bed? Can't you really red-flag "torturing small animals" as the serial-killer behavior? Do we need the other two? That's like saying, "The only thing we know about serial killers is that when they were little kids they all loved ice cream, cartoons, and masturbating around dead people ... we think those are the three."—Jesse Joyce

They televised the Jeffrey Dahmer trial, and his mom was in the audience. What's she gonna say? "That's my boy. The cannibal thing, it's a phase. Uncle Jack ate people till he was 60/65. He'll outgrow it."—Larry Amoros

On my way here I walked by a car, and I guess I got too close because the car alarm went off. I didn't want the people who owned the car to be confused, so I threw a brick through the windshield. I figured that would explain what had happened.—Jessica Delfino

I cannot pee if I know someone is watching me. It's not a psychological thing; it's the terms of my probation.—Bruce Cherry

Make 'Em Laugh

Remember, telling a joke to friends or at a party is quite different from telling one in a speech. You can take some risks in casual social settings; much less so in a public speaking situation. Laurie Rozakis, in her book *The Complete Idiot's Guide to Public Speaking* (Alpha Books, 1999), shares a golden rule for determining if a joke is appropriate for a speech: "When in doubt—cut it out."

Mike Tyson is in the news again. Last week Tyson jumped on the hood of a car and started attacking it. Not surprisingly, the car knocked Tyson out in two rounds.—Conan O'Brien

The police in this town have a very tough sobriety test. Not only do they make you blow up a balloon, but then you have to twist it into a giraffe.—Author unknown

I'm a slow reader, and it sucks being a slow reader, because it will never hold up in court. "I'm sorry your honor, I now know it says 'Speed Limit 55,' but at the time all I read was 'Speed.' At least you didn't catch me going through the 'St' sign."—Deric Harrington

At a high school in South Dakota this week, an undercover police officer roamed the halls with an unloaded gun to test the response. The school passed with flying colors when concerned students spotted the officer and shot him. —Tina Fey

I was feeling crazy the other day and decided to do a drive-off at a gas station. You should've seen the look on the guy's face when I prepaid for 10 bucks and drove off on "E."—Greg Volk

Hackity Hack _____

You already know not to drink and drive. Well, here's a new one—don't drink and joke. "Try not to be too drunk when you're telling a joke," says comedian Lisa Lampanelli, "because then you'll slur your words, and people will be like, 'what?' The punch line is really lost when you have to say 'what?'"

I got pulled over for tailgating an Escalade for an hour and a half. I said, "Officer, I'm just trying to watch the movie."
—Phil Mazo

Goldilocks—I don't like that one, because she breaks into these people's house. She comes into the bears' house, she's eating their porridge, she's like, "Ooo, this is too hot." B*tch, this ain't your food.—Tony Woods

Why does man kill? He kills for food. And not only food—frequently, there must be beverage.—Woody Allen

Authorities believe that the seven Texas prison escapees who have been on the run since December may now be in New York. The men are filthy, violent, and deranged and have evaded New York police by blending into the beer line at a Rangers game.—Tina Fey

If you ever see me getting beaten by the police, put the video camera down and help me.—Bobcat Goldthwait

Who Made the Funny? _____

Bobcat Goldthwaite once had his own bizarre interaction with the police—starting, of all places, on *The Tonight Show*. During an interview with Jay Leno, Goldthwaite set *The Tonight Show* couch on fire (a move he later said Leno knew about in advance). This led to his arrest on arson charges, for which he was sentenced to appear in public service announcements. And the ongoing feud with Leno got so silly that, according to Goldthwait, when he and Leno were later featured in the same episode of *The Simpsons*, Leno insisted that Goldthwait be drawn out of the scene.

Because they found him sane, they put Jeffrey Dahmer in jail instead of in a mental institution. At least now we don't have to worry about that prison overcrowding problem.
—Larry Amoros

7

Dating

Have I Got a Joke for You!

I always met men who weren't right for me. That's why I feel that after you date someone, you should be able to stamp them with whatever's wrong with them. So the next person doesn't have to start from scratch.—Rita Rudner

I'm thinking my new dentist has been trying to seduce me. I just don't believe there's always rose petals floating in the spit sink.—Joanna Parson

I don't have a girlfriend. I just know a girl who would be really mad if she heard me say that.—Mitch Hedberg

I just broke up with someone, and the last thing she said to me was, "You'll never find anyone like me again." And I'm thinking, *I should hope not. If I don't want you, why would I want someone like you?*—Larry Miller

Who Made the Funny?

Larry Miller's sense of the bizarre was notable early on. A classically trained musician, his school thesis was "A Harmonic Analysis of Frank Zappa."

I fell in love with this woman, so I wrote her a poem. Isn't that romantic? I poured my heart out into this poem, and all she could say was, "Well, Bruce, you misspelled 'Nantucket.'"—Bruce Cherry

I'm dating a woman with a kid. The kid's name is A. J., which stands for Cock-Block.—J-L Cauvin

I'll never go on another date with a vegan. Why? I discovered *vegan* is Latin for *freak*. We couldn't find *one* restaurant that adhered to all her *absurd* rules and regulations, and ended up getting coffee. I politely asked, "Do you want any sugar?" She replied, "I don't *believe* in sugar." Then I said, "B*tch, it exists!" You can say you don't *believe* in the Easter Bunny or you don't *believe* in Jesus, but you *have* to believe in sugar. It's on the table! They don't have little packets of Jesus. They have packets of sugar that say, "*real sugar!*"—Dan Allen

I know my limits. I can never get a hot-looking white guy. I can always get a chubby, ugly, disgusting white bastard, or a hot black guy. I can get LL Cool J, or Jared from Subway.—Lisa Lampanelli

Machiavelli said, "It is better to be feared than loved." Does this work with women? Because if so, I am a helluva ladies man. They're scared to death of me.—Jeremy Hsu

I've been on so many blind dates, I should get a free dog.—Wendy Liebman

I met a girl who had a real hourglass figure ... but that was just her head. The rest of her was grandfather-clockish. Just boxy and wooden.—Larry Getlen

Who Made the Funny?

Wendy Liebman owes her career in comedy to a postal service screw up. When a catalog for the Cambridge Center for Adult Education was delivered to her apartment by mistake, she kept it and later signed up for one of the courses it offered—a course on stand-up comedy.

My sister, when she was in high school, went out with the captain of the chess team. My parents loved him, 'cause he was the captain of the chess team. They figured any guy who took 3 hours to make a move was okay by them.
—Brian Kiley

I don't have a girlfriend, but sometimes I like to pretend I do. I just stand in my apartment screaming, "Hey! No! No, that's *not* what I said! No! I didn't say that! Excuse me—put down the knife. Put it down!"—Dave Attell

I'm single. I think the older you get, the lower your standards get, 'cause you're too tired to really give a crap anymore. I used to be real picky, like, "When I get married, he's gonna have to be tall, dark, handsome, educated, wealthy ...." Now I'm down to "registered voter."
—Kathleen Madigan

The only difference between a date and a job interview is, there's not many job interviews where there's a chance you'll end up naked at the end.—Jerry Seinfeld

I tried personal ads and I did the Internet, and the great thing about that is I learned that I'm not alone. I'm not the only one who enjoys fine dining.—Maria Bamford

You know, a lot of girls go out with me just to further their careers ... damn anthropologists.—Emo Philips

I dated one girl who had a beauty mark like Cindy Crawford. We get to kissin' and stuff, I took a look at it— it was a tick.—Larry the Cable Guy

Blatant Lies

While mankind is descended from apes, scientists have determined that Emo Philips is actually descended from an awkward encounter between Magilla Gorilla and Grape Ape.

My girlfriend and I went to Hana, Hawaii, which is the most romantic place in the world to have a fight. You're yelling; the trees are swaying in the background; the ocean's there; there's a sunset, you look at it, then you pick up where you left off.—Garry Shandling

I want to date a suicide bomber. At least they can commit.—Jennifer Dziura

To me, being single is a struggle between loneliness and euphoria. It's loneliness right before you go to bed at night and euphoria the entire rest of the day.—Ted Alexandro

I am single. I don't drink. It's kinda hard to get a woman buzzed when you don't drink. You'd be like, "I'll have a glass of water, and, you want a shot of Jager? You want eight of 'em?"—Jim Gaffigan

I broke up with my boyfriend because he was taking me for granted. He still hasn't noticed—still hasn't called.—Catie Lazarus

You have to fib a little to get women in Hollywood. I told this girl I had an agent, so she went home with me. The fib? My agent works for State Farm.—Michael J. Nelson

Scientists estimate that the average American male spends a full four days of his single life hearing the phrase, "Pull the car over, a**hole. I'm walking."—Dennis Miller

There's very little advice in men's magazines, because men don't think there's a lot they don't know. Women do. Women want to learn. Men think, "I know what I'm doing, just show me somebody naked."—Jerry Seinfeld

I was single for a long time and it was fun. But sooner or later, you get tired of driving your car without a woman sitting next to you making you so tense you can feel your colon tying itself into a square knot.—Richard Jeni

Married people underestimate how hard it is to date. My mother keeps asking me, "What's your problem? Pretty women are a dime a dozen!" Well, the problem is, that's in Thailand—and it's wrong! —Moody McCarthy

Who Made the Funny?

During Jay Leno's tenure as host of *The Tonight Show*, Richard Jeni has made more appearances on the show than any other stand-up comic.

Every woman I meet, for some reason, I end up being the friend. Having a woman as just a friend is like having $19 in the bank and looking at your ATM card. You can see it. You know it's there. You just ain't getting to it.—Alonzo Bodden

I love my gay male friends, but when I was a little girl, I always wished that I would be constantly surrounded by gorgeous guys, and now I am. I should have been more specific.—Margaret Cho

When I was 18, I thought I was in love—first time, good feelin'. So I asked my father, "Dad, is love real?" And he said, "No—but herpes is, so watch your ass."—Greg Fitzsimmons

Making a relationship work is a lot like getting a fitted sheet over your mattress. You try to pull it over, it doesn't want to stay. After a while you get frustrated and start stomping on it and slashing it into pieces. —Molly Anderson

Blatant Lies

After writing this joke, Molly finally found a man who didn't fill her with the need to slash things, and the couple were recently married. So congratulations to Mr. and Mrs. Crispin Glover!

Looking to men for stability is like looking to Crispin Glover for psychoanalysis.—Dennis Miller

Me and my last girlfriend didn't see eye to eye, so I got my eyes checked. Apparently I'm clutter-blind.—John Heffron

I believe that for every person, there's another person they're meant to be with. I feel like I'm always just missing my special person. I'll be in a bank; she's in a deli. I'll go to a strip club; she's not working that night.—Dave Attell

You want a criteria for a relationship? Drive cross-country together. Along about Nebraska, most people just say, "You know, I'd rather just walk." That's how they settled the Midwest. It was just people who had to get the hell out of the car.—Jeff Cesario

Don't get me wrong, the girls I go out with all have nice personalities. Some of them have two or three nice personalities.—Bruce Cherry

I'm single because I have a fear of commitment. I can't seem to commit to just one woman to stalk. It's a big pattern with me: I'll be perfectly happy stalking one woman. I'll convince myself she's the only woman I want to stalk for the rest of my life. And then along comes some other girl who is just so uninterested in me that, well ... I think I should stalk other people.—Jason Reich

Who Made the Funny?

Sadly enough, the premise of Larry Getlen's joke is completely true.

I had a date set up last week, and the woman cancelled on me at the last minute because she said she was feeling melancholy. What do you say to that? "That's okay, I'm just getting over my gout."—Larry Getlen

A good date ends with, "I had a great time," or, "I'd love to see you again." A *great* date ends with "God, I feel like such a whore."—John Westerhaus

Men are attracted to a woman with a raspy voice. We think, "Hey, maybe she's all done yelling."—Moody McCarthy

I'm tired of girls going for a**holes. So on my next date, instead of trying to get to know the girl first, I'm gonna start by slapping her around a little bit. "How'd you like that, b*tch?" And if that doesn't work, I'll apologize profusely.—Greg Volk

My boyfriend's black, and two days ago, we celebrated our two-year anniversary. He's the nicest guy, supportive, and makes a little less money than me. So I call him Steadman.—Lisa Lampanelli

My girlfriend's not that bright. She called me up yesterday; she said, "John, the light bulb in the bathroom burned out. I don't know how to change it." I said, "First, you fill the tub with water ...." I called today. There's no answer. —John Fox

I asked a girl I work with why she left her boyfriend, and she was like, "Beats me."—Bri Cowan

I was in an abusive relationship once. I didn't realize it until we were out in public one night, and he hit me in the back of the head, and I said, "Ow! Can't you wait till we get home?"—Debbie Shea

Girls have broken up with me for all sorts of reasons, but my all-time favorite is, "You're just too nice." What am I supposed to do? Apologize? "I'm sorry. I never meant to hurt you. I guess I just never took a minute to find out exactly how big an a**hole you're looking for."—Michael "Ziggy" Danziger

Hackity Hack

Stand-up is one of those crafts that sounds natural only after years of practice. Which means that if you're not a pro, don't try to sound like George Carlin your first time out. "Many amateur joke-tellers make the mistake of trying to sound like a comedian, which is not advisable," says veteran comedian Brian McKim, who publishes (along with his comedian wife, Traci Skene) the popular stand-up comedy website SHECKYMagazine.com. "You're not a comedian; don't try to sound like one. Try to sound as conversational as possible. It's a wildly unnatural situation, but everyone is cognizant of that fact. Avoid any affectations, quirks, dialects, or doing physical shtick unless you know you can handle it. Keep it simple, streamlined, and low-key, and let the actual joke do the heavy comedy lifting. Your recipients will thank you for it."

I dated a guy who went off to L.A. to become a P.A. For those of you who don't know, P.A. stands for "cheater."
—Kimmy Gatewood

I love to scare people. This past weekend I snuck up to the windows of each and every one of my ex-boyfriend's houses dressed as commitment.—Molly Anderson

I saw a light switch with a sticker on it that said, "Turn me off when you're done using me." Then I looked over my shoulder to see if anyone had put one of those stickers on my back, because that would explain a lot about my social life.—Jennifer Dziura

I read that girls are less interested when a man orders a salad on a date. They like men who order manly things. That's why I only order steak. Steak and titties.—Jeremy Hsu

Just because you look at another woman, it doesn't mean you're gonna do anything. If you're at a restaurant and food comes to another table, you're not gonna dive over and start eating it. It's not like I look at another woman and then at my girlfriend and go, "I wish I'd gotten that. Why didn't I get what he's having?"—Garry Shandling

I dated a balding man once. It wasn't so bad because he was really hairy everywhere else, so that was nice. He used to wear this scent I really liked. It was called Love My Carpet.—Debbie Shea

I can't tell how young women are anymore. I went out on a blind date. She ordered "'pascetti." Then she walked to the ladies room and her sneakers lit up.—Moody McCarthy

Ladies, guys like playing video games because we can eventually figure them out and win. We can't do that with women. I can't go online and find a cheat code to deal with you b*tchin' at me. I can't hold a controller at you and go, "triangle, square, up down two two" and have you blink and disappear.—John Heffron

We're never gonna understand women, because they're mysterious. And they're never gonna understand us, because they can't handle the truth.—Jake Johannsen

I met a woman on the Internet who described herself as "voluptuous." I assumed that meant "busty" until I tried to download her picture and my computer ran out of memory.—Eric Deskin

Death and the Afterlife

Last Call—No, *Really!*

Last week, my aunt passed away. She was cremated. We think that's what did it.—Jonathan Katz

I always live every day as if it were my last. Which is why I sleep on a bedpan with a tube up my nose.—Bill Maher

HA HA HA Make 'Em Laugh
If you're preparing to tell a joke to a group and you're tempted to utter that old saw, "Stop me if you've heard this before ..." think again. "'Stop me if you've heard this' is bad," says comedian Steve Hofstetter, "because if one of ten people has heard it, why should you stop?"

For three days after death, hair and fingernails continue to grow—but phone calls taper off.—Johnny Carson

In her will, my grandmother stipulated that she wanted to be buried with all of her favorite possessions. Her cat was not happy about that decision.—Tom Cotter

I don't think that the Grim Reaper is that scary. I mean, his weapon of choice is generally used for farming, and he's holding it upside down. I don't run away from people who don't know how to wield a rake correctly.—Elie Saltzman

The key is to not think of death as an end, but as a very effective way to cut down on your expenses.—Woody Allen

Death is the last thing everybody does, and it's the first thing a lot of them do correctly.—Gene Perret

My grandma just passed away. 104 years old—but they saved the baby.—Larry the Cable Guy

---

🚫 **Hackity Hack** _____

You wouldn't date someone you didn't like, eat food you didn't like, drive a car you didn't like—why tell a joke you didn't like? "This is a really weird thing people do sometimes—they'll tell a joke that didn't really make them laugh just because they remembered it," says comedian Mitch Fatel. "The power of one strong joke is so powerful and sticks with people for a long, long, time, whereas you leave a bad taste in their mouths with a bad joke. So if it annoyed you and didn't make you laugh, don't tell it."

I'm working on a new book called *How to Commit a Murder-Suicide.* Chapter One: "Do the Murder First."
—Tim Cavanagh

Suicide is man's way of telling God, "You can't fire me— I quit."—Bill Maher

The other day a man died on the New York City subway, and his body rode around for five hours before anybody noticed. Apparently just before the man passed away, he saw a bright light, and he went through a long tunnel that smelled like urine.—Conan O'Brien

When I die, if the word *thong* appears in the first or second sentence of my obituary, I've screwed up.—Albert Brooks

They say that when you die you see a bright light at the end of the tunnel. I think my father will see the light, then flip it off to save electricity.—Ed Marques

On the plus side, death is one of the few things that can be done just as easily lying down.—Woody Allen

The guy who writes the obituaries passed away. But nobody knows.—Myq Kaplan

Hackity Hack

When you want to tell a joke that contains a profanity or two—or three or four—but the occasion calls for more propriety, some people think they can just censor the joke. Don't. "Don't clean it up for your audience," says creator of *The Aristocrats*, Penn Jillette. "There are very good clean jokes, but there are no dirty jokes that are good cleaned up. So don't try to do that. Don't say, 'and he slaps her on the rear end.' You sound like a radio DJ if you do that." And Penn doesn't mean that as a compliment.

Cryogenics is the science of freezing your body until they find a cure for what killed you. What if you die from frostbite?—Mike Morse

Food

Oral Pleasure

McDonald's is going to be phasing out beef with antibiotics in it. Which should be easy since their beef has now been phased out of beef.—Conan O'Brien

I like refried beans. That's why I wanna try fried beans. Maybe they're just as good, and we're wasting time. —Mitch Hedberg

I used to eat while I was in the supermarket. I guess I didn't consider it stealing 'cause I took it out inside my body.—Arsenio Hall

My cooking is so bad my kids thought Thanksgiving was to commemorate Pearl Harbor.—Phyllis Diller

I saw this wino. He was eating grapes. I was like, "Dude, you have to wait."—Mitch Hedberg

Who Made the Funny?

Phyllis Diller is a virtuoso not just of the joke, but of the piano as well. She has appeared as a soloist with more than 100 symphony orchestras in the United States and Canada.

If God did not intend for us to eat animals, then why did he make them out of meat?—John Cleese

When they first introduced bottled water, I thought it was so funny. I was like "Bottled water! Ha ha, they're selling bottled water! I guess I'll try it … ahhhhh … this is good. This is more watery than water. Yeah, this has got a water kick to it."—Jim Gaffigan

Ever been looking through the refrigerator and come across an empty plate? That starts me to wondering. I think, "Did something eat something else?"—George Carlin

The makers of Hostess Twinkies are going out of business. Seems Twinkies could survive everything except for bankruptcy.—Ben Schwartz

Starbucks released a previously unavailable album from Bob Dylan. A spokesman for Starbucks said that Dylan was the perfect partner for them, since if Starbucks coffee can make Bob Dylan sound awake, then it proves they truly are the world's greatest coffee.—Larry Getlen

Parsley is the Paris Hilton of herbs. They both have no purpose on this earth; they're only here for show; and I don't want either one of them spread on my food.—Vic Alejandro

It says on the container that a serving size of ice cream is a half a cup. Is that a joke? I think a serving size of ice cream is when you hear the spoon hit the bottom of the container.—Brian Regan

KFC is being criticized for their new ad campaign that touts the health benefits of fried chicken. They want you to believe that fried chicken is good for you. Oh yeah, I think that's true. Most health food is served in a bucket.—Jay Leno

Who Made the Funny?

During his early days, nationwide headliner Brian Regan performed at the same comedy club where he worked as a cook and would often fulfill both duties in the same evening, finishing his comedy sets quickly so he could grill up some burgers for the audience.

I bought a box of animal crackers. It said, "Do not eat if seal is broken." I opened it up—sure enough …—Brian Kiley

Fettuccini alfredo is macaroni and cheese for adults. —Mitch Hedberg

I used to be a chocoholic. Fortunately, they don't sell chocohol around here.—Geoff Holtzman

I'm not a vegetarian because I love animals. I'm a vegetarian because I hate plants.—A. Whitney Brown

I went to a pizzeria. I ordered a slice of pizza, and the f*cker gave me the smallest slice possible. If the pizza was a pie chart for what people would do if they found a million dollars, he gave me the "donate it to charity" slice. "I would like to exchange this for the 'keep it.'"—Mitch Hedberg

My whole family's lactose intolerant. When we take pictures, we can't say cheese.—Jay London

A pizza place in my neighborhood has a sign in the window that says, "Say aloha to pineapple pizza." Which means, they now have pineapple pizza … or, they're getting rid of it.—Pat O'Shea

Waiters and waitresses are becoming nicer and more caring. I used to pay my check, and they'd say, "Thank you." That graduated into, "Have a nice day." That's now escalated into, "You take care of yourself, now." The other day I paid my check and the waiter said, "Don't put off that mammogram."—Rita Rudner

I don't know what's going on with cranberries, but they're getting in all the other juices. Whoever the salesman is for cranberries, he's doing a great job. "What do you got, some apples? Put some cranberries in there, call it cran-apple! What do you got, grapes? Call it cran-grape! Mangoes, cran-mango. Pork chops, cran-chops!" Back off, cranberry man.—Brian Regan

Make 'Em Laugh

As with any art, comedy involves many judgment calls. How much you should personalize a joke is a good example. "Add some personal details and make a joke your own if you want to, but don't add so much that it becomes a chore for people to listen to it," says comedian Christian Finnegan. "People have short attention spans, so you don't want to tax them too much. That said, detail generally helps."

Ever notice on a box of cookies it says, "Open here." What do they think you're gonna do—move to Hong Kong to open their cookies?—George Carlin

I can't eat spaghetti—there's too many of them.—Mitch Hedberg

I just signed my first endorsement deal with powdered milk. "Try the great taste of powdered milk. It's the other white powder."—Deric Harrington

I ate at an Ethiopian restaurant. You go there and you serve them food.—Danny Hirsh

I put fruit on top of my waffles, 'cause I want something to brush off.—Mitch Hedberg

What is Dr Pepper a doctor of? Would you still drink it if I told you he was a proctologist?—Bob Reinhard

We're the only country on the planet with all-you-can-eat restaurants, the only people on the planet to whom that concept is even *remotely* appealing. "You mean for the price of a regular, filling meal, I can gorge myself till I'm in a blinding sugar coma? Bon appétit!"—Jeff Cesario

We're lazy. We used to have breath mints. Now we have breath strips. They just dissolve on our tongue for us. How lazy. Can we not suck anymore?—Ellen DeGeneres

Mr. Pibb is a replica of Dr Pepper, but it's a bullsh*t replica, because the dude didn't even get his degree. Why'd you have to drop out and start making pop so soon?—Mitch Hedberg

Who Made the Funny?

Mitch Hedberg was one of those bright lights who left us way too soon. A master of the blasé non sequitur, he was 37 at the time of his death in March 2005, and many people felt he was on his way to becoming comedy's next great superstar. If you're unfamiliar with his material, do yourself a favor and pick up his two releases, *Mitch All Together* and *Strategic Grill Locations*. You won't regret it.

Throwing pasta against a wall is a good way to tell if it's done—or, if the paint job isn't.—Myq Kaplan

I like Chef Boyardee, but they have some stuff I've never seen in the real Italian food world. Ever been in a nice Italian restaurant, "Hi, how are you? I'd like to start with a nice bottle of Chianti, and a couple of Caesar salads to get started, and I'm gonna have the Beefaroni. And some Teenage Mutant Ninja Turtles for the lady."—Brian Regan

McDonald's has announced a talent contest to showcase its employees' skills. The contest favorite is Jim, who can fit over 10 human body parts in one chicken nugget.—Ben Schwartz

They say the recipe for Sprite is lemon and lime, but I tried to make it at home. There's more to it than that. "Want some more homemade Sprite?" "Not till you figure out what the f*ck else is in it."—Mitch Hedberg

I had what I thought was an orange the other day. But it was really a tangelo. That's a cross between a tangerine and Maya Angelou. I didn't like it—it tasted sweet enough, but it was too sanctimonious.—Jeremy Hsu

I saw this guy on the side of the road with a sign, "Will work for food." So I gave him a coconut.—Dwight York

The worst thing you can find in the refrigerator is something you can't identify. "Is it meat? Is it cake? I've never seen anything like it. It looks like ... meatcake!"—George Carlin

I just read that apparently the number-one condiment in Canada is chewing gum. Number two? Gastric bypass surgery.—Geoff Holtzman

Hackity Hack _____

This seems so logical and yet people screw it up—be sure your joke makes sense. "I saw a comedian do a joke about how women never fart, followed directly by a joke about how women always fart at the worst times," says comic Steve Hofstetter. "I couldn't listen to anything he said after that. Not only was he relying on fart jokes, but they were contradictory fart jokes. How terrible is that?"

I recently had some food that disagreed with me. When food disagrees with you, you're sick. But when you disagree with food, you're crazy. Unless it's a fortune cookie.—Myq Kaplan

I think that french fries were invented because someone's mother would not let them eat catsup straight out of the bottle.—Elie Saltzman

I wanna have my face on the cover of a Rice Krispies box. Snap, Crackle, Mitch, and Pop. "Hey, how did he do that?" In Hollywood, it's all who you know, and I know Crackle. —Mitch Hedberg

An apple a day keeps the doctor away. But eating 365 apples in 1 day will kill you.—Jeremy Hsu

Baking soda is the most versatile product on the market. You can scrub toilets, do laundry, and even cook with it. My mom used to make us chocolate chip cookies with Arm and Hammer. We'd wash it down with a refreshing glass of ammonia. Good times.—Shane Lou

I'm trying to drink more water 'cause you're supposed to drink 8 glasses a day, but I'm really bad about it because I'm lazy and I forget. So now I just try to get it done all at once … in the shower.—Debbie Shea

HA HA HA   **Make 'Em Laugh** _____

Jokes succeed and fail based on the sound and rhythm of the words. If you tell a joke and the rhythm feels wrong to you—like, for instance, if you can't say the punch line without running out of breath—don't be afraid to change it. Shortening a punch line or throwing an extra pause into a sentence often works to enhance the joke. Don't be afraid to experiment.

In Judaism, pork is not kosher. In the South, pork is a vegetable.—Michelle Ferguson-Cohen

Bulimia is the only way you can actually have your cake and eat it, too.—Myq Kaplan

I went to a restaurant and ordered a chicken sandwich, but I don't think the waitress heard me, 'cause she asked how I'd like my eggs. So I tried answering her anyway. "INCUBATED! Then hatched, then raised, then beheaded, then plucked, then cut up, then put onto a grill, then put onto a bun … it's gonna take a while. I don't have the time. Scrambled!"—Mitch Hedberg

Diners will serve you whatever you want—you don't even need a menu. Once I ordered a "fruit cobbler"—a gay guy came out and fixed my shoes.—Moody McCarthy

10 Gender Relations

Sugar and Spice, My Ass ...

Women are the most powerful magnet in the universe, and all men are cheap metal. And—we all know where North is.—Larry Miller

Rap music is the first music to be honest about the male agenda. It's not a lot of bullsh*t about, "I will be with you on a mountaintop." It's, "Back that ass up." You gotta admire the honesty.—Bill Maher

Women have a big problem communicating with men, because you ask us questions we cannot answer. The number one question we cannot answer—"Do you remember …?" No! I don't remember! I'm a man. I cannot remember. Look—we invented instant replay because we forgot something we just saw.—Alonzo Bodden

Who Made the Funny?

Groucho Marx died in 1977. Even though he was considered the comic genius of his age, his death was overshadowed in the press by the death of another legend three days earlier—Elvis Presley.

Anyone who says he can see through women is missing a lot.—Groucho Marx

Women are always looking for men who don't exist. "I want an outdoorsy guy who's hilarious." What? If you combine those two things, you would not like it—rodeo clowns. Outdoorsy, hilarious, alcoholic, and wanted. Then there's the girl, "I just want a guy who will give and give and give, and not want sex in return." I actually know this guy. His name's Grandpa—and he has your nose.—Dave Attell

Women have confidence with love. Women know about love. When a woman says "I love you," it means something—it means, "We're committed, we're together, we're gonna make it." When a man says, "I love you," sometimes it just means, "I'm done talking now—can we wrap it up?"—Nick Griffin

The boys I grew up with were so dumb and fratty. If they were smart enough to date rape they would have, but they couldn't figure it out.—Catie Lazarus

What were they doing with a car on the moon? You're on the moon already! Isn't that far enough? There is no more male idea in the history of the universe than "Why don't we fly up to the moon and drive around?"—Jerry Seinfeld

We have women in the military, but they don't put us in the front lines. They don't know if we can fight, if we can kill. I think we can. All the general has to do is walk over to the women and say, "You see the enemy over there? They say you look fat in those uniforms."—Elayne Boosler

Who Made the Funny?

Elayne Boosler learned comedy from the best—and bizarrest. Her mentor in the clubs was Andy Kaufman, whom she dated for three years.

To judge from the covers of countless women's magazines, the two topics most interesting to women are: (1) Why men are all disgusting pigs, and (2) How to attract men. —Dave Barry

How do men look at women? Women think they know, which amazes me. Women will always say, "Hey, we look at guys sexually, too." You have no idea. It's like the difference between shooting a bullet and throwing it. Trust me ladies, if you had any idea, even for a second, of how we really looked at you, you would never stop slapping us.—Larry Miller

I was reading an article in the paper about [serial killer] Ted Bundy being on trial in Florida. In the article, it said, "The courtroom was filled with women waiting to give him flowers, love letters, and *wedding proposals!*" And I'm afraid to say that the first thing that entered my head was: "And *I'm* not getting laid?!?"—Bill Hicks

I was at a baseball game last summer, and this plane flew overhead with a banner that said, "Ann, Will You Marry Me? Dave." Apparently, Ann said no, because another plane showed up and shot the first plane down.—Brian Kiley

My boyfriend ran off with the decorator. It's okay, I hated her color schemes. She wanted to do the bedroom in sea green. I preferred yellow and black—and crime scene tape.—Joanna Parson

When women are depressed, they either eat or go shopping. Men invade another country. It's a whole different way of thinking.—Elayne Boosler

Who Made the Funny?

Tim Allen knows of what he speaks. After a 1979 arrest for selling cocaine, the affable actor was incarcerated for two years.

Women now have choices. They can be married, not married, have a job, not have a job, be married with children, unmarried with children. Men have the same choice we've always had: work or prison. —Tim Allen

Your only job on Earth is to love yourself as you are. If your boyfriend doesn't think your breasts are big enough, ladies, maybe you should get a new boyfriend. Maybe a midget with tiny hands? He'll think they're huge.—Nick Griffin

The problem in movies is not violence, it's romance. Because what's every movie with a romantic plot? Guy meets a girl, she hates him, but he's gonna get her no matter what. Well, in real life, that's called "stalking."—Bill Maher

Growing Old(er)

Where Are My Keys?

You know you're going bald when your conversations with your barber keep getting shorter and shorter. I sit down, and he's like, "Nice day. You're finished." I'm like, "Well, take a tip." "No son, that would be stealing."—Dave Attell

Who Made the Funny?

Bob Hope's real name is not Bob or Robert. It's Leslie. His full name is actually Leslie Townes Hope.

My secret for staying young is good food, plenty of rest, and a makeup man with a spray gun.—Bob Hope

First you forget names, then you forget faces. Next you forget to pull your zipper up, and finally you forget to pull it down.—George Burns

We all admire the Rolling Stones for keeping at it in their 50s, but their fans are too old to be buying souvenirs. Even if you did, would you really want to get that colostomy bag with the big red tongue on it?—Bill Maher

I remember when my attitude was "Look all you want, just don't touch." Fast-forward 20 years, and now I'm like, "Touch all you want, just don't look!"—Kelly Smith

I have one neighbor I loved, an elderly woman, about 85, and I found myself in a politeness contest with her. We tried to out-nice each other. I turned my stereo down, so she turned her radio down. I stopped talking on the phone late at night, so she unplugged her phone. Then I stopped waking up to my alarm, so she died in her sleep.—Laura Kightlinger

There's one advantage to being 102 years old. There's no peer pressure.—Dennis Wolfberg

I want to be a rock star. Doesn't look like that's gonna happen—39, no band. Plan's got some gaping holes in it. —Greg Behrendt

Hackity Hack

Unless your name is Jim Carrey, leave the funny faces and voices at home. "Sometimes, people feel like they have to act funny when they're telling a joke, use crazy voices, or be really expressive with their faces or hands. Most of the time, that ruins jokes," says comedian Christian Finnegan. "Usually, jokes are funnier if you tell them with a straight face. Just because you're telling a joke, it doesn't mean you have to act 'funny,' because that's when you look like a summer camp counselor at a talent show."

I had long hair, and I was going bald. There's no way to do both of those things and look cool. Every year I looked more and more like Ben Franklin.—Bobcat Goldthwait

Why did the menopausal woman cross the road? *To kill the chicken!*—Jane Condon

My brother called me last night to complain that his teenage daughter dresses too sexy, 'cause she doesn't wear a bra, and she should; her shirt never covers her belly; half the time her butt crack is exposed. It made me realize that my dad dresses too sexy. Dad, you're a ho.—Brian Kiley

I am officially middle-aged, which is fine with me. I don't need drugs anymore. Now I can get the same effect just by standing up really fast.—Jonathan Katz

I can tell I'm getting older, because now when I see a porno movie, I go, "Wow. What a great house."—John Marshall

I went to see a concert, and the security guard goes, "Excuse me. I'm gonna need to take that chain wallet from you." I'm like, "Why, because of the recent terrorism, and the war, and the upgrades in security?" He goes, "Nope. Because you're 38."—Greg Behrendt

You know you're not hip anymore when your car gets broken into and they don't steal your tapes.—Moody McCarthy

Blatant Lies

Among the tapes in Moody's car: *Steve and Eydie's Bar Mitzvah Hoedown;* Herman's Hermits sing *The Best of Bread;* and Bread sings *The Best of Herman's Hermits.*

You can only be young once. But you can always be immature.—Dave Barry

I got some bad news in the mail. I got my high school reunion coming up. That's a lot of pressure. You get that letter in the mail, and right away you feel like you only have six months to make something of yourself. "Come on, seven! Daddy needs a new career!"—Drew Carey

Now that I'm moving out of my college dorm I have my sight set on the perfect neighborhood. It's located right in the basement of my parents' house.—Danny Hirsh

My grandmother started walking 5 miles a day when she was 60. She's 93 today, and we don't know where the hell she is.—Ellen DeGeneres

Who Made the Funny?

In real life, popular talk-show host Ellen DeGeneres is actually a lesbian! Who knew?

It feels great to be 95. I mean, for those parts of me that still have feeling.—Bob Hope

Is it rude to tell a balding man you want to run your fingers through his hair?—Debbie Shea

You know you're getting old when your blood type's been discontinued—Phyllis Diller

You're at a concert, you're 16, having a good time—oh, who's that? Creepy old guy. Creepy, old, rockin' solo—I'm that guy. But I know I have 39-year-old brothers and sisters that also rock, 'cause I've seen them tattooed and pierced at the Pottery Barn. There's a grunge brother, pickin' out an area rug. Right on, dude.—Greg Behrendt

I'm 57, and I'm hot—it just comes in flashes.—Linda Sweig

We sent my grandma on a cruise before we put her in the nursing home, so we didn't get cut out of her will. I thought I did good. I found her this three-month cruise to Alaska. But she didn't like it. All she did was complain. "The captain was mean, the nets were too heavy, all I did was gut fish ..."—Mike Storck

> **Blatant Lies**
>
> Contrary to popular belief, the character of "Jerry Seinfeld" Jerry Seinfeld portrayed in the hit sitcom Seinfeld was based not on Jerry Seinfeld, but on Watergate conspirator G. Gordon Liddy.

I can't drive in Florida with the old people. They drive slow and sit low. The state flag of Florida should just be a steering wheel with a hat and two knuckles on it, and that left turn signal on from when they left the house that morning. That's a legal turn in Florida. It's known as an eventual left. You can signal this week, and turn any year of your life.—Jerry Seinfeld

I'm at that age where I see the commercial for the Craftmatic Adjustable Bed and go, "Sweet! You mean I can sleep in the shape of a U?"—John Heffron

Gettin' old's a b*tch, man. Young dudes here are look-ing at me like, "I ain't going out like that, bro." Yeah, motherf*cker—you are. Sittin' there with your tight skin and your judgment. Don't get cocky. Get yourself a skin-care program, 'cause it won't stay that way.—Greg Behrendt

I'm supposed to go to my high school reunion, but I'm not going, and I'll tell you why. If I wanna see one of the losers I hung out with in high school, I'll get a pizza delivered. —Dave Attell

Health

It Hurts When I Do This ...

I saw my doctor last week. I said, "Doc, every day I wake up and look in the mirror, and I want to throw up. What's wrong with me?" He said, "I don't know, but your eyesight is perfect."—Rodney Dangerfield

They have disposable douche. I'm wondering, who would want to keep it in the first place?—George Carlin

I had a cold a few weeks ago, and the entire wall of the drugstore is cold medication. It's so hard to figure out what to use. "This one's quick acting. This one's long lasting. Hmmm. When do I need to feel good, now or later?"—Jerry Seinfeld

I have a bad photographic memory. I remember everything, but my thumb is in the way.—Craig Sharf

HA HA HA Make 'Em Laugh

Jokes aren't funny if it sounds like your mouth is full of marbles. *Tonight Show* host Jay Leno reminds us that if you're trying to be funny, "Speak clearly and enunciate—you need to be understood."

I lost 31 pounds. Yeah. Crystal meth is amazing. I lost it in four hours, and my apartment was spotless.—Ant

My father's allergic to cotton. He has pills he can take, but he can't get them out of the bottle.—Brian Kiley

Studies show that you lose seven minutes off your life for every cigarette you smoke. I think that's fantastic. I'm going to start smoking 10 packs a day and go back in time. I'd time travel back to the year 1872, walk into a saloon, and order a shot of whiskey. The bartender would ask, "Where you from, city slicker?" After a long, unhealthy spat of coughing and wheezing, I would whisper, "The future!" —Dan Allen

Researchers at Yale have found a connection between brain cancer and work environment. The number-one most dangerous job for developing brain cancer? Plutonium hat model.—Jimmy Fallon

We have some fat people in this country, and I am fed up with the little denial phrases they have. "I'm not fat. I'm husky. I'm portly. I'm big-boned." You're big-*ssed, okay? Dinosaurs are big-boned. Put the fork down.—Denis Leary

I flew back from Los Angeles, and on the plane was a *Time* magazine. And there was a 30-page article about diabetes, and I read the entire thing. By the time that plane landed, I had diabetes.—Lewis Black

My uncle just had angioplasty done. The weird thing is, his doctor's a part-time clown. When he pulled out the catheter, the balloon was twisted into a dog.—Tim Cavanagh

There was a fella at Disneyland who had an epileptic fit, and three kids jumped on his back—thought he was a new ride. Threw me off twice.—Redd Foxx

I went to the doctor the other day. All this guy did was suck blood out of my neck. Never go to see Dr. Acula.—Mitch Hedberg

Happiness is your dentist telling you it won't hurt and then having him catch his hand in the drill.—Johnny Carson

Where did this sudden fear of germs come from in this country? It's ridiculous, and it goes to ridiculous lengths. In prisons, before they give you a lethal injection, they swab your arm with alcohol! Wouldn't want some guy to go to hell *and* be sick.—George Carlin

HA HA HA Make 'Em Laugh

Hear a joke you like but don't think you'll be able to remember it? Write it down and save it in a file.

We have an obesity epidemic in the United States. One out of every three Americans weighs as much as the other two.—Richard Jeni

If you say you didn't know smoking was bad for you, then you're lying through the hole in your trachea.—Dennis Miller

What's the difference between me and O. J.? O. J. walked. —Christopher Reeve

I have bad luck with doctors. The last one I went to wrote out a prescription for me. It was for cigarettes.—Gene Perret

When I quit smoking my sense of smell came back, which was nice. Because I had completely forgotten about that hooker in the closet.—Mike Storck

I went to the video store the other day and rented *Philadelphia, Angels in America, The Band Played On,* and *An Early Frost*. They wanted cash up front.—Steve Moore, HIV+ comedian

Whenever they need money, they raise the tax on booze and cigarettes, 'cause all the people who don't drink and smoke say we have to pay for the health insurance. But we also have an obesity problem. So how about a fat tax? How about we make a jar of mayonnaise $13? And how about some warning labels on the food and the booze, like they do on cigarettes? On the side of cigarettes, it says "You'll get cancer if you smoke these." So put on the side of a Whopper box, "If you keep eating these, no one's gonna f*ck you anymore."—Jim Florentine

Dr. Kevorkian's my man. He's the doctor who helps people die, who are so sick they just wanna get out of here. I can't say I blame them. I've had the runs and written a suicide note.—Richard Jeni

Hackity Hack

"Ethnic jokes don't go over as well as they used to," reminds Conan O'Brien writer Brian Kiley. "There are times people tell me a racist joke, and I'm shocked, but I'm also embarrassed for them, like, you just made a fool of yourself." So if you want to tell a joke that's off-color, save it for people you know for a fact will appreciate it.

I have a friend who's a dyslexic-paranoid. He always thinks he's following somebody.—Dwight York

I have a friend who was obese. She just lost 150 pounds, which is great, because I can finally call her chubby. —Carmen Lynch

I'm color-blind. The worst thing about being color-blind— going to the buffet and putting chocolate pudding on your mashed potatoes—Roland A. Duby

I'm sick of hearing about health. I know cholesterol's bad. Big deal. I smoke three packs of cigarettes a day, I breathe the air in New Jersey, and I have sex without condoms. A slab of butter is not gonna make that much difference. —Rich Vos

My girlfriend has an eating disorder, but I'm very support- ive. I hold her hair.—Geoff Holtzman

My friend Marlene used to be bulimic. To save money, she converted to anorexia.—Craig Sharf

When it comes to pain relievers, nobody wants less than extra strength. You can't even get "strength"—"strength" is out now. Extra strength is the absolute minimum. Some people aren't satisfied with extra, they want maximum. "Give me the maximum allowable human dosage. Figure out what will kill me and then back it off a little bit." —Jerry Seinfeld

I'm really bad with names. Last night, I saw a guy choking. I performed the Kevorkian maneuver on him.—Craig Sharf

I have a bumper sticker on my car that says, "Lose weight now ... ask me how!"—Steve Moore, HIV+ comedian

I used to stutter. In fact, I stuttered for almost 20 years. I finally finished the sentence on Tuesday.—Geoff Holtzman

I said to my doctor, "My penis is burning." He said, "That just means someone's talking about it."—Garry Shandling

13 Holidays

When Relatives Attack

Santa Claus? You have to look very carefully at a man like this. He comes but once a year? Down the chimney? And in my sock?—Professor Irwin Corey

Who Made the Funny?

The remarkably zany Professor Corey has actually graced more serious stages than most would expect, performing in both *Taming of the Shrew* and *Hamlet* at the Stratford Shakespeare Festival.

I celebrated Thanksgiving in an old-fashioned way. I invited everyone in my neighborhood to my house, we had an enormous feast, and then I killed them and took their land.
—Jon Stewart

Let us not forget the true meaning of Thanksgiving. The Pilgrims came to this country so they could practice religious freedom. And so they could wear big hats made out of black construction paper.—John Marshall

It's Halloween! Today I saw one of those scenes you only see in New York. There was a kid carving a jack-o-lantern and after he finished he wiped the fingerprints off the knife.—David Letterman

You know what was a very tricky time for me? Halloween. 'Cause all my life my parents said, "Never take candy from strangers." And then they dressed me up and said, "Now go beg for it." I didn't know what to do. I'd knock on people's doors and go, "Trick or treat—no, thank you."—Rita Rudner

It's Halloween! I didn't have enough time to find a costume, so I just put a few cats in my hair and went as Nick Nolte.—Craig Kilborn

The one thing I remember about Christmas was that my father used to take me out in a boat about 10 miles offshore on Christmas Day, and I used to have to swim back. Extraordinary. It was a ritual. Mind you, that wasn't the hard part. The difficult bit was getting out of the sack. —John Cleese

Probably the worst thing about being Jewish at Christmas time is shopping in stores, because the lines are so long. They should have a Jewish express line: "Look, I'm a Jew, it's not a gift. It's just paper towels!"—Sue Kolinsky

New Year's Eve, when old acquaintances be forgot. Unless, of course, the tests come back positive.—Jay Leno

HA HA HA　**Make 'Em Laugh**

This may be the most important piece of advice in the entire book. In the name of all that is holy, *memorize your jokes before telling them!* According to the perpetually silly Dave Barry, "Many people—and I am not going to single out any one particular gender, but I am talking about women, and particularly my mother-in-law—will launch into a joke, only to realize they have forgotten the punch line. Or sometimes they will *start* with the punch line, and, having gotten that bit of baggage out of the way, proceed to reconstruct the joke." So unless you want Dave trashing you in a column—or your friends walking away from you in frustration—memorize your jokes.

Easter is my new favorite holiday. I celebrated a little differently this year. I had an egg hunt ... in my womb. It was great. A lot of people came.—Debbie Shea

I'm not cheap. That's not recycled Christmas wrapping paper—that's the Bat Mitzvah Elk.—Joanna Parson

I love the New Year's celebration, but it's a little bizarre that we're drunk, counting backward. When did this tradition start? Did they have it back in ancient times, like in ancient Rome: "X ... IX ... VIII ... VI ... IV ... I'm out! Happy New Year, Hopocles! See you at the vomitorium!" —Ted Alexandro

Home Sweet Home ... or Not

Wherever I Hang My Hat ...

I bought a two-bedroom house, but I think it's up to me how many bedrooms there are, don't you? "F*ck you, real estate lady, this bedroom has an oven in it."—Mitch Hedberg

A friend told me that her apartment was so messy, she had dust bunnies. I just laughed. I'm *way* beyond dust bunnies. I have a dust John Goodman. He just floats around my apartment drinking all my beer, then takes off once a week to make a real sh*tty movie.—Larry Getlen

People in glass houses shouldn't hang pictures.—Geoff Holtzman

I saw a mouse the other day in my apartment, and it freaked me out ... which is weird, because I love surprises.—Carmen Lynch

> ### Hackity Hack
> Jokes are meant to be fun—not to get revenge or use as a weapon, says *Tonight Show* host Jay Leno. He advises not to tell a joke about something you really have hostile feelings about, because the hostility will come across and ruin the joke. "If you have something you're really angry about or mad about, the anger will come across more than the humor," says Leno. "You just wanna be funny—tell jokes, have a laugh, and have a good timo."

I'll give you an idea how bad my cooking really is. Last Christmas the family chipped in and bought me an oven that flushes.—Gene Perret (written for Phyllis Diller)

They have a new candle out called Home Sweet Home. I don't know what home this is coming from. It doesn't smell anything like sloppy Joes or bathtub meth.—Bri Cowan

A friend of mine gave me a feng shui book. It was just what I needed, just the right thickness—because my coffee table has a wobbly leg.—Mike Storck

There have been a lot of robberies in my apartment building lately. I feel so bad for my neighbor because her dog and VCR got stolen. Nothing else, just the dog and the VCR. I wonder what the burglar was thinking? *I'd really like to rent a movie, but I don't want to watch it by myself.*
—Debbie Shea

I've lived in NYC for almost seven years, and it occurred to me that I cannot live anywhere else. Because if I move to another city, I could get ripped off and not even know it. I'd be looking at a house and the realtor would say, "It's a lovely house, but there's no roof, no electricity, and you're going to have to replace all the plumbing. The owners want $950,000 for it." And I'd be like, "Whoa, wait a minute … you get the entire *house?*"—Gayle Crispin

My boyfriend really wants us to move out of the city. He says, "It'll be great that we'll have grass and trees, and we can start a garden and grow our own vegetables." I say, "Have a salad. It'll pass."—Pat Galante

A man needed to get a stain out of his pants, so he put gasoline into his washing machine. It caused an explosion and burned down his home. See, this is what happens when you let a man do housework.—Craig Kilborn

I don't make my bed. Why would I? When you come home at night and take your shoes off, do you put little bows in them so they look good in the closet when you're not using them?—Jeremy Greenberg

I do a lot of volunteer work with Habitat for Humanity, building houses for people who otherwise couldn't afford one. I like working with Habitat because I'm a do-it-yourselfer, and every once in a while it's nice to go screw up someone else's house.—Tony Deyo

Blatant Lies

Tony was recently barred from working for Habitat for Humanity after the recipients of one house found that they could not use their shower, as it was blocked by the porch.

My neighbor makes a lot of noise. One night it was so loud that I threw a 5-pound weight against the wall. The cat didn't deserve that.—Kai Ajaye

I've combined the homeless problem with the health-care crisis. In my plan, we send the homeless to medical school.

Now, they've all got good jobs, and whenever you need a doctor you won't have to make an appointment 'cause they're just out walking around.—Jake Johannsen

It was reported that the preserved body of a homeless man kept in the studio of the late British artist Robert Lenkiewicz may have been there for 20 years. But at least it was 20 years where he had a home.—Larry Getlen

It always makes me feel bad to see homeless people with dogs. I always think: *That poor dog. I hope he knows if worse comes to worst, he can eat that guy.*—Jessica Delfino

You never see homeless people in the country with signs saying, "Will work for food." Farmers would drive by, saying, "What the hell you think we're doing?"—George Wallace

I was homeless for a while. I didn't want people to know, so I slept in front of a Ticketmaster.—Dwight York

Make 'Em Laugh

The art of self-deprecation doesn't come naturally to everyone. If you're one of those people it doesn't come naturally to, but you want to be funny, it's a skill worth developing. The best way to do that is to tell true, funny stories where *you're* the butt of the joke. "A good rule of thumb is that 'jokes' demean someone, making you look like an a**hole," says former *National Lampoon* editor Tony Hendra, "Whereas 'true' jokes work quite the other way around, where you suggest that you're the a**hole, but people realize that you're quite the opposite."

I'm afraid of the homeless, because I've heard they steal, and I'm afraid that one day they might try to steal my home.—Jessica Delfino

People always tell you, "Don't give the homeless money; they're just gonna spend it on booze or drugs." But I kinda feel like, hey, the guy lives in a box. Maybe he could use a drink.—Jake Johannsen

Just Bizarre

What the ...?

I wanna make a jigsaw puzzle that's 40,000 pieces. And when you finish it, it says, "Go outside."—Demitri Martin

I was attacked by a shark today, but I poked it in the eye and got away. All I have to say is, "Thank you, Viagra!" —Craig Kilborn

HA HA HA **Make 'Em Laugh**

For those of you who love telling jokes but can't seem to keep the details in mind, Philip Van Munching makes a great suggestion in his book *How to Remember Jokes* (Workman, 1997). "Cast the parts," says Van Munching, meaning think about the joke as if it's really happening to people you know. In addition, "Imagine a place you know as a joke setting." Giving the joke a real location and staging it in your mind with real people greatly increases the chance you'll remember it.

I wonder what the most intelligent thing ever said was that started with the word *dude*. "Dude, these are isotopes." "Dude, we removed your kidney. You're gonna be fine." "Dude, I am so stoked to win this Nobel Prize."—Demetri Martin

When I look into your eyes, I see beauty. Then I realize, "Hey, that's my reflection," and I wish your eyes were bigger.—Debbie Shea

I like being ahead of the game, but I wish it would stop staring at my ass.—Joanna Parson

I went to a friend's house. He said, "You have to sleep on the floor." Damn gravity, got me again. You know how bad I wanna sleep on the wall.—Mitch Hedberg

On the bathroom wall, somebody always has to write, "Mike was here." But then someone else puts an arrow, and writes, "Mike is a faggot." Like Mike is coming back to check it out. "What the f*ck is this? I was here, but not as a faggot!"—Dane Cook

I don't like alarm clocks. They have no empathy. Just once I'd like my alarm clock to stress out about not going off on time. "Am I on radio or buzzer? What if I am on radio but not tuned to a radio station? My work will go unnoticed."—Jeremy Greenberg

> **Make 'Em Laugh**
>
> *King of Queens* cast member Patton Oswalt offers two simple but crucial pieces of advice for telling a joke: "Make sure to be heavily medicated," he says, and, "Don't burst into tears." Wiser words were never spoken. Thanks, Patton!

If a rain forest has a forest fire, does it put itself out?
—Craig Sharf

Here's a bit I like to do at parties. Next time you're invited to an elegant dinner party, you arrive late, so everyone's there. You walk in, and throw all the food on the floor. I did this at the last party I went to—about six years ago ...
—Steve Martin

Sticks and stones may break my bones, and that's why I hate nature.—Geoff Holtzman

It's been a rough day. I got up this morning, put on a shirt, and the button fell off. I picked up my briefcase and the handle came off. I'm afraid to go to the bathroom.
—Rodney Dangerfield

I know a lot about cars. I can look at a car's headlights and tell you exactly which way it's coming.—Mitch Hedberg

My grandmother spends all her time out in the garden—'cause, that's where we buried her.—Tom Cotter

The Loch Ness Monster is actually a submarine. Driven by Bigfoot.—Bill Hicks

You know what burns me? Matches.—Jay London

How come the people that snore are always the first to fall asleep?—George Wallace

If I were punctuation, I'd be a semicolon, because nobody understands what I mean.—Geoff Holtzman

When I'm offstage I'm very quiet; I don't say very much. But I hang around people who just talk nonstop, just talk talk talk talk talk. So any time I can get a word in edgewise I say, "Hey, man, you want some taffy?"—Mitch Hedberg

"Sort of" is such a harmless thing to say. *Sort of.* It's just a filler. *Sort of.* It doesn't really mean anything. But after certain things, "sort of" means everything. Like after "I love you," or, "you're going to live," or, "It's a boy."—Demitri Martin

How come no one can spell my name? It's three letters. I'm booking a flight, and this lady said, "Spell your name." I said, "V-O-S." She said, "V-L-S?" Yeah, my last name has no vowels. "My first name is Rich—R-Z-K."—Rich Vos

If these walls could talk, I'd run like hell, because that's some scary stuff.—Geoff Holtzman

My brother says "hello"—so, hooray for speech therapy. —Emo Philips

Make 'Em Laugh

If telling a joke at a party or other boisterous event, it's easy to get distracted by the madness around you. But if you do, you'll kill the joke. After you start telling a joke, it's essential to stay focused. "Once you're in the process of telling a joke, do not get distracted by your drunken friends who are making rabbit ears or manipulating their genitals," say comics Jesse Joyce and Kevin Miller—speaking, no doubt, from experience.

A man who was attempting to walk around the world ... drowned today.—George Carlin

I recently took up ice sculpting. Last night I made an ice cube. This morning I made 12—I was prolific.—Mitch Hedberg

Bad poetry is poetry that lacks feeling. Or letters.—Geoff Holtzman

I bought a house on a one-way dead-end road. I don't know how I got there.—Steven Wright

I like to wear a "Do Not Disturb" sign on my neck so that little kids can't tell me knock-knock jokes. "Hey, how ya doin', nephew?" "Knock knock!" "Read the sign, punk!" —Mitch Hedberg

I just finished writing my one-man show. It's about a guy who battles the bureaucracy at a public television station. It's called, "You Jerk-Offs Owe Me a Tote Bag."—Larry Getlen

You know who really got screwed over? The guy who invented the patent.—Geoff Holtzman

I did a radio interview, and the DJ's first question was, "Who are you?" I had to think—is this guy really deep, or did I drive to the wrong station?—Mitch Hedberg

I was thrown out of college for cheating on the metaphysics exam. I was caught looking into the soul of the boy sitting next to me.—Woody Allen

Hackity Hack

"Own up to petty larceny," says Mark Katz. "If you are 'borrowing' a time-honored joke, let it get the laugh it deserves before offering up a bibliography. For example: 'I am two with nature ... [uproarious cackling] ... Remind me to send Woody Allen a residual check for the use of that joke.'"

Know how you can tell when a moth farts? He flies in a straight line.—George Carlin

I said, "Officer, I'm speeding because I'm taking my mom to the hospital. She OD'ed on reducing pills." He said, "I don't see any woman in the car with you." I said, "I'm too late."—Emo Philips

When butterflies are nervous, what's in their stomachs? —Myq Kaplan

I have a fertile imagination. That's because I'm full of sh*t.—Craig Sharf

I like writing short stories, because I hate writing.—Geoff Holtzman

Today I dialed a wrong number .... The other side said, "Hello?" and I said, "Hello, could I speak to Joey?" They said, "Uh, I don't think so ... He's only 2 months old." I said, "I'll wait ..."—Steven Wright

Aquaman's super power is that he talks to fish. Not great for fighting crime, but he'd make an awesome waiter at Red Lobster. "Hey Aquaman, how's the catch of the day?" "Pissed off."—Mike Bobbitt

Don't you hate it when you're in a time machine, and you get off at the wrong year? You think you're going to, like, 1986. You have on a gold chain with a big cross on it; your boom box is blasting; you step off that time machine, and someone says, "Shh. They're crucifying Jesus. And this is a library."—Geoff Holtzman

People have dreams and they wanna tell them to you, but the thing about a dream is—didn't happen. So it's a long story about something that didn't really happen, and the ending is always the same unless you pass away in your sleep: you woke up.—Greg Behrendt

My fake plants died because I did not pretend to water them.—Mitch Hedberg

One time the power went out in my house. I had no lights. Fortunately, my camera had a flash. I went to make a peanut butter sandwich and took 60 pictures of my kitchen. My neighbors called the police. They thought it was lightning in my house.—Steven Wright

Blatant Lies

Wright was recently awarded an exhibit of his photography by the prestigious Museum of Modern Art. The exhibit was titled, "Steven Wright, and the World's Most Annoying Photo Exhibit."

When I can't fall asleep, I count cloned sheep—1, 1, 1 … —Craig Sharf

If you hit a midget in the head with a stick, he turns into 40 gold coins. But be careful—if you lose a fight to a midget, you become one.—Patton Oswalt

I had a dream that midgets were trying to assassinate me, so I bought a bullet-proof car. But since they were midgets, I bought a convertible.—Steven Wright

I don't know how to speed-read. Instead, I listen to books on tape on fast forward.—Craig Sharf

Some people are opposed to free speech, but you don't hear much from them.—Myq Kaplan

People who are threatened by jokes are the same people who tend to refer to actors on the soap operas by their character's name.—Dennis Miller

I have friends in very high places. I hope the police can talk them down.—Craig Sharf

What if everything is an illusion and nothing exists? In that case, I definitely overpaid for my carpet.—Woody Allen

They say some shampoo causes "no more tears," but I've found that's not true, especially if you jam the bottle directly into someone's eye.—Myq Kaplan

I think it's interesting that "cologne" rhymes with "alone."—Demitri Martin

Blatant Lies

While George has managed to avoid the dreaded beernuts, he was recently diagnosed with cotton balls, and barely survived a horrific case of aqualung.

If it's the thought that counts, why is it only a penny for your thoughts?—Craig Sharf

I'd rather have pussyfoot than woodpecker. Or beernuts. That must be awful.—George Carlin

For the longest time I thought that stuffed animals had feelings. When I finally realized they didn't, I let them have it.—Debbie Shea

I have a bad memory, and here's how I know. Sometimes, I pick up something, like my keys, and I'm holding them in my hand, and ten seconds later, I forget to breathe.—Geoff Holtzman

I don't like the term "best friend." I think it's mean. You're saying, "This is my best friend, and you all suck a little more than she does."—Carmen Lynch

The difference between spit and drool is just a matter of motivation.—Myq Kaplan

A group of geese on the ground is a gaggle; a group of geese in the air is a skein. A group of geese sh*tting on your face are a**holes.—Mike Cotayo

As the poet said, "Only God can make a tree"—probably because it's so hard to figure out how to get the bark on. —Woody Allen

I figured out what earthquakes are. See, the earth is a ball suspended in space, and every once in a while God comes by and grabs the earth and says, "Cough."—Richard Belzer

This is embarrassing. I found out I scream exactly the same if a great white is gonna attack me or if a piece of seaweed touches my foot. There's a moment I want back. "Get me in the boat!" "What's the matter?" "Yucky toes!"—Kevin James

Who Made the Funny?

One of the brilliant comics involved in the *National Lampoon Radio Show* and good friends with John Belushi, Richard Belzer, served as the warm-up comedian for the audience at the tapings of NBC's *Saturday Night* (later known as *Saturday Night Live*) during the show's first season.

Marriage

Till Death Do Us Part—Which Will Be on Tuesday

My husband and I are either going to get a dog or have a child. We haven't quite decided if we want to ruin our carpet or our lives.—Rita Rudner

If variety is the spice of life, marriage is the big can of left-over Spam.—Johnny Carson

I can't relax. The other night I felt like having a few drinks. I went to the bartender, and I said, "Surprise me." He showed me a naked picture of my wife.—Rodney Dangerfield

> **Blatant Lies**
>
> Julius Marx decided on his nickname, Groucho, only after rejecting a slew of other suggestions, including Crotcho, Stasho, Flipper, Sasquatch, and Juicy.

Marriage is a wonderful institution, but who wants to live in an institution?—Groucho Marx

My wife will say this to me— "Honey, I want you to tell me if I start getting fat." And I say, "All right, and you tell me if I start getting retarded."—Jeff Foxworthy

According to a new study, women in satisfying marriages are less likely to develop cardiovascular diseases than unmarried women. So don't worry, lonely women, you'll be dead soon.—Tina Fey

My boyfriend and I were talking about getting married. I'm not sentimental at all, but I think for me, it would mean something to be able to call friends and relatives and be able to say, "It's official. We can start referring to it as spousal abuse."—Laura Kightlinger

They say the two biggest things that couples fight about are sex and money. But I'm lucky—my wife has been charging the same rate for years.—Brian Kiley

I never cheated on my wife; I just never said the right thing. One time my wife said to me, "My grandfather used to tell my grandmother she was the most beautiful woman in the whole world every day of their marriage." Yeah. Back then, they didn't have cable. He didn't know.—Nick Griffin

My mom's always looking for new ways to keep excitement in her marriage. She took up belly dancing once. In order to make it appear like she was moving, my dad and I had to jiggle the furniture in back of her.—Rita Rudner

If you're going to be married, it's very important that you pick the right person. Because this is the person you won't be having sex with for the rest of your life.—John Marshall

---

Hackity Hack _____

"If you say the first line of a joke, and someone says, 'Oh, I heard that one already,' they probably didn't—they just don't wanna hear the joke," advises Jim Florentine, who says that when that happens, you should take it as a sign that that person's not a receptive audience. "Get the hint. Stop it. Don't go, 'Oh, I got another one then,' because it means the guy doesn't wanna hear any of your jokes. If he stops you the first line in, cut your losses there."

My wife told me I was one in a million. I found out, she was right!—Rodney Dangerfield

Marriage is nature's way of keeping people from fighting with strangers.—Alan King

Same-sex marriage? What's the problem? My husband and I have had the same sex for 26 years. It's not a problem. —Jane Condon

It's a sad fact that 50 percent of marriages in this country end in divorce. But the other half end in death. You could be one of the lucky ones!—Richard Jeni

My wife and I have been married 20 years. Remember that first year, when you'd pick a fight just so you could make up and have sex? Twenty years later, you pick a fight just so they'll sleep in the other room.—Bill Engvall

I am not the boss of my house. I don't know how I lost it. I don't know when I lost it. I don't think I ever had it. But I've seen the boss's job, and I don't want it.—Bill Cosby

Who Made the Funny?

Before he became a legendary stand-up comic and then sitcom star, Bill Cosby made television history as the first African American man to star in a television series—the 1965 spy drama *I Spy*.

The other day, my little boy talked back to my wife. She told him to do something, and he said "No. I don't want to." I pulled him aside and said, "Listen—you gotta teach *me* how to do that."—Brian Kiley

I told Fang he could watch half of *Laverne and Shirley*. So he watched Shirley.—Phyllis Diller

My planning of my wedding was intense. I don't know much about women, but I do know that they all wanna get married in fairyland by King Neptune. And as a guy, you're the ass who's trying to bring that in under budget.—Jake Johannsen

I got no sex life. My wife cut me down to once a month. I'm lucky. Two guys I know, she cut out completely. I met one of the guys. I told him, "Who told you you could fool around with my wife?" He said, "Everybody."—Rodney Dangerfield

Lately I think my wife has been fooling around, because our parrot keeps saying, "Give it to me hard and fast before my husband Jonathan Katz comes home. And yes, I'd love a cracker."—Jonathan Katz

I like being married. I don't like arguing, though. Know what I do now? When we get into an argument, I just take her side against me. It's easier. She's like, "What's wrong with you?" and I'm like, "I know! Dammit!" She's gonna win anyway—I wanna be on the winning side occasionally.—Louis C. K.

They say marriage is a contract. No, it's not. Contracts come with warrantees. When something goes wrong, you can take it back to the manufacturer. Your husband starts acting up, you can't take him back to his momma's house. "Uhh, he's broke. He just stopped working, just lying around, making a funny noise."—Wanda Sykes

Marriage is the roughest thing in the word. Nelson Mandela endured twenty-seven years in a South African prison, but once he got out, it only took two years before his marriage busted his ass.—Chris Rock

Who Made the Funny?

After graduating college, Wanda Sykes worked for the National Security Agency. She was later quoted as saying, "Everyone at the NSA has a side job, selling candy or making crafts at their desks," because they had so much free time—which is, without question, the most frightening fact in this entire book.

In the planning of my wedding, I was the least important person. If my wedding were the United Nations, I would be Guam.—John Marshall

My wife thinks I'm too nosy. At least that's what she keeps scribbling in her diary.—Drake Sather

My wife and I tried to spice up our sex lives by making one of those lists of people we could have sex with without getting into trouble if we ever had the opportunity. I could have sex with Shania Twain or Pamela Anderson. She could have sex with Brad Pitt, or this attorney that works in her building.—David Ridings

One time, while I was having an out-of-body experience, my body went to Vegas—with all my credit cards! Had some kind of fling with a $500-a-night hooker. But do you think I could explain that to my wife? No! Women see what they want to see.—Jim Carrey

Blatant Lies

Jim Carrey's Fire Marshall Bill character from *In Living Color* was based on the real fire marshal from Jim's hometown of Newmarket, Ontario, a dyslexic who read the fire marshal's manual backward and mistakenly thought his job was to set fires, not put them out. The town of Newmarket retired him after only 3 weeks on the job, rewarding him with a flaming gold watch for his service.

Basically, my wife was immature. I'd be at home in the bath, and she'd come in and sink my boats.—Woody Allen

My wife tried to sue McDonald's. She put a 16-ounce cup of hot black coffee between her legs, and it froze.—Billy Bingo

The difference between a divorce and a legal separation is that a legal separation gives a husband time to hide his money.—Johnny Carson

I'm not worried about hell. I was married for *two years!* Hell would be like Club Med!—Sam Kinison

This story will warm you up. In Jamaica, there is a group of couples that are going to have an all-nude wedding. Now, that's every girl's dream—to walk down the aisle and be given away by your nude dad.—David Letterman

Who Made the Funny?

Many comedians had strange, uncharacteristic jobs early in their careers, but David Letterman might take the cake. He served as a weatherman for a TV station in his native Indiana.

My wife and I were happy for 20 years. Then we met. —Rodney Dangerfield

I'm arguing with my wife on the cell phone, and I say, "Look, I gotta go—you're wasting my minutes." She said, "No, remember—we get free minutes when we talk to each other." I said, "No, I mean the minutes of my *life!*"—Mick DiFlo

It serves me right for keeping all my eggs in one bastard. —Dorothy Parker

I don't go out with my single friends, 'cause I never have fun. We'll go to a club, and a guy comes over, "Can I buy you a drink?" They're like, "No, she's married." I'm like, "Yeah, I'm married, but I'm thirsty. Why don't you shut the hell up and let me have a free drink?"—Wanda Sykes

I pee in the shower all the time. My ex-husband used to get all annoyed. I guess because he was taking a bath at the time.—Lisa Lampanelli

Single or married. I think it's a close choice. You know what it boils down to? Whether you want to be lonely or annoyed.—Richard Jeni

I married Miss Right. I just didn't know her first name was Always.—Author unknown

Blatant Lies _____

"Author unknown" spent seven years as a private bodyguard for author J. T. Leroy. Since then, he has spent all his free time writing pithy jokes and lists of "reasons you know you're old" for distribution on the Internet and e-mail solicitations about cheap pharmaceuticals and penile size. Long-spread rumors that he was the journalistic source known as "Deep Throat" have since been disproved.

Married men live longer than single men. But married men are a lot more willing to die.—Johnny Carson

I'm married, and my wife and I don't see eye to eye on everything. I say "tomato," and she says, "Oh, shut the f*ck up!"—Dennis Miller

Sex is an important part of marriage. I don't want to say it's a job, but some women fake orgasm. I fake sleep.—Jane Condon

I saw something today that came close to truth in advertising, because the DeBeers people are almost saying what they mean. Their new slogan is, "Diamonds—render her speechless." Why don't they just go ahead and say it? "Diamonds—that'll shut her up."—Ron White

My wife dresses to kill. She cooks the same way.—Henny Youngman

Now that I'm married, friends ask me which form of birth control I use—rhythm? pill? condom? diaphragm? Actually, I've found that frigidity works best.—Julia Gorin

The other night, in front of my house, I saw a guy jogging naked. I said, "How come?" He said, "Because you came home early."—Rodney Dangerfield

My wife just got me into role-playing in the bedroom. I'm playing the role of a celibate monk.—Vic Alejandro

HA HA HA **Make 'Em Laugh** _____

If you do feel compelled to tell a joke after you've had a few, keep it brief. "People tend to tell jokes when they're drunk. If you're gonna do that, do a short joke, like a quick one-liner," says Jim Florentine, the voice of Special Ed and Bobby Fletcher on Comedy Central's *Crank Yankers*. "Don't tell long, drawn-out stories, 'cause no one has the attention span for it, and you'll look like an a**hole when you go on for ten minutes and everyone's just staring at you."

My girlfriend gets mad at me because I still play video games. Women will never understand this. We play for the suspension of disbelief; it's stuff we'll never get to do in real life. It's the same reason she watches those TV weddings.
—Tony Liberati

I bought my wife a new car. She called and said, "There was water in the carburetor." I said, "Where's the car?" She said, "In the lake."—Henny Youngman

My marriage works because we don't take each other for granted. Every morning for 14 years I ask my wife how she takes her coffee. It's a small thing, but it is annoying.—Jonathan Katz

Instead of getting married again, I'm going to find a woman I don't like and give her a house.—Lewis Grizzard

Who Made the Funny? _____

When Lewis Grizzard died in 1994, he was cremated. Then, per his wishes, some of his ashes were scattered at the 50-yard line of Sanford Stadium, the home field of the University of Georgia football team.

I finally found the right woman. Finally found a wife. Turns out she's from New Zealand—which is why I had trouble finding her. She started off on the other side of the damn earth.—Jake Johannsen

A study says that being married actually reduces the risk of heart attack—or anything exciting, really.—Jonathan Katz

You have to look at marriage like you've been in a car accident and lost the use of your legs. You can't get around the way you used to, but now you get to have a really cool van.—Jeremy Greenberg

My parents just celebrated their forty-third anniversary. If I get a divorce, my parents don't wanna hear that. "Things get rough, you just throw in the towel? Let me tell you something—your father and I had a shoot-out. He took one in the arm. Harry, show her where I shot you. See, that's love, right there. He was wrong, I shot him— you move on."—Wanda Sykes.

My wife had a mirror put over her bed. She told me she likes to watch herself laugh.—Rodney Dangerfield

I think my wife was having an affair. I came home unexpectedly and found a smoldering cigarette sitting out by the Jacuzzi. I said, "Hey ... where did this Jacuzzi come from?" She was sleeping with a plumbing contractor.—Bruce Cherry

I'm divorced. I had such a tough time letting go when she left me. She cleaned out the house. There was no electricity, no running water, no furniture, no food, no phone, nothing. I'm sitting on a mattress with a candle burning, going, "She'll be back. She's just trying to teach me a lesson."—Rich Vos

Before marriage, there is 69. After marriage, it looks more like a 96.—Julia Gorin

HA HA HA Make 'Em Laugh

How Not to Introduce a Joke, by Tim Cavanagh

The joke experience actually begins before you start telling the joke. So be aware of what you say to introduce it:

When You Say ...	Your Listeners' Visceral Response Is ...
"I heard the funniest joke ..."	"The funniest joke? I doubt it."
"You're not Catholic, are you? ..."	"I'm offended already."
"Did you hear the one about the cat? ..."	"The cat joke. Hmm, that narrows it down."
"I hope I'm not too drunk to get through this joke ..."	"I hope you don't projectile vomit."
"Did you hear the one about the guy who fell out of a tree while raking leaves?"	"That's the punch line, you moron."
"Now, I've got nothin' against gay people ..."	"Stop!"

My wife and I have been married five years. The sex is still shockingly good, although it's obviously not like when we first met—there are nights when I have to fake an erection.—Dennis Miller

When you get married, you say, "till death do you part." The divorce rate is sky high, so everybody's just lying their asses off. Why don't we just come clean? Instead of saying, "till death do you part," let's just go, "I'll give it a shot." —Wanda Sykes

My mother buried three husbands—and two of them were just napping.—Rita Rudner

I have an uncle who's been married 35 years. I said, "Where are you going on summer vacation?" and his wife said, "The Bahamas." He just moved his lips. It was like a ventriloquist act. They're a year away from her just sticking her hand up his ass and working his head.—Garry Shandling

My wife and I went to Disneyworld on our honeymoon. It was a big mistake. The last thing you want your new bride to hear when you're getting undressed in front her is, "It's a Small World After All."—Mike Morse

In marriage at some point, I don't care how powerful the initial attraction, the lust is replaced by this incredible longing for sleep.—Jonathan Katz

Money

The Best Things in Life Are Free—with Just a Quick, Three-Hour Tour of This Magnificent Timeshare

My grandfather always said, "Don't watch your money, watch your health." So one day while I was watching my health, someone stole my money. It was my grandfather. —Jackie Mason

Money cannot buy health, but I'd settle for a diamond-studded wheelchair.—Dorothy Parker

The phone rings, and a voice on the other end says, "How would you like to be this year's vodka man?" I said, "No. I'm an artist, I do not do commercials. I don't pander. I don't drink vodka, and if I did I wouldn't drink your product." He said, "Too bad. It pays $50,000." I said, "Hold on. I'll put Mr. Allen on the phone."—Woody Allen

Blatant Lies

Mason caught his grandfather after a three-day manhunt and exacted his revenge, subjecting the man to four days of nonstop kvetching. Mason's grandfather was buried in a quiet ceremony.

The IRS sent back my tax return saying I owed $800. I said "If you'll notice, I sent a paper clip with my return. Given what you've been paying for things lately, that should more than make up the difference."—Emo Philips

The stock market's not doing well for me, especially my mutual funds: the Stunted Growth Fund and the Malignant Growth Fund. I think it's the broker I'm using: Infidelity. —Craig Sharf

I got something in the mail today. It said, "This is not a bill." I opened it up, it said, "That was the envelope—*this* is the bill."—Brian Kiley

A man who won the $100 million lottery said he was gonna go back to his job teaching. Apparently he doesn't teach math.—George Wallace

Whatever you do, make sure it makes you happy. If it don't make you happy, take it out yo' life. Pray over it and let it go. That's why I don't pay credit card bills no more. I prayed over it and Jesus told me, "Let it go."—Dominique

If you want to know what God thinks of money, just look at the people he gave it to.—Dorothy Parker

HA HA HA **Make 'Em Laugh**

You don't talk the same way to your friends that you do to your grandmother, do you? Then don't tell them the same joke, or at least not the same joke the same way. "In order to know what would make your audience laugh, you probably have to know a little bit about them and speak their language," says comedian Wendy Liebman. Be sure you understand if your potential audience is the type who would relate to and enjoy the joke you plan to tell. (And if your grandmother *is* the type to enjoy the same jokes as your raunchy friends—well, rock on, Grandma.)

I came home one night, and my house was robbed. I called the insurance company. They said, "What type of policy are you carrying with us?" I said, "Fire and theft." They said, "You have the wrong policy. You should have had fire *or* theft." According to their claims, the only way you can get any money is if the house is robbed *while* it's burning down.—Alan King

I had eight credit cards, every one of them maxed out. I lost my wallet, and I didn't give a sh*t. You can charge something with these? God bless you, go right ahead. —John Henton

I went to see a psychic the other day. I could tell right away that she was no damn good. She took one of my checks. —Dwight York

You think when they asked George Washington for his ID, he just took out a quarter?—Steven Wright

Gas prices are so high that people driving Hummers have other things to worry about other than penis size.—Ben Schwartz

Movies

If the Screen Really Was Silver, Mickey Rourke Would Look His Age

The number one movie over the weekend was *X-Men*. It took in over $50 million! That's outstanding, considering that no one at the movie had a date.—Craig Kilborn

Hollywood does what it does for financial reasons alone. If Hitler walked into this town and said, "I've figured out how to do *Die Hard* in a hot-air balloon!" he'd have a three-picture deal before you could say Carrot Top.—Dennis Miller

The cold weather continues to spread across the United States. In fact, down south it was so cold that people were shaking like Jerry Falwell watching *Brokeback Mountain*. —Jay Leno

The light saber used by Mark Hamill in the original *Star Wars* sold for $200,600 in an auction. For $10 more, Mark Hamill will come over and clean your gutters.—Ben Schwartz

Bill Cosby was accused of drugging and molesting 12 women. Cosby insists that he never molested the women, saying that drugging them was the only way to get them into theaters to watch the *Fat Albert* movie, thereby doubling the film's box office take.—Larry Getlen

It was reported that Guy Ritchie has cast his wife Madonna in a small walk-on role in his new movie, *Revolver*. Madonna will play the part of the woman who ruins the film.—Tina Fey

Hackity Hack

There's nothing sadder than watching someone make a joke on the backs of the vulnerable. Ever watch a terrible comedian make a joke at the expense of an old person or someone handicapped? It's a sad, pathetic sight and the mark of a sure amateur or hack. Someone like Jon Stewart, on the other hand, makes his jokes at the expense of those in power. It's a good model to follow in your own joke-telling. "An enormous number of jokes are told at the expense of the weak, by people who are worried about whether they're strong," says *This Is Spinal Tap's* Ian Faith, Tony Hendra. "The best jokes are told by the supposedly weak about the supposedly strong."

Today, the controversial new movie *Brokeback Mountain* opens, about two gay cowboys. Apparently, you can tell the characters are gay because they're dressed like cowboys. —Conan O'Brien

Did you see *The Piano?* About somebody getting his fingers chopped off. I said, if this is what *The Piano* is about, I'm not going to see *The Nutcracker.*—George Wallace

Brokeback Mountain leads the SAG Awards with four nominations. The biggest one, the best male performance by a male lead in another male lead.—Jay Leno

I watched a movie called *The Greatest Story Ever Told.* It got two stars.—Chad Lehrman

I rented *The Panic Room*—the story of a 15-year-old boy whose mom walks in his room while he's jerking off. Then I saw *XXX*—a film about how Vin Diesel signs his name. —Larry Getlen

Every western movie you ever seen, a lady has a baby on the prairie, and there's always one cowboy who takes charge. He goes, "All right, we need some soap, some rags, some buckets of hot water." "She gonna have the baby here?" "No, we're gonna wash the truck and take her to town."—John Fox

The big winners at the Golden Globes were *Brokeback Mountain, Capote,* and *Transamerica.* All movies with gay themes. I think this is God's way of punishing Pat Robertson.—Jay Leno

Did you watch the Golden Globes? They were so long that Dick Cheney taped it and is using it to torture detainees. —David Letterman

A movie theater in Utah abruptly canceled a screening of the movie *Brokeback Mountain.* They felt it was inappropriate for the community standards. Instead they ran *Deliverance.*—Jay Leno

President Bush was asked by someone in the audience if he'd seen *Brokeback Mountain.* The president said he hadn't seen it, but he'd be happy to talk about ranching. Then he added, "*Ranching* still means gay sex, right?"—Conan O'Brien

Music

I Believe in Music—Of Course, I Also Believe That Drinking Certain Brands of Beer Makes Me More Attractive to Girls

I don't like country music—but don't mean to denigrate those who do. For those who like country music, *denigrate* means "to put down."—Bob Newhart

Eminem should lighten up. My mom was a bitch, too, but I don't go writing songs about it.—Triumph the Insult Comic Dog

Heavy metal bands can be sued because people's kids commit suicide. Does this mean I can sue Dan Fogelberg for making me into a pussy in the mid-seventies? I dated Catholic girls. Between him and James Taylor, I didn't have sex till I was 31.—Denis Leary

Who Made the Funny?

When he's not being surly onstage, Denis Leary is actually quite the charitable guy. His Leary Firefighters Foundation has raised more than $6 million to provide firefighters with the most up-to-date equipment and training. Learn more at www.learyfirefighters.org.

The music I listen to is mostly cult classics—like "Helter Skelter."—Geoff Holtzman

I know for a fact that Axl Rose can still belt out the tunes. I hear him every other Wednesday when he's skimming my neighbor's pool. —Dennis Miller

My sister joined a hip-hop dance group called "Funk Without Limit." It sounds like athlete's foot to me. I'm concerned they might war with a rival group, "Ointment."—Joanna Parson

They just released the complete works of Johann Sebastian Bach. It's 179 CDs—that's 10 straight 24-hour days of music. What occasion would you ever have to listen to that? "Hey guys, I'm just going to toss on some background music while I grow a beard."—Jesse Joyce

You know, if you play New Kids On The Block albums backward ... they sound better. Gives them that edge they're missing.—Bill Hicks

I keep a lighter in my back pocket all the time. I'm not a smoker; I just really like certain songs.—Demitri Martin

This week the Supreme Court will hear a case about Internet music piracy. Regardless of the outcome, one thing is certain: it will be the first time Chief Justice William Rehnquist has said the word *Hoobastank*.—Craig Ferguson

I saw a band in New York City. The singer got on the microphone and said, "All right, how many people feel like human beings tonight?" And then he said, "All right, how many people feel like animals?" And everybody cheered after the "animals" part. But I cheered after the "human beings" part, because I did not know there was a second part to the question.—Mitch Hedberg

HA HA HA Make 'Em Laugh

In Jon Macks's book *How to Be Funny* (Simon & Schuster, 2003), Jay Leno relays a sage piece of advice about expectations. However big a laugh you think you'll get, cut your expectations by half. "If you have a great joke, count on a good laugh," says Leno, and "if you expect a good laugh, count on a chuckle."

I'm telling you, my singing voice is in full bloom. Which explains why my neighbors need a Claritin.—Joanna Parson

So you're The Strokes, yes? Look how cute you are. You're like the Monkees with a drinking problem.—Triumph the Insult Comic Dog (to The Strokes)

I used to have a record collection, but now somebody else has a bigger one.—Geoff Holtzman

Dave Matthews Band and Hootie and the Blowfish—never has a CD purchase spoken more volumes about a person. You don't rock, as a rule, but when you do, it's in a very VH1 kinda way. You like the show *Friends* a *lot*, and you wish that Meg Ryan and Tom Hanks could star in *every* movie—not just as a loving couple, but as a functionally retarded couple.—Janeane Garofalo

Parents and Parenthood

The Reason You're Like This, *Part Deux*

Don't you think we should stop celebrating spawning? It's not a virtue anymore. There's six billion people. Every Mother's Day, they give an award to some maniac who sh*tted out 20 kids and then they have the nerve to say it's a miracle from God. It's a miracle from Pfizer.—Bill Maher

I want to have children, but my friends scare me. One of my friends told me she was in labor for 36 hours. I don't even want to do anything that feels good for 36 hours. —Rita Rudner

When my wife first got pregnant, I didn't realize. She wasn't feeling well. I didn't think anything of it. Then she started throwing up every morning and putting on weight. Then it occurred to me—she's got a drinking problem. —Brian Kiley

My wife and I have a son now—we had a child so we could pre-board airplanes. I don't wanna say my wife's biological clock was big, but Harold Lloyd was hangin' off the minute hand.—Dennis Miller

I've been married 18 years. It did not dawn on me until year five that she was training me. We were in bed, reading, and my wife said, "I'm hot." I closed *my* book. Got out of bed. Turned on the ceiling fan. I was almost back to the bed, and I went, "*Whoooaaaa*." I wasn't hot.—Jeff Foxworthy

I have a 5-year-old daughter and twin 2-year-old boys. Two 2-year-olds at my house. I make excuses to get out. I offer myself up. "You need anything from anywhere? Anything from the motor vehicle bureau? Let me register something. It's on my way."—Ray Romano

I got the greatest mother in the world, Joyce Underwood. I love her. Black mothers are always on your side. I could kill three people, and she would go, "What did they do to you, baby?"—Sheryl Underwood

HA HA HA   Make 'Em Laugh

If you're telling a joke at a party or other crowded affair and your audience gets momentarily distracted—pause. No sense talking on if they're not listening. Don't say, "Hey, I'm over here," or look annoyed. Just pause exactly where you were when you lost them. In a few seconds, they'll hopefully look back. If they do, and seem like they're ready for the rest of the joke, pick up right where you left off. If they break into discussion groups and it seems you've lost them, cut your losses and move on. Once momentum is gone for good, there's no fighting it. There will be other jokes and other audiences.

No kids, don't have any kids. Kids, c'mon. If I want something that's mine forever that I can't control, I'll get another credit card.—Nick Griffin

I have twin boys. One overly sensitive mom told me, "You know, you shouldn't dress your boys the same. They're individuals." I guess she's right. So now, I always dress one of them as a girl.—Kerri Louise

Last night at bedtime, my 8-year-old told me he hates his teacher; she's an idiot; and she's out to get him—which is the last thing you wanna hear when your kids are home-schooled.—Brian Kiley

I think I'd be a good mother. Maybe a little overprotective. Like, I would never let the kid out—of my body.—Wendy Liebman

I think kangaroos have a good deal. I like that pouch setup. I'd have a baby if it would mature in a handbag.—Rita Rudner

Talking to kids is hard. My son asked me, "Dad, where do babies come from?" I said, "You know, son, my dad never told me, but I'm gonna tell you straight up. Mommy bends over like this. Here, just watch the tape. You're on it. Sorta. Good swimmer. Proud of ya, boy."—Basil White

I did everything a father should do for the preparation for my baby. I went to Lamaze classes. My job was to remind my wife to breathe. Think about that for a second; you realize just how worthless I am in this thing. When was the last time you had to be reminded to breathe? That's like saying, "Digest!" or "When I put my fingers in your eye, blink!"—Robert Klein

Always be nice to your children, because they are the ones who will choose your rest home.—Phyllis Diller

My mother has always been a very cautious person. She was in her high school marching band. She played the rape whistle.—Todd Levin

I wanted to get some edible underwear, but I accidentally got the kind that makes you kill your father and marry your mother.—Myq Kaplan

I'm very loyal in a relationship. Even with my mom. I don't look at other moms. I don't go, *I wonder what her macaroni and cheese tastes like.*—Garry Shandling

Make 'Em Laugh _____

When not ruining movies with that god-awful rating system, former Motion Picture Association of America head Jack Valenti was a frequent public speaker and, previously, speechwriter for President Lyndon Johnson. In his book *Speak Up with Confidence*, Valenti explains that if comedy is timing, then the key to timing can be as little as a split-second pause. "It is the pause, the 2–3-second hesitation between the speaking of one sentence and the beginning of another, that can become a speaker's high moment," writes Valenti. "Just before you deliver a punch line ... pause."

It gets harder to have children when you get older. Not only having them, but naming them, 'cause by the time you're in your 30s, every name you think of reminds you of someone you hate. We have to hurry—we're down to Jethro and Nefertiti.—Rita Rudner

Like a lot of dads, it's my dream that my son will grow up to be the next Tiger Woods. I don't even care if he plays golf. I just want him to marry a hot Swedish model.—Brian Kiley

I'm the proud father of two little girls, and my brother has three girls. My mother has nine grandchildren—all girls. I live in the Estrogen Ocean, in the middle of the nekkid Barbie Woodstock, nekkid Barbies as far as the eye can see. There are days I have fantasies about being G.I. Joe on a 3-day pass.—Jeff Foxworthy

Blatant Lies _____

Foxworthy, already the best-selling recorded comedian of all time, was recently given another honor for this joke. He is now the proud recipient of the "Most Disturbing Visualization Award" from the American Psychiatric Institute.

If a woman has to choose between catching a fly ball and saving an infant's life, she will choose to save the infant's life without even considering if there is a man on base. —Dave Barry

My mom suffered from depression. It sucked, because every Thanksgiving, she'd only put the turkey's head in the oven.—Mike Morse

My wife and I just bought a video camera, and we've been videotaping our kids a lot. We think they've been stealing from us.—Brian Kiley

> **Make 'Em Laugh**
>
> "Always remember that specific is better than general," says veteran comedy writer Jon Macks in his book *How to Be Funny*. He further points out that, "Saying you went to Hooters is always funnier than saying you went to a strip club."

I have a 16-year-old daughter. She's growing up, and I don't know when it happened. I came home the other day and I'm helping my wife fold clothes. I pick up a little pair of skimpy underwear, and I go, "Hey, hey, when you gonna wear these for me?" She goes, "I can't. They're your daughter's."—Bill Engvall

I remember my dad told me, "You don't know what it's like to be a real man until you hold your baby in your arms." And I thought, that sounds cool, but I don't buy it. But then I got my own baby, and I'm holding her, and I did, I felt like a real man—'cause I could crush that kid. —Louis C. K.

When my daughter made me a grandma, I wrote her a poem:

> Roses are red
> Violets are blue
> Now you will know
> What I just went through.—Linda Sweig

What really chaps my *ss are the people who take fertility drugs. When you see them interviewed, they say, "It's a blessing. God wanted us to have eight healthy 2-pound babies." Well, I say, what about when they weren't able to have kids in the first place? How could God be any clearer than that? That was a sign from God that your particular line is one he's trying to phase out.—Laura Kightlinger

Don't tell your kids you had an easy birth or they won't respect you. For years, I used to wake up my daughter and say, "Melissa, you ripped me to shreds. Now go back to sleep."—Joan Rivers

If you were to open up a baby's head—and I am not for a moment suggesting that you should—you would find nothing but an enormous drool gland.—Dave Barry

We had a teacher's conference, and every time the teacher pointed out one of my son's faults, it coincidentally happens to be one of my faults. "He's a terrible listener." "I see." "And he daydreams all the time." "Uh huh." "And he puts everything off till the last minute." I'm like, "Does he also make bad financial decisions?"—Brian Kiley

I have twin 2-year-old boys, and they're cute no matter what, because they're 2. But when they become adults, I hope they're handsome, because if they're even slightly ugly, there's two of them. If you see one slightly ugly man, that's no big deal. But if you see that same ugliness right behind him? "Look at that. I didn't think he was that ugly until I saw it again."—Ray Romano

My son's 2 and a half now, always active, always moving, working, eager to please. I just wanna lean in and go, "Whoa, whoa, whoa—you've got the job. Kick back, take a poop, unwind. You're here."—Dennis Miller

My dad was a real leather-necked hell-raiser. He actually bombed Germany during the war … the Korean War. The Germans were understandably upset.—Bruce Cherry

When we were trying to have a baby, every day I would take my wife's temperature, and every time it was 99 or above, we'd make love. This went on for 3 months, until she caught me—stirring my coffee with the thermometer.—Brian Kiley

> **Hackity Hack**
>
> Reason number two not to say, "Stop me if you've heard this before"—it's old hat. John Marshall, writer for Chris Rock, Colin Quinn, and others, puts it bluntly: "'Stop me if you've heard this before' is as out-of-date as 'groovy' or 'jive turkey.'"

Every family has one person who's pleasant all the time. In my family it's my father. He could say something nice about anybody. I got sick of it one day. I said, "All right dad, what about John Wayne Gacy. Killed 35 people, buried them under the house. What about him?" "Well, he's not lazy. And he's a homeowner."
—Larry Amoros

In the natural childbirth classes my wife and I took, the birthing process was represented by a hand puppet being pushed through a sock. So at the actual birth I was shocked to see all this blood. The thing I had prepared myself for was a lot of lint.—Steve Skrovan

I come from a long line of cowards. My family crest is a picture of a mighty lion disappointedly eating a meal it didn't order.—Todd Levin

I was almost thrown out of my daughter's basketball game for yelling at the ref. After the game, the coach is like, "You gotta calm down. Your daughter's here to have a good time." I'm like, "What good time is my daughter gonna have when her daddy loses $1,500?"—Rich Vos

Parents always make ridiculous predictions about their kids. The day my little boy was born, a friend of mine called me. His little girl was born the day before, and he said, "Who knows? Maybe they'll end up getting married." My little boy's a day old. His daughter's 2 days old. He's not gonna marry someone twice his age.—Brian Kiley

I'm from a very large family. Nine parents.—Jim Gaffigan

My wife and my mother-in-law are trying on bathing suits. My mother-in-law walks out in her bathing suit, my youngest daughter says, "Gamma, you shouldn't draw on your legs with a blue magic marker."—Jeff Foxworthy

There's one word they never use in the Lamaze class—*pain.* They refer to it as "discomfort." Discomfort, to me, is, "This mosquito bite is giving me a lot of discomfort," or "This underwear will simply never do." But, *"Noooooo! I can't go through with it!"* is not discomfort to me.—Robert Klein

My parents were typical Jewish parents—always putting pressure on me, always using Jewish guilt. My dad had a bumper sticker on his car that said, "If my son worked just a little bit harder, I, too, would have an honor roll student at Jefferson High School."—Joel Chasnoff

My mom had her backseat driver's license revoked. Got caught giving out advice while intoxicated.—Craig Sharf

Make 'Em Laugh

When telling a joke, keep it as conversational as possible. "Comics create the illusion that they are just talking, while people telling a joke go, 'I'm going to tell you a joke,'" notes popular comedian Eugene Mirman. You would do well to make your jokes seem like part of the conversation, not a separate and larger entity.

We picked out old-fashioned names for our kids. Our little boy is Hunter. And our little girl is Gatherer.—Brian Kiley

My mother always told me I wouldn't amount to anything because I procrastinate. I told her, "Just wait."—Judy Tenuta

One of my favorite TV shows of all time is *I Dream of Jeannie*. My mom reminds me of Jeannie because she lives in a bottle, too.—Debbie Shea

My mother always lied to us kids. One time she told us that the music the ice cream truck plays is to let us know they are out of ice cream.—Terry Johnson

When you see a big family, that's not a family that loves children—they're trying to get one that's right. They get one that's right, and they cut them off from the rest. "You're gonna be all right; forget them—they're not gonna make it."—Sinbad

Why do new parents send out cards when they have a baby telling you how big the baby is? I'm not going to sew the kid a pair of pants. I got one card: "It's a boy! 7 pounds, 4 ounces, 19 inches!" I wrote back: "I just put up some shelves! 60×24×15! When are you gonna come see them?"—Jason Reich

I had dinner with my dad tonight and made a classic Freudian slip. I meant to say, "Can you pass me the salt, please," but it came out, "You prick, you ruined my childhood."—Jonathan Katz

Who Made the Funny?

Before starting his stand-up career in the early 1980s, Jonathan Katz was a songwriter and musician, and in 1979 served as the musical director for another famous stand-up comic—Robin Williams.

My dad used to say all the time, "I slept wrong." I'd be like, "How did you f*ck that up? That's just a lay-down thing, isn't it?" They don't even put instructions on a bed, that's how simple it is. You got a pillow there to remind you where your head would go, but even if you did that wrong, your feet would be there. That'd be it.—Greg Behrendt

Last week, we brought our kids to the art museum. And we're looking at the paintings, and every time they see a nipple, they have to point and laugh. 'Cause they're at that age where they have to copy everything I do.—Brian Kiley

I asked my 11 year old the other day, "You want me to help you with your homework?" She started laughing. She said, "Daddy, I can fail on my own."—Rich Vos

I have something of an Oedipus Complex. Whenever I'm around my mother, I want to blind myself by jabbing sharp needles into my eyes.   Jason Reich

They say people with pets live longer. So I'm trying to figure out a way to get rid of my mother's cat.—Debbie Shea

Know how to get a grown kid out of your house? They can't take the parents naked. While he's eating breakfast, just walk in the kitchen naked. Smack your wife on the butt—"Your mom's a freak!" They will run out your house and never come back. —Sinbad

My twins are finally sleeping through the night. Well, I don't know if they are, but I am.—Kerri Louise

Like any parent, I want my kid to have all the advantages in life that I never had, so we started putting money aside—for his hair weave.—Brian Kiley

My dad's a doctor, and he had the worst handwriting. He wrote me a note once excusing me from gym class. I gave it to my teacher. She gave me all of her money.—Rita Rudner

I have good kids. I don't spank them. Don't have to spank them. I find that waving the gun around gets the same job done.—Denis Leary

Pets

Rubbing His Nose in It

With my dog I don't get no respect. He keeps barking at the front door. He don't want to go out. He wants me to leave.—Rodney Dangerfield

The ASPCA has filed a criminal complaint against a man who was keeping tropical fish in a moving blender. The man says it is true, but that he never turns the blender above "mix." The ASPCA claims he's had it up to "whip" and "purée" several times.—George Carlin

I had a professor who said that man's ability to use language makes him the dominant species on the planet. Maybe so, but I think there's one other thing that separates us from the animals—we aren't afraid of vacuum cleaners.—Jeff Stilson

I was riding a horse, and its leg was broken, so I had to shoot it. Everybody on the carousel freaked out.—Tom Cotter

Dogs can't wait to get in the car, and they can't wait to get out of the car. I think you can let them in one side of the car and leave the door open, and they'd run right through. I don't think you'd have to leave the driveway.—Garry Shandling

I bought my grandmother a seeing-eye dog. But he's a little sadistic. He does impressions of cars screeching to a halt. —Larry Amoros

A man who had a heart attack while he was alone in his house was saved when his dog brought him the phone so he could call for help. However, it should be noted that for every one of these heartwarming stories, there's a million others where the dog just sits there like a moron and watches you die.—Tina Fey

Experts say the way your animals behave around the house can sometimes predict earthquakes. I believe it. The night before the last big earthquake in Los Angeles, my German Shepherd took the car keys and drove to Arizona.—Gene Perret

The annual cat festival began today in Belgium. It got off to a rocky start. Right at the beginning, somebody turned on a vacuum cleaner and cleared the place out.—Jay Leno

I have nothing against dogs. I just hate rugs that go squish-squish.—Phyllis Diller

They say dog is man's best friend. Well, that was until man discovered drugs.—Bob Reinhard

I found out why cats drink out of the toilet. My mother told me it's because the water is cold in there. And I'm like, how did my mother know that?—Wendy Liebman

This one friend said to me, "You know what, Jake? Dogs are never depressed." What kind of advice would a dog give you? "Have you tried lying in the sun until you're really hot, then going to lie in the shade? Feels pretty good." —Jake Johannsen

I took my dog in for a cat scan. They found three in his stomach.—Myq Kaplan

Some stories are really difficult to pull off. Next time you wanna talk about your dog, if in your dog story your dog doesn't explode or speak Spanish, maybe you don't tell it. —Greg Behrendt

Hackity Hack

If you love telling jokes but only know a few by heart, don't be greedy. Tell the jokes you know, and don't bother with the rest. "Just have a couple of favorite ones, rehearse them, and do what you gotta do," says comedian Jim Florentine. "People hear a joke and then 3 days later they wanna repeat it. It's a 4-minute joke, and they forget half of the thing in the middle. I wouldn't do it if I didn't know the joke."

I was walking a dog in Times Square, and this cop stopped me. He was like, "What the hell are you doing? You can't bring animals here." And then he rode off on his horse. —Jeremy Hsu

When I play with my friend's dog, I feel like I'm cheating on my dog. I've got dog hair all over me, and my dog goes, "Where the hell have you been?" I'm like, "I was at the barbershop. This is human hair … all right. I threw the ball once."—Garry Shandling

I was watching *Pet Emergency* on Animal Planet and a dog was in the hospital for smashing into a full-length mirror. The good news is he's all right. The bad news is he now has 49 years bad luck.—Tony Liberati

My dog is blind. His name is Blind Spot.—Craig Sharf

Remember, if you want to love your dog or cat, have him spayed or neutered first.—Greg Volk

A woman in Auburn, Washington, was injured when an explosion ripped apart a storage container, freeing hundreds of her exotic flying squirrels. Viewers can see scenes from this incident in the new film, *Bullwinkle Goes to Hell*.—Larry Getlen

I was kissing my dog on the face, saying "You're a good boy," and he was licking me and getting into it, and we both got homosexual panic at the same moment. "Does this count?" "No, no, we're different species, it's all right. But we should just shake from here on out."—Garry Shandling

Physical Fitness

My Body Is a Temple—My Mind, the Ark of the Covenant—My Spirit, the, Um ... Ghost of Poseidon? HELP ME, METAPHOR POLICE!

Now everybody's doing yoga. That's not for me. If I want my legs behind my head, I'll just go to jail.—Dave Attell

Being in California and being fat, I'm trying to get into this California life. I went to the beach the other day. Every time I laid down, someone tried to push me back into the water.—Louie Anderson

Big people, now, if you fly Southwest Airlines, you have to buy two seats. Problem is— they're not together.—Robin Williams

Who Made the Funny?

Louie Anderson was given his start in the business by a true comedy pioneer. When he won the 1981 Midwest Comedy Competition, the host of the event was the king of the one-liners, Henny Youngman, who was so impressed with young Louie that he gave him a job as a writer.

Jews don't exercise. If God had wanted me to bend over, he would have put diamonds on the floor.—Joan Rivers

I finished the New York City marathon in under an hour. It would have been faster, but I had to stop for gas.—Craig Sharf

I've been trying to get in shape by doing 20 sit-ups every morning. It may not sound like a lot, but you can only hit that snooze alarm so many times.—J. Scott Homan

Who Made the Funny?

Kevin James spent his high school years as a wrestler. While he didn't stick with it, one of his high school teammates did—pro-wrestling star Mick Foley.

When you're big, you don't need a reason to sweat. My friends cannot grab a hold of this concept. They come up to me all the time, "Geez, what are you doing, jumping rope in the attic?" "No, I peeled an orange … about an hour ago. Why?"—Kevin James

One of the airlines, Southwest, is charging people double if they can't fit in a seat. I don't think that's fair. You get a big fat guy can't fit in a seat, just prop him right in front of the cockpit door. No one's gonna get through him. You picture a guy pulling a knife, running up there and seeing a fat guy, he's like, "By the time I cut through him, my blade's gonna be dull."—Jim Florentine

I'm not into jogging. Not because I'm against the jogging, but joggers are always the ones who find the dead body. You never find a dead body sitting at home eating ice cream, watching porno, do you? "I was changing tapes, and I saw a foot. I dropped the lube and called the cops."
—Dave Attell

Guys will "spot" you at the gym. But they yell at you, like "All you! All you!" I'm struggling, like "Some you! It's too heavy! A little bit me, mostly you!"—Ted Alexandro

When you have a fat friend, there are no see-saws. Only catapults.—Demitri Martin

The airline industry in the United States spent an extra $375 million over the last 10 years on jet fuel because Americans are more overweight than they used to be. Americans are so fat now that we have to chip in for gas on a jet. I wouldn't be surprised to find out that days are now 26 hours long because Americans are so fat that the earth is rotating slower.—Jesse Joyce

The other day I had a really hard time hauling a heavy garbage bag to the trash. The really sad thing was, the bag wasn't near breaking. This means one thing—I am weaker than a Glad Bag.—Bob Reinhard

Pilates is not really exercise. It's a bunch of already skinny bitches pointing their legs in the air and pretending they're 5-year-old ballerinas. If they had a class like that for men, you'd go to the gym, oil yourself up, look in the mirror, and just go, "Flex! Flex! You are so butch!"—Jennifer Dziura

Politics and World Events

The Leaders We Deserve

We have a two-party system. The Democratic Party, which is a party of no ideas, and the Republican Party, which is a party of bad ideas. A Republican stands up in Congress and says, "I got a really bad idea!" And the Democrat says, "And I can make it sh*ttier."—Lewis Black

Bill Clinton has spent a lot of time jogging around Washington. I'm not saying he doesn't look too good in his jogging shorts, but the Lincoln statue has its hands over its eyes.—Bob Hope

History buffs probably noted the reunion at a Washington party a few weeks ago of three ex-presidents: Carter, Ford, and Nixon—See No Evil, Hear No Evil, and Evil.—Bob Dole

Today was President Bush's inauguration, and security was tight in Washington, D.C. The Bush twins were stopped by margarita-sniffing dogs.—David Letterman

Hackity Hack

It's the hackiest, most overworn joke form in the world at this point, but people won't stop using it—the Top Ten List. "I can give you nearly a dozen funny-ish reasons why not to, but I won't," says Mark Katz, former joke writer for President Bill Clinton. "There is only one person who walks the planet today who can hold a Top Ten List in his hand and not seem like an amateur, and his name is David Letterman."

If anybody comes up to you and says, "My kid is a conservative. Why is that?" You say, "Remember in the sixties when we told you if you kept using drugs your kids would be mutants?"—Mort Sahl

Condoleezza Rice was confirmed by a vote of 85 to 13 despite a contentious but futile protest vote by Democrats. By the way, for a fun second-term drinking game, chug a beer every time you hear the phrase "contentious but futile protest vote by Democrats." By the time Jeb Bush is elected, you'll be so wasted you won't even notice the war in Syria.—Jon Stewart

New York City has been found to be the city least likely to help strangers. In fact, the only time New York City has helped out a stranger was when Hillary Clinton was elected to the Senate.—Conan O'Brien

HA HA HA **Make 'Em Laugh**

"Watch how your favorite comedians connect with a crowd while telling a joke," advises Comedy Central's *Premium Blend* veteran Ted Alexandro. "There's a lot more going on than the words coming out of their mouths, like pace, eye contact, and body language." Making use of the same will help you absorb your listeners in the joke.

The Chevron Corporation has reached a deal to buy Texaco. The $45 billion deal will give Chevron full control of Texaco, the Caltex Corporation, and George W. Bush. —Tina Fey

President Bush says he needs a month off to unwind. Unwind? When the hell does this guy *wind?*—David Letterman

Rush Limbaugh is very popular with the homeless community in this country, 'cause there always seems to be a new refrigerator box in his trash bin.—Dennis Miller

People wanna know what President Bush knew before 9/11. I'm like, he didn't know a damn thing. Remember— he didn't get smart until after 9/11.—Wanda Sykes

You know we armed Iraq. During the Persian Gulf War, those intelligence reports would come out: "Iraq: incredible weapons—incredible weapons." How do you know that? "Uh, well … we looked at the receipts."—Bill Hicks

John Edwards announced today that he is running for president. Don't kid yourself, the guy is desperate. Today he had a queer makeover.—David Letterman

All these Enron guys and these CEOs were robbin' everybody blind. The stock market, boy. That's why I got out. I called my broker, I'm like, "Hey, put all my money in weed."—Wanda Sykes

Bill Gates was in Washington today talking to a congressional committee. He was supposed to talk about visas for skilled foreign workers and technology to improve education, but of course, these were congressmen. He wound up spending four hours answering questions about whether e-mails from a mistress can be traced.—Bill Maher

You know what's good about these Dixie Chicks' [CD] burnings? It's a wonderful, wonderful way for really stupid people to hook up. They meet, they throw some things on the fire, they talk about Vin Diesel, they tell stories about who their favorite Fox anchor is, they exchange phone numbers, and in some cases it's led to marriages.—Janeane Garofalo

The NRA has this cute little bumper sticker—"You'll get my gun when you pry it from my cold dead hands." Whatever.—Dennis Miller

Stalin killed many millions—died in his bed. Pol Pot killed 1.7 million Cambodians, died under house arrest, age 72. The reason we let them get away with it is they killed their own people. We're sort of fine with that. Help yourself. Hitler killed people next door. Stupid man. After a couple of years, we won't stand for that.—Eddie Izzard

In Washington last week, officials from the National Rifle Association met with a group of 200 high school students. There were no survivors.—Tina Fey

I am, and always have been, pro-death. I'm pro–death penalty; I'm pro-choice; I'm pro–assisted suicide; I'm pro–regular suicide—I'm for anything that gets the freeway moving faster.—Bill Maher

The CIA predicts that by the year 2020 the two biggest superpowers in the world will be China and India. Which means every day we will be bombarded ... with menus. —John Marshall

Embarrassing moment for President Bush today. He called the pope to wish him a happy Passover.—Jay Leno

Today is Veteran's Day. President Clinton celebrated this Veteran's Day just like he has every Veteran's Day. He flew to England and lit up a joint.—David Letterman

The economy is in trouble. In a speech, President Bush said that the economy is recovering from a hangover of the '90s. He also went on to say that he is recovering from his hangover from the '80s.—Conan O'Brien

The American political process—every four years, candidates running for president put together educated position papers, announce detailed policy changes, hire Ivy League advisers—and then go to Iowa to suck up to farmers.—Bill Maher

Make 'Em Laugh

"If you're going to tell a joke that's making the rounds, try to make it your own," says Firesign Theatre veteran Phil Proctor. "For instance, when I pass on a funny story in my Planet Proctor mailings, it's always trimmed, polished, and punched up as if I was actually telling it to someone."

Osama bin Laden's brother has been arrested in Paris for money laundering. I tell you, it's things like that that could give the bin Laden family a bad name.—David Letterman

Al Gore talked to the astronauts onboard the space shuttle today. Gore asked them what zero gravity is like, and they asked him what zero charisma is like.—Conan O'Brien

George W. says he reads the Bible every day. He's 56 years old—finish the book.—Gregg Rogell

You can go to Dealey Plaza, where Kennedy was assassinated, and go to the sixth floor of the Schoolbook Depository. It's a museum called "The Assassination Museum." They have the window set up to look exactly like it did on that day. And it's really accurate, 'cause Oswald's not in it.—Bill Hicks

Hackity Hack

Think you can do great impressions? Think again. "If you do impressions, ask someone you trust if you're good at it," advises popular comedian Mitch Fatel, "because everybody thinks they're good at doing somebody, and pretty much everybody's bad at it. Everybody thinks they can do Marlon Brando, everybody thinks they can do Rodney Dangerfield, and they probably can't. So don't do impressions if you can't."

President Bush is out on the campaign trail more and more. Most Republicans wanna see him serve four more years ... while the National Guard wants to see him serve at least two years.—Jay Leno

I believe that Ronald Reagan can make this country what it once was—an Arctic region covered with ice.—Steve Martin

Pope Pius XII apologized for the Spanish Inquisition. He said it was far too inquisitive. It was supposed to be the Spanish Casual Chat.—Eddie Izzard

My sister married a German. I'm at a deli with her husband, and he says, "Emo, I can't get a good bagel back in Germany." I said, "Well, whose fault is that?"—Emo Philips

Democrats look at half a glass of water and think it's half empty. Republicans look at half a glass of water and think, "Who the hell drank half my water?"—Jeff Cesario

A new poll shows that Senator Kerry's support in the South is strongest amongst blacks. Kerry's appeal to Southern blacks is obvious. He is a white man who lives far, far away.—Dennis Miller

Vice President Cheney went duck hunting in South Dakota. He wants to show that despite the fact that he has a heart condition, he's still able to bring down defenseless birds with a cannon.—David Letterman

Everybody's like, "You have to get behind your president," Well, yeah. That's a given, a**hole. We're gonna get behind the president; we're at war. That's the deal. It's not like I have a choice between him and Yosemite Sam.—Lewis Black

This week First Daughter Jenna Bush was given community service after pleading no-contest to underage drinking charges. Her father insists Jenna is going through a rebellious phase and just like him, she'll grow out of it in 27 years.—Tina Fey

It's been over a year since they graduated, but neither of the Bush twins has been able to find work. Why don't they sign up for the army? Do they hate America, or just freedom in general?—Bill Maher

President Reagan wanted to take sex education out of the schools. He said he believed sex education caused promiscuity, that if you had the knowledge, you'd use it. Hey, I took algebra. I never do math.—Elayne Boosler

Give a gun to a monkey, and let him into Charlton Heston's house. Then lock the doors, and film it through the window. They'll have to change the line to "Guns Don't Kill People, People Kill People—and monkeys do, too, if they have a gun."—Eddie Izzard

Pat Buchanan proudly says he does not believe in evolution—and he's not too sure about gravity. He thinks it might be a plot by Jews to get people to drop spare change.—Bill Maher

The military announced this week they're planning to use trained sea lions and seals to guard our ships in the Persian Gulf. That's when you know you don't have any allies—when you have to turn to other species for help. "You, fish—can you give us a hand?"—Jay Leno

HA HA HA Make 'Em Laugh

It's a cardinal rule of show biz—always leave 'em wanting more. "If people laugh at your joke, then go out on a laugh," says *Tonight Show* correspondent Mitch Fatel. "Once you get a big laugh, don't go to another joke. Give up while you're ahead."

George Bush went for 18 days on his vacation without catching a fish. I didn't know that many bass were Democrats. —Bob Hope

Jesse Jackson admitted this week to fathering a child with an employee in May 1999. Jackson said the reason he waited two years to reveal the pregnancy is because he couldn't think of a word that rhymed with "broken condom."—Jimmy Fallon

American Taliban fighter John Walker Lindh is supposedly gay. Do you know what that means? The Taliban is more tolerant than the Boy Scouts.—Jay Leno

Bush the younger has two things going for him that his father never had. One: an easy charm with regular people, and two: the power to make them disappear without a trial.—Bill Maher

I was led to believe that the Iraqi people were going to welcome us with open arms. Turns out it was just arms.—Mike Storck

I picked up a book at the mall today. I'm reading *The Rise and Fall of the Third Reich*. Fifteen hundred pages. I had to take a spotter with me to get it home. I'm not too far into the book—Hitler is still a Mary Kay rep.—Dennis Miller

Al Gore said that they market candidates the way they do dog food and soap suds, which isn't true—because you can't lie about dog food. –Bill Maher

They always throw around this term "liberal elite." And I kept thinking to myself about the Christian right: what's more elite than believing that only you will go to heaven?—Jon Stewart

Al Gore—there's some stiff body language. Guy makes Ed Sullivan look like an auto fellatio freak.— Dennis Miller

President Bush says he now wants to simplify the tax code. Only those in the blue states will pay.—David Letterman

I walk past a little gang-banger, I don't even blink. But if I see a white dude with a *Wall Street Journal*, I haul ass. Before I walk through the Arthur Anderson building, I cut through the projects—you might just lose what you have on you that day, but I ain't never been mugged of my future.—Wanda Sykes

Hillary Clinton will receive $8 million from Simon & Schuster to write her memoirs. Mrs. Clinton has said she'll use the money from the book to, quote, "Pay off all the legal bills incurred by my husband's five hummers." The book is tentatively titled *Why I Throw Things.*—Tina Fey

I love talking about the Kennedy assassination. I'm fascinated that our government could lie to us so blatantly, so obviously, for so long, and we do nothing about it. People say, "Bill, quit talking about Kennedy, man. It was a long time ago; just let it go, all right?" I'm like, "All right. Then don't bring up Jesus to me. As long as we're talking shelf life here …"—Bill Hicks

HA HA HA **Make 'Em Laugh**

"If you want to strike people as funny, tell a joke on yourself, involving something that made you look like an idiot, but never use words or phrases that suggest you are, in fact, an idiot," advises Tony Hendra, who directed the likes of John Belushi and Christopher Guest in *National Lampoon's Lemmings* stage show. A list of Hendra's idiot phrases include "so like," "like, like … then," "you won't believe what happened then …" "I was, like, so freaked," and "it was so weird, man." The intelligent joke teller will leave such phrases for Pauly Shore.

In a battle between corporate profits and the environment, the environment has about as much a chance of coming out on top as Pat Buchanan does of winning a *Soul Train* lifetime achievement award.—Dennis Miller

It's being reported that Janet Reno's campaign in Florida is low on money. I guess their Janet Reno Swimsuit Calendars aren't selling.—Conan O'Brien

If I had nickel for every time Bush has mentioned 9/11, I could raise enough reward money to go after bin Laden. —Jon Stewart

Sometimes I think war is God's way of teaching us geography.—Paul Rodriguez

Saying that evolution and intelligent design are the same because they're both theories is like saying Britney Spears and Ella Fitzgerald are the same because they're both singers.—Larry Getlen

Who Made the Funny?

Whatever Paul Rodriguez accomplishes, his son can ride rings around him. Paul Rodriguez Jr. is a champion skateboarder, and in 2004, he won a gold medal at the X Games Skateboard Street Competition.

I got into a morbid conversation with a construction worker—big guy. We start talking about nuclear war. I say, "The missiles are on their way, you have 20 minutes to live. What are you gonna do?" He says, "I am gonna f*ck anything that moves." He asked me what I was gonna do, I said, "I'm gonna try and keep perfectly still." —Jonathan Katz

John Ashcroft, in his home state, lost an election to a dead man. The voters of his state, when faced with that choice, were like, "Oooo ... that is tough. Do I go with the right wing, religious, fundamentalist nut, or the rotting, maggot-infested corpse? This is truly a lesser of two evils. Okay—gotta go with the corpse."—David Cross

We just live in a terrible time right now. We have the terrorist attacks, India and Pakistan might be going to war, and the stock market is crazy—sometimes don't you just wish you were like President Bush and knew nothing of any of this?—David Letterman

Attorney General John Ashcroft has stepped down. He wants to spend more time not dancing with his wife.—Jay Leno

President Bush is going to establish elections in Iraq. He's going to rebuild the infrastructure. He's going to create jobs. He said if it works there, he'll try it here.—David Letterman

What I love about Bill Clinton is how amazed we are that he can play that saxophone. We can't believe we actually have a president who can do something! We're just lookin' up at him, like, "He can play that! If he can speak Spanish, I'll sh*t myself!"—Dennis Miller

Please explain to me why John Kerry sounds more dickish telling the truth than Bush sounds when he's lying. How is that possible?—Jon Stewart

As soon as September 11 happened, everyone in this country had that little moment where they went, "Oh, well, that really f*cks up my plans." Everybody did it. Even the Christians were going, "Oh, now I won't be able to read to the blind woman. *F*ck!*"—Lewis Black

The radical right is so homophobic that they're blaming global warming on the AIDS quilt.—Dennis Miller

Monica Lewinsky has agreed to host a new Fox reality show called *Mr. Personality*. Lewinsky says this way, when people ask her the most degrading thing she's ever done, she'll have a new answer.—Tina Fey

There are people who think our gas consumption doesn't have anything to do with why we invade other countries. I don't understand it. People who drive a gas-guzzling SUV and put a flag on it, that's like a whore wearing a rosary.—Paul Gilmartin

Charlton Heston was re-elected president of the NRA for the third term, and they made an exception, because their charter, their constitution, says you can only have two terms. But they changed it. Ah. So constitutions can be changed … interesting.—Bill Maher

I come from a stupid family. During the Civil War, my great uncle fought for the west.—Rodney Dangerfield

Does it seem like Iraq has a more stable government than we do?—David Letterman

When they said Bush was president and then brought out Ashcroft, I went out and got me four abortions. I was like, "I'm stockin' up." The doctor said, "M'am, you're not pregnant," and I'm like, "Shut up and do your job. I'm exercising my right."—Wanda Sykes

The president has a new puppy in the White House. The Senate expects rapid confirmation.—David Letterman

Make 'Em Laugh

Some people mistake strange and inaccessible for cutting edge. Just because a joke is weird doesn't make it funny. Take it from master showman, rock legend, and radio host David Lee Roth. "There is such a thing as going too far out," says Roth. "Just because nobody understands you doesn't mean you're an artist."

Democracy means that anyone can grow up to be president, and anyone who doesn't grow up can be vice president.—Johnny Carson

President Bush is in Japan today, and the prime minister took Bush on a tour of a temple. There was an awkward moment on the tour when Bush said to the prime minister, "You don't look Jewish."—Conan O'Brien

The names of our military weapons here in the U.S. enrage me—Tomahawks, Blackhawks, and Apaches. We eradicated an entire nation of Native Americans, ripped off their names, slapped them on our bombs, and eradicated another nation. God bless America! The Australians wiped out the Aborigines, but they don't drop Didgeridoo bombs or shoot Boomerang bullets. And God forbid Germany becomes another superpower and the Fourth Reich begins. They would be armed to the teeth with Hasidic grenades and Hebe-seeking missiles.—Dan Allen

Are you watching the Olympics? They have the bobsled, the luge, and now the skeleton. One event you lie on your back, one on your stomach, the other you sit down. I don't have a punch line for this joke, but if I did—it'd have the name Clinton in it.—David Letterman

In his first news conference after being elected governor of California, Arnold Schwarzenegger promised to "clean house" in Sacramento. He also threatened to molest the energy crisis and date rape the deficit.—Tina Fey

The president is making a six-nation tour of Asia, traveling throughout the Far East to make friends. If it works, he may try it in this country.—Bob Hope

I just want to say to the French girl who dumped me—I am prepared to go it alone.—Craig Kilborn

President Bush is being criticized by right-wing groups because his Christmas cards to friends this year did not say "Merry Christmas." Instead, they said, "Sorry about the indictment."—Conan O'Brien

This weekend, the Democratic National Committee elected former governor and one-time shoe-in Howard Dean as their new party chairman. You know, there's something stirring about the peaceful transfer of no power.—Jon Stewart

Politics is the art of looking for trouble, finding it every-where, diagnosing it incorrectly, and applying the wrong remedies.—Groucho Marx

The new governor elected in the state of Minnesota is pro-fessional wrestler Jesse "the Body" Ventura. He ran on the "hookers and malt liquor" ticket.—David Letterman

A car bomb exploded in Beirut. It killed 10 innocent people and 20 guilty ones.—Craig Sharf

Ralph Nader is asking for a recount of all the votes in New Hampshire. Today an election official in New Hampshire agreed to the recount and said, "One, two ... yup, that's it."—Conan O'Brien

Make 'Em Laugh

Author Jonathan Ames is one of our premiere public story-tellers and has some advice for giving your jokes a cohesive flow and making them relatable to all who listen: "My jokes are usually in the form of embarrassing stories from my life, so I like to apply simple storytelling rules: start at the beginning and build to the end, and be real clear with the timeline and chronology of the story. Since the comedic stories I tell are about myself, this requires honesty and vulnera-bility about my toibles and neuroses. If you want to tell this kind of joke/story, don't hold back—nothing gets people laughing more than the truth."

GOP strategists hope the revelation of Kerry's wealth might debunk his status as a "man of the people" and reveal him to be a bit of a fat cat. Unlike the president, who—as we all know—before attending Andover and Yale, was a Cockney matchstick girl dying of tuberculosis.—Jon Stewart

Here's something frightening—this report came out today. It said al Qaeda had a plot to assassinate President Bill Clinton while he was in Malaysia in 1998. They were going to use a suicide fat girl.—Jay Leno

The two-party system has undergone a lot of changes from Camelot to today, from John F. Kennedy's "Ask not what your country can do for you," to Teddy Kennedy's "Let's go someplace quiet."—Bill Maher

At a Democratic fund-raiser, Barbra Streisand sang a parody of her song "The Way We Were," changing the lyrics to make fun of Republicans. In response, Vice President Dick Cheney sang a song of his own, titled, "Shut the Hell Up, You Loud-Mouth Liberal Whore." —Larry Getlen

Bush is amazing. He's against abortion but for capital punishment. Spoken like a true fisherman—throw 'em back, kill 'em when they're bigger.—Elayne Boosler

Howard Dean was criticized because during his 11 years as governor he never appointed a single black person to his Cabinet. Dean said that he tried, but in 11 years he couldn't find a single black person in Vermont.—Conan O'Brien

The Democrats seem to be basically nicer people, but they have demonstrated time and again that they have the management skills of celery.—Dave Barry

I just don't get the Arabs in the Middle East. Who'd think men who could have as many wives as they want would have the energy to go to war?—Bob Hope

The United States Central Command of the Armed Forces has asked Geraldo Rivera to leave Iraq. It should also be noted that the only three other people that the U.S. military has asked to leave Iraq are Saddam Hussein and his two sons.—Jon Stewart

The U.S. Army announced that during the first part of the 1960s, they performed LSD tests on human beings that destroyed their minds. However, they claimed that none of the victims has been promoted beyond the rank of lieutenant colonel.—George Carlin

> **Who Made the Funny?** _____
>
> If you think George Carlin and the U.S. military would be a bad match, you're right. Airman Third Class George Carlin was court-martialed from the Air Force three times, including once for getting high in the crawlway of a B-47 bomber and telling his commanding officer to go f*ck himself.

Condoleezza Rice, national security adviser. I knew that was a problem. C'mon, now, you know a black woman can't keep no secrets. She probably at the beauty parlor tellin' all our business. "Look, I can't be in here all day, we bombin' Iraq at 2. Just give me a quick pedicure, I wanna look cute when we put our foot up Saddam's ass."—Wanda Sykes

My mom said she was voting for Bush 'cause he was a God-fearing man. I said, "Well, he has a lot to fear God about."—Nick Tarr

In a speech to the Amish, President Bush said that, "I trust that God speaks through me," which sounds reassuring until you realize, that's what Courtney Love has been saying.—Jay Leno

Flag burning is truly bipartisan. What other political act annoys veterans and damages the ozone layer at the same time?—Bill Maher

Washington could not tell a lie; Nixon could not tell the truth; Reagan cannot tell the difference.—Mort Sahl

If evolution is true, then I'll be a monkey's nephew.—Craig Sharf

Here's the slogan for this country: "America—20 million illegal aliens can't be wrong."—Richard Jeni

I heard Dennis Kucinich say in a debate, "When I'm president ..." and I just wanted to stop him and say, "Dude ..."—Jon Stewart

Who Made the Funny?

One of Bobcat's earliest comedic endeavors came when he was 18. He formed a comedy troupe called "The Generic Comics" with fellow Boston comic Tom Kenny—better known today as the voice of SpongeBob SquarePants.

Oliver North always confused me, because he was in the military, but then he was dismissed. But when he went on trial, he'd wear his uniform. I've been fired from a lot of jobs, but you don't see me toolin' around in my Burger King outfit.—Bobcat Goldthwait

They don't make 'em like Hubert Humphrey anymore—but just to be on the safe side, he should be castrated anyway.—Hunter S. Thompson

Waterboarding—that's what America does to its prisoners now. Dunking them in water until they confess. Of course, you have to remember—we uncovered a lot of witches that way. So credit where credit is due.—A. Whitney Brown

There was a big salute to World War II veterans on TV, and the singers were John Schneider and Tom Wopat from *The Dukes of Hazzard*. Great. Let's honor the men who defeated Adolph Hitler with the guys who could barely outrun Sheriff Buford T. Pusser.—Larry Getlen

Why do people oppose gay marriage but still get drunk and sing "YMCA" at their own wedding?—David Ridings

If you're a parent, hold on to your hats. The federal government's gonna give you $400 for each child you have. So if you've got a thousand kids—you're on easy street. —Lewis Black

I think you should be allowed to own a Humvee. But when you go to buy it, you should be hit on the back of the neck with a roll of quarters in a sock and then wake up in Iraq with a gun and have to get the oil yourself.—Patton Oswalt

According to the latest poll, 66 percent of Americans believe Dick Cheney has been given too much power by President Bush, and the other 34 percent think President Bush has been given too much power by Dick Cheney. —Jay Leno

Donald Rumsfeld is giving the president his daily briefing. He concludes by saying, "Yesterday, three Brazilian soldiers were killed in an accident." "*Oh no!*" the president exclaims. "That's terrible!" His staff sits stunned at this display of emotion, nervously watching as the president sits, head in hands. Finally, the president looks up and asks, "How many is a Brazillion?"—Author unknown

> **HA HA HA Make 'Em Laugh**
> A joke's frame of reference must match that of the audience you're telling it to. So for example, if you're telling a joke to a crowd that's mostly 60 and over, a *Saved by the Bell* reference is probably not the best way to go.

We got the death penalty in Massachusetts. That's kind of a hassle. 'Cause now if you wanna kill somebody, you have to go up to New Hampshire or down to Rhode Island.—Barry Crimmins

You have to be either stupid or a liar for the people to like you. They can't actually think Reagan meant what he was saying. His economic theory was called trickle-down. They're actually saying, "We're pissing on you." That's the theory—"We have all the money. If we drop some—that's yours."—Bill Maher

There was a beautiful irony in the fact that we had female pilots dropping bombs on the Taliban. They should have had little pamphlets as they dropped that said, "This bomb was brought to you by Jennifer, who enjoys drinking, smoking, and premarital sex."—Paul Gilmartin

Our government told us that we could protect ourselves from a chemical attack with duct tape. The only way duct tape protects you from a chemical attack is if you have enough to wrap it around yourself and suffocate before the chemicals kill you.—Lewis Black

President Bush said that our country needs to stick together as a team. And we all know there is no "I" in "team." That must be why he calls it "Amerca."—Jeremy Hsu

Hackity Hack

Public speaking often makes people nervous, and when people are nervous, they talk faster. But Pulitzer prize–winning funnyman Dave Barry reminds us that if you tell a joke too fast, you'll kill it. "In front of a crowd, DON'T RUSH THE JOKE," screams Barry through capital letters. "Take a little time to set it up clearly, and pause a second before you deliver the punch line."

I have this feeling that whoever is elected president goes into a smoky room with the 12 industrialists who got him in there, a guy says, "Roll the film," and it's a shot of the Kennedy assassination from an angle you've never seen before. And then the lights come up, and they go to the new president, "Any questions?"—Bill Hicks

Bush did nothing about the prisoner abuse scandal for a month, then finally said, "Here's what I'm gonna do. I'm tearing down the Abu Grahib prison." Which I thought was great. Because clearly, it was the building that was the problem. So now, I'm gonna use that logic in my own life. I haven't gotten laid in a while—so, I'm tearing down my apartment.—Larry Getlen

When Hurricane Katrina struck, Continental Airlines donated all of their luggage trucks to carry the survivors. Only problem is, I've flown Continental, and they're probably going to lose those people.—Veronica Mosey

Despite his infirmities, Strom Thurmond showed up to work every day and did not miss a Senate vote in his final year, though no one is sure if a shouted "Bingo!" counted as a yea or a nay.—Jon Stewart

One time I was watching the World Series, and during the National Anthem they had a bald eagle fly around the stadium to represent our freedom. Then, at the end of the anthem, it flew back to its owner.—Bri Cowan

In Michigan, an 18-year-old high school student was elected mayor, ousting a 51-year-old incumbent. An 18 year old replacing a 51 year old. In Beverly Hills, that's called a second marriage.—Jay Leno

The Bush administration said it will classify fetuses as "unborn children" under a government-funded health program. In a related story, it was announced that the text of the president's speeches will from now on be classified as "unborn words."—Larry Getlen

Some people think there's no separation between church and state. But that can't be true, because then it would just be called "Sturch" or "Chrate."—Myq Kaplan

Last night we had Carol Moseley Braun on the program. She's explaining to me why she should be the next president of the United States. I get home that night, check the Internet, and she dropped out of the race. My guess is this whole presidential run was a ruse to get on this program. Gore did the same thing.—Jon Stewart

Governor Arnold Schwarzenegger signed a bill outlawing necrophilia in California. The law makes necrophilia a felony punishable by up to eight years in prison, with a reduced sentence of two to four years for "under the shirt, over the bra."—Jason Reich

Senator John McCain, who spent over five years in a Vietnamese POW camp, publicly released 1,000 pages of medical records. Now people are left with only one nagging question: what kind of freak has 1,000 pages of medical records?—Jon Stewart

Going to Vassar College when Bush was elected president was like living at a nudist colony if pants were elected president.—Geoff Holtzman

HA HA HA   **Make 'Em Laugh**

The key to comedy is surprise, so it's essential to not give away the surprise by signaling what comes next—especially if describing a scenario in which the main character is you. "It is crucial when telling a joke about yourself to keep a straight face," says best-selling author of *Father Joe*, Tony Hendra. "Do not laugh along with the good parts; do not nod enthusiastically before you get to the good parts; in fact, don't signal the good parts. You must maintain the fiction that, for you, the good parts were the bad parts. Lenny Bruce said, 'comedy is tragedy plus time.' You must present your own 'tragedy' (misery or humiliation) as something your audience can laugh at and will love you for."

I'm not an activist, but I did get arrested for protesting the Vietnam War. By robbing a gas station. In 1997. So the message was muddled, but it's important to stand up for what you believe in.—Bruce Cherry

The week President Reagan died, President Bush's poll numbers skyrocketed. So for a month afterward, Bush was on the phone with his advisers—"Is Gingrich sick? Scalia with a head cold, maybe? How's Dad?"—Larry Getlen

Galileo looked at the stars and said, "I think that the earth goes around the sun." And the pope was overjoyed at the truth of his words—and put him under house arrest for 20 years. That pope has been renamed, Pope Sh*t-for-Brains the Ninth.—Eddie Izzard

President Bush is on his Asian tour. He'll visit Japan, China, South Korea, Mongolia. Once again, he's skipping Vietnam.—David Letterman

I can say one nice thing about Osama bin Laden—he's a great hiker.—Jayson Cross

Hackity Hack

No matter how funny a line is, if it's told out of order, it won't work. Be sure you've not only memorized all the funny lines in your joke, but memorized them in the right order. "One common mistake is when you forget to give the listeners a key piece of information," says *Miami Herald* columnist Dave Barry, "and then, when they fail to laugh at the punch line, you say, 'Oh, I forgot to tell you: the guy had a third hand sticking out of his forehead.'"

Jesse Helms had heart surgery—so, there goes a theory of mine.—Bobcat Goldthwait

The FBI has us totally freaked out—it's yellow, it's orange, it's purple. They tell us to be on the lookout for anything unusual. Anything out of the ordinary. So I called 'em. I'd never seen a black guy on figure skates. All of a sudden, I'm the big a**hole.—Paul Gilmartin

Last quarter, the economy showed no growth. So we're now officially mired in what financial experts call a "Gary Coleman economy."—Larry Getlen

You realize Hitler only had one ball? What do you think of a man who only has one ball? You think he has two strikes against him? Maybe he's got one ball and two strikes. But Hitler only had one ball. A lot of people don't know that. They say, "Hitler, he had a lot of balls." Nope. One.—George Carlin

Vice President Dick Cheney told reporters that our nation must rise to defend the principles laid down by our founding fathers. "As a nation born in revolution, we know that our freedom came at a very high price. We have no intention now of letting it slip away," Cheney said. And then, to illustrate the strength of his resolve, he turned to a random news reporter and ate his brain.—Larry Getlen

I don't understand the whole gay-marriage controversy. Who cares? One politician actually said, "Gay marriage will lead to insurance fraud." Like we're all going to run out and take it up the butt for dental.—Eric Deskin

Saddam Hussein used to watch CNN. So on top of every other horrible thing he did, he had an illegal cable hookup. They should have told the cable company he wasn't paying his bill. They would have gone in and got him.—Garry Shandling

Put-Downs

With a Face Like That, Who Needs Enemies?

You're letting this place run down, and what's the result?
You're not getting the class of people you used to.
Why, you've got people in here now that look like you.
—Groucho Marx

Who Made the Funny?

Groucho Marx's impact on our culture was so great that when he stopped by the New York Stock Exchange for a tour one day in the 1950s—singing, dancing, and telling jokes—the Wall Street ticker was blank for 15 minutes. Groucho so enthralled the traders that he stalled the entire stock market.

What a soulful voice. You're like a white Celine Dion.
—Triumph the Insult Comic Dog (to an *American Idol* contestant)

Abe Vigoda, Freddy Roman, Alan King ... I've seen younger faces on cash.—Jeffrey Ross

She should get a divorce and settle down.—Jack Paar on Zsa Zsa Gabor

He is to acting what Liberace was to pumping iron.—Rex Reed on Sylvester Stallone

You went from being in a movie with Robert DeNiro and Dustin Hoffman to being in a TV show with Lenny Clarke and me! Next stop, Quaker State.—Adam Ferrara to Denis Leary

That singer before me. Who was it? It was very courageous of MTV to start the show with a genuine transvestite; he was very convincing. It was only his hands and his testicles that gave it away.—Borat, after an appearance by Madonna

Nervous? He's tighter than Pat Buchanan's sphincter muscle at a 4th of July soirée on Fire Island.—Dennis Miller

When you go to a nightclub and the DJ says, "Everybody say HO!" do you think you're being paged?—Ant

Donald, you're not my type. Too egomaniacal and narcissistic. I can't be involved with a man who calls out his own name when he's climaxing.—Susie Essman to Donald Trump

Not an attractive man … when he goes to the park, dogs sniff his face.—Triumph the Insult Comic Dog (about Gilbert Gottfried)

He may look like an idiot and talk like an idiot, but don't let that fool you—he really is an idiot.—Groucho Marx

HA HA HA Make 'Em Laugh

Ever find the way a joke's worded uncomfortable, and feel tempted to change it? Go ahead and give it a shot—as long as you're not messing up the punch line or making the joke longer. It's okay to try to make a joke feel more natural, because you'll be more at ease when you tell it. After all, great comedians are great because they have a unique voice. So why not add a little bit of your own voice to your jokes? "A joke that a comic does is specific to their persona," reminds veteran comedian Wendy Liebman. "When I read a great comic's joke, I can usually hear their voice in my head." Make it the same for your jokes.

Isn't it possible for them to get a real fascist instead of this guy who plays one on TV?—Mort Sahl (about Sean Hannity)

Paula Jones—this chick could make a strap-on go limp. —Bill Maher

She ran the whole gamut of emotions from A to B. —Dorothy Parker (about Katherine Hepburn)

She turned down the role of Helen Keller because she couldn't remember the lines.—Joan Rivers (about Bo Derek)

Drew Carey is to comedy what Mariah Carey is to comedy.—Jeffrey Ross

I haven't seen someone so overmatched since Mike Tyson tried to recite the alphabet.—Dennis Miller

I didn't like the play, but then I saw it under adverse conditions—the curtain was up.—Groucho Marx

Boy George is all England needs—another queen who can't dress.—Joan Rivers

So you're French and Canadian—you're obnoxious *and* dull.—Triumph the Insult Comic Dog (to a random Canadian)

Al D'Amato is a waste of an apostrophe.—Dennis Miller

She's a vacuum with nipples.—Otto Preminger (about Marilyn Monroe)

She's so old her vagina has mice.—Jeffrey Ross (about Dr. Ruth)

I never forget a face—but in your case, I'll make an exception.—Groucho Marx

How did you learn that breath control? How did you learn to sing and suck at the same time?—Triumph the Insult Comic Dog (to an *American Idol* contestant)

HA HA HA **Make 'Em Laugh**

Tony Hendra, one of our finest humorists, firmly believes that a story about something that actually happened is always funnier than a standard joke. "Wherever possible, tell a story," advises Hendra. "Be honest. Take chances. If you like, exaggerate to make yourself look even more ludicrous and loserlike than you actually were, but keep it honest and real. There are almost no jokes as compelling as stories involving insane things that happened to you. Even if you boost the details some, these are still true stories, and people will love you for them. They're revealing and universal. Jokes involving tortured situations that would never occur (three guys are adrift on a raft in the pacific) are not stories, and they are *never* truly funny because such jokes are *not real*."

Now there's a man with an open mind—you can feel the breeze from here!—Groucho Marx

Elizabeth Taylor's so fat, she puts mayonnaise on aspirin. —Joan Rivers

Why, you're one of the most beautiful women I've ever seen, and that's not saying much for you.—Groucho Marx

Psychologists have proven that when you play Jeff's humor to a baby when it's in the womb, it'll eventually be wearing a hockey helmet and sh*tting its pants at 40.—Nick DiPaolo (about Jeff Foxworthy)

I've seen women pee standing up with better aim.—Dennis Miller

The only genius with an IQ of 60.—Gore Vidal (on Andy Warhol)

I can see you and I married. I can see you bending over the stove. I can't see the stove!—Groucho Marx

She speaks five languages and can't act in any of them.—Sir John Gielgud (about Ingrid Bergman)

You're in a vampire movie. Finally, a role that *requires* you to suck.—Triumph the Insult Comic Dog (to Jon Bon Jovi)

The closest thing to Roseanne Barr's singing the national anthem was my cat being neutered.—Johnny Carson

Race

Two Jews *Don't* Walk in to a Bar ...

I'm a white guy with a black sister. How could I be racist? "I can't stand black people. They're always reading my diary." And I know I just told you I keep a diary. But before you judge me, let me say that if you were a white, Jewish kid with a black sister, you'd start writing things down, too.—Steve Hofstetter

They claim that in certain parts of the South, this is the coldest it's been in a hundred years. I can't go along with that. I remember when I was a kid back home, it got so cold one night the Ku Klux Klan tried to burn a cross on our front porch, and we opened the door and told 'em, "Bring it inside." And they did.—Dick Gregory

According to recent census figures, whites are now officially a minority in New York City. And you know what? I am getting *sick* of being hassled by the man.—Dennis Miller

Now they're calling taking drugs an epidemic—that's 'cause white folks are doing it.—Richard Pryor

I think it's perfectly okay to have Indians as sports mascots. I know it offends some of them, but if they're *that* offended they should just go back where they came from.—David Ridings

Last time I was down South I walked into this restaurant, and this white waitress came up to me and said, "We don't serve colored people here." I said, "That's all right. I don't eat colored people. Bring me a fried chicken."—Dick Gregory

Hackity Hack

Nothing's worse than a bad imitation—unless it's a bad *racial* imitation. Then, not only are you being a hack, but now you're a hack in some hot water. "The worst thing you can ever see is a white guy imitating a black guy or a black guy imitating a white guy," says comedian Mitch Fatel. "It's just the most obvious, racist, stupid-sounding thing you could do, and everybody will hate you."

What do you call a Jamaican man with glasses? Rasta-Four-I. —Josh Filipowski

I love Mexicans, because if you ever forget a Mexican dude's name, you can just read his necklace.—Ralphie May

In this day and age, can you believe people still stare? One day we're sitting in the car minding our own business when this white devil couple comes up to us. I said, "Don't worry honey, I'll handle this." I said, "That's right, bitch. I'm white, he's black. What the hell you got to say about it?" They're like, "Why are you in our car?"—Lisa Lampanelli

Movies can tell us a lot about race and history in America. That's why I like the *Rocky* movies—or as I like to call them, *What White People Were of Afraid of That Year.* —J-L Cauvin

Not only was the last blizzard an inconvenience, but the Reverend Al Sharpton charged that the snow was 98 percent white.—Bill Maher

Every town has two malls. The white mall, and the mall white people used to go to. They don't got nothing in the black mall but sneakers and baby clothes. Guess that's all they think we doin'—runnin' and f*ckin'.—Chris Rock

All the white people wanna be black, all the white kids. It's a hip-hop thing. They wanna be black, then the cops show up, and they're like, never mind. I can't take the beating. — Alonzo Bodden

A group of white South Africans recently killed a black lawyer because he was black. That was wrong. They should have killed him because he was a lawyer.—A. Whitney Brown

HA HA HA **Make 'Em Laugh** _____

Sure, three guys walked into a bar. But what if one of those guys was you? Well, it would probably make the joke funnier. "What most people perceive as a joke is something that's very impersonal, whereas comedian bits are very personal," says *Conan O'Brien* staffer Brian Kiley. "Even when Jerry Seinfeld talks about restrooms at the airport, it's still personal to him, because he's still in the bit as an observer." The more you can make a joke personal, the funnier it will be.

I was arrested at the Las Vegas airport. This Latino guy with a bald head and a tattoo across his neck goes, "Hey homes? They arrested you because you're Arabic?" "I guess, yeah." "So they think you're a terrorist?" "I guess, yeah." "Well, then blow this place up and get us out of here."—Ahmed Ahmed

That random screening they say they do at the airport—there's nothing random about it. You get to the gate, and they're standing there with a Sherwin Williams paint chart. If your ass is darker than khaki, you're getting searched.—Wanda Sykes

White supremacists want their own state. I say, give it to 'em. Give 'em 5 acres inside Compton.—Jeff Cesario

African American. Why don't they name most black people after someplace they actually been, like, Compton Americans, or Inglewood Swap Meet Americans, Vietnamese Nail Salon Americans—someplace black folk actually go.—Ralphie May

The USO sent me to Greenland. You have any idea what it's like to be black in Greenland? When you get there you have to tag the other black guy, tell him he can leave. Polar bears looking at you like, "Ooo, chocolate."—Alonzo Bodden

Who Made the Funny?

Alonzo Bodden was the grand-prize winner of NBC's *Last Comic Standing 3*. There was just one problem. Due to poor ratings, NBC cancelled the show with only one episode to go—the episode that showed Bodden's victory.

I don't know if Jesse Jackson is trying to appeal to a broader audience, but I just saw him doing a commercial for Wonder Bread.—Bob Hope

I am really enjoying the new Martin Luther King Jr. stamp—just think about all those white bigots, licking the backside of a black man.—Dick Gregory

I was reading the paper, and it said that 80 percent of the people in New York are minorities. Don't you think we should stop calling them minorities when they hit 80 percent? You could put one white guy in a room with 50,000 black people and 20,000 Puerto Ricans, and he'd still be going, "Look at all these minorities! I'm the only majority here."—Louis C. K.

I love listening to hip-hop music in my car. But when a black guy gets into my car, I'm faced with a dilemma. I can either: a) continue playing the music, but then he might think I'm doing it for him, or b) switch to the classic rock station, but then I'm not being true to myself. That's why I generally choose c) don't let black people in my car.—Phil Mazo

Black people don't care how good you do; they always got a cousin who could do what you do as good or better. You can drive up with a $380,000 Bentley, "Man, my cousin got that same one in teal green." You're watching basketball, Kobe make a great shot, "My cousin made that same shot on PlayStation."—Jamie Foxx

I love how New York is so multi-cultural. I wish I was ethnic. 'Cause if you're Hispanic and you get angry, people are like, "He's got a Latin temper." But if you're a white guy and you get angry, people are like, "That guy's a jerk."—Jim Gaffigan

Blatant Lies

Indiana native Jim Gaffigan earned a prestigious honor in 2002, when he was officially named Earth's Whitest Man. Congratulations, Jim!

Black people don't hijack planes. We steal a lot of stuff, but we do not hijack planes. In the history of aviation, a black person has never even attempted to hijack a plane. Want to know why? Because you can't sell an airplane.—Alonzo Bodden

I never believed in Santa Claus because I knew no white dude would come into my neighborhood after dark.—Dick Gregory

In kindergarten, the teacher used to ask us, "Who stole the cookies from the cookie jar?" Everybody started singing and stuff, but me, I just stared at the black kid and asked him why he did it.—Chris Cardenas

Who Made the Funny?

D. L. Hughley was one of the four stars of *The Original Kings of Comedy*, which captured one of comedy's most successful tours ever on film. The movie had a sharper, more inventive look than most stand-up comedy films, and with good reason— it was directed by Spike Lee.

Remember the crayon box with the flesh-colored crayon? Little white kids were like, "I'm gonna draw my mother and father." Black kids were like, "I don't know nobody look like this. I mean, don't throw it out. I can use it to draw the police.—D. L. Hughley

I am, in fact, black. I'm not African American. I don't make that kind of money yet.—Alonzo Bodden

I've been trying to pitch my own TV show in Hollywood. The first idea I had, the title was gonna be *Middle Eastern Eye for the Midwestern Guy*. What you do is get five Arabs or Muslims to bust into a white guy's house and teach him how to make bombs and hate women. I'm kidding. Midwestern guys already know how to do that.—Ahmed Ahmed

I was born a suspect. I can walk down any street in America and women will clutch their purses tighter, hold onto their mace, lock their car doors. If I look up into the windows of the apartments I pass I can see old ladies on the phone. They've already dialed 9-1- and are just waiting for me to do something wrong.—Chris Rock

Khalid Muhammad's speech got him in some hot water with Louis Farrakhan, because it is strictly against the Islamic code to hate white after Labor Day.—Bill Maher

There is a growing controversy over the issue of reparations, or a formal apology to African Americans for slavery. I'm not sure what to think, as my ancestors weren't even in this country during slavery. They were back in Europe financing the whole thing.—Eric Deskin

Latinos outnumber black people now. I'm not too happy about it. It's only a matter of time before we lose our month. Soon as they figure it out they're gonna have Latino History Month, and all we'll have left is Cinco de Negro.—Alonzo Bodden

Who Made the Funny?

Alonzo Bodden is one handy comic. He spent nine years as a jet mechanic for Lockheed, then McDonnell Douglas, and his first assignment was the "top secret" Stealth Fighter. Which makes sense, because if there's anyone the U.S. government should trust the safety and security of our best military weapons to, it's a stand-up comic.

Red Necks and Blue Collars

Where Buckshot Falls from the Sky like Teeth from Your Sister ...

My father is the mayor of our town. It's a small town, so eventually everyone gets to be the mayor. They elect the mayor by radio, and last year, Dad was the fifth caller. —Jake Johannsen

Three rednecks met me after a show. "Hey buddy, we're Christians. We don't like what you said." I said, "Then forgive me."—Bill Hicks

It's hard to be cool with a Southern accent. You can take a Southerner to a nude beach on the French Riviera, they'd be goin', "Damn, this looks like a good place to fish, here. Ed, bring the cooler, I found a spot." Goin' up to naked women, "You don't know where we can pick up some red wigglers, do you?"—Jeff Foxworthy

I come from a part of the world where the Egg McMuffin would be a heritage object.—Bill Bryson

I used to go to a lot of monster truck rallies as a kid. Now I go to a lot of monster truck rallies as white trash.—Deric Harrington

If you surveyed a hundred typical middle-aged Americans, I bet you'd find that only two of them could tell you their blood types, but every last one of them would know the theme song from the *Beverly Hillbillies*.—Dave Barry

I grew up in a mobile home. You learn a lot when you grow up in a mobile home. Did you know that the average Jehovah's Witness can run 35 miles an hour?—Brian Kiley

Blatant Lies

Young Jeff was a finalist in his tenth-grade spelling bee, losing in the last round to the only boy in school who knew that *phone* didn't begin with the letter F.

My entire childhood we had the letters m-a-l-e painted on the side of the mailbox. By the time I was in eleventh grade, I was like, "That ain't right. That M is supposed to be capitalized, isn't it?"
—Jeff Foxworthy

Is there anything more pathetic than an Elvis imperson-ator? There is. The *wife* of an Elvis impersonator.—Susie Essman

My sister wanted to be an actress, but she never made it. She does live in a trailer. She got halfway. She's an actress; she just never gets called to the set.—Mitch Hedberg

The average Southerner has the speech patterns of some-one slipping in and out of consciousness. I can change my shoes and socks faster than most people in Mississippi can speak a sentence.—Bill Bryson

I am the only person in the history of Moreland, Georgia, to ever be on *The New York Times* best-seller list. I'm the only person in the history of Moreland, Georgia, who ever *heard* of *The New York Times* best-seller list.—Lewis Grizzard

Here's a redneck word for you—*mayn'aise*. "Mayn, aise a lot of people here this eve'nin." Here's a new one—*aorta*. "Aorta cut that grass down by the ball field so the kids don't get hurt."—Jeff Foxworthy

Auto racing is boring except when a car is going at least 172 miles per hour upside down.—Dave Barry

You might be a redneck if ...

you think Dom Perignon is a Mafia leader.

you think a Volvo is part of a woman's anatomy.

you think possum is "the other white meat."—Jeff Foxworthy

You might be a Jewish redneck if …

> your game of dreidel decides whose turn it is to shave Grandma.

> you were circumcised with a hunting knife.

> cleaning for Passover means taking your house to the car wash.
> —Elie Saltzman

You might be a redneck Jedi if …

> you say "These are not the beers you are looking for."

> you call Hank Williams Jr. "Master."

> you have ever used a lightsaber to light the barbecue grill.
> —author unknown (George Lucas, maybe? Nyah, probably not.)

Religion

The God Question—Why Did God Cross the Road?

In the Christian faith, God created Adam in his own image. But 65 million years before that God created the dinosaurs, using the image of his cousin Ted.—Eddie Izzard

If you're going to war over religion, now you're just killing people in an argument over who has the better imaginary friend.—Richard Jeni

Hackity Hack _____

There's nothing more embarrassing—or less funny—then starting to tell a joke only to mess up the words, stumble, or otherwise get it wrong. "Don't start a joke until you know *exactly* how you're gonna say it," advises veteran stand-up and VH1 commentator Christian Finnegan. "There's nothing worse than starting a joke and having to backtrack, or say, 'Oh wait, I forgot to tell you this.' At that point, you're screwed. Go over the joke in your head first, and get it down before you open your mouth. You have to have a mastery of the joke you're telling."

You have these nuns beating your knuckles bloody and then telling you they were the sisters of God, and I felt like, "I don't want to meet your brother."—Joe Bolster

If the Old Testament were a reliable guide in the matter of capital punishment, half the people in the United States would have to be killed tomorrow.—Steve Allen

A lot of people say to me, "Why did you kill Christ?" I dunno ... it was one of those parties that got out of hand, you know?—Lenny Bruce

The nation of Dubai banned the movie *Charlie's Angels* because it's "offensive to the religion of Islam." Apparently, the religion of Islam is offended by anything without a plot.—Jon Stewart

Who Made the Funny? _____

Jon Stewart attended The College of William and Mary, which awarded him an honorary doctorate in 2004. In giving the commencement address, Stewart talked to the graduates about "the real world," saying, "I wanted to bring this up to you earlier about 'the real world,' and this is as good a time as any. I don't really know how to put this, so I'll be blunt—we broke it."

My friend Al was trying to get his life in order, so he was born again. But he was three months premature, and there were complications. He ended up an atheist.—Craig Sharf

So I was watching that show ... oh, what the ... that show where there's a guy onstage, and everyone in the audience believes he has contact with the dead, and spirits talk to him? Oh—it was "church."—David Cross

Know who had it rough in school? Jesus. How would you like to have a mom who was famous for being a virgin? 'Cause let's face it, kids are cruel. "Hey Jesus—you're mom's so messed up even your dad won't screw her." —Larry Getlen

Stay in a Marriott Hotel, you don't get the Bible. You get the Book of Mormon. I look at that book and I think, you know, it's one thing that Catholics don't read the Bible, but at least we didn't just make one up. It says right on the front, "another testament of Jesus Christ," like, "Oh— here's the sh*t we forgot."—Kathleen Madigan

The secret of a good sermon is to have a good beginning and a good ending, then have the two as close together as possible.—George Burns

If only God would give me some clear sign—like making a large deposit in my name in a Swiss bank.—Woody Allen

I belong to a reform congregation. We're called Jews R Us.—Dennis Wolfberg

I believe in being proactive. Yesterday, I found a Jehovah's Witness neighborhood and went door to door telling them I wasn't interested.—Craig Sharf

My grandmother told me that there was a passage in the Bible that says, "It is better to spill your seed in the belly of a whore than to spill it on the ground." So I tried both. And the Bible's right! It's *way* better. That's one of the reasons they call it the good book.—A. Whitney Brown

I was walking past a church with my 5-year-old son. He said, "What's that?" I said, "It's a church." He said, "What goes on in there?" so I said, "Those people worship God, and they go in and pray to their god." And he said, "I heard Paddington Bear was the son of God." And I thought, that sounds just a plausible as the nonsense I'm about to tell you.—Ian Stone

At the Last Supper, how come no one sat at the other side of the table?—Gilbert Gottfried

Ever been in an argument with somebody and they start quoting the Bible on you? I'd have more respect if you quoted Hall and Oates. At least I know they walked the earth. Or awkwardly danced it.—Paul Gilmartin

Blatant Lies

The quoting of Hall and Oates is actually a recognized affliction in the medical community, categorized by the senseless worship of musical acts dominated by one partner who far overshadows another. This is known in the medical community as Garfunkel syndrome.

If you switched the stories in the Bible with the ones in your fairy tale books as a kid, would you know the difference? If it was religion that Jack went up a Beanstalk, and a fairy tale that Jonah lived in a whale; Delilah, Repunzal, a talking wolf, a talking snake? There's a poison apple in the Garden of Eden, and there's one in Snow White. Does it matter? Who cares?—Bill Maher

In the Islamic religion if you want to get divorced you just have to say, "We are divorced, divorced, divorced!" It's like Beetlejuice Divorce Court. Wouldn't it be cool if that worked for other things in life? Like with your girlfriend: "You are *not* pregnant, pregnant, pregnant. Or at least it's not mine, mine, mine."—Vic Alejandro

Three out of four people now believe in angels. You know what I think it is? I think it's a massive, collective, psychotic, chemical flashback from all the drugs smoked, snorted, shot, and absorbed rectally by all Americans from 1960 to 1990. Thirty years of adulterated street drugs'll get you some f*cking angels, my friend.—George Carlin

What do atheists scream when they come?—Bill Hicks

Some people read the Bible too much. Too much of anything isn't good for you—that's why you have fanatics who misinterpret the Bible, from reading it 150,000 times. You read *Green Eggs and Ham* 150,000 times, you'll come up with all sorts of twisted ideas. "I will not eat it in a house, I will not eat it with a mouse. Jews are the Devil."—Gregg Rogell

Bless me, Father, for I have sinned. I did an original sin. I poked a badger with a spoon.—Eddie Izzard

A lot of Christians wear crosses around their neck. You think when Jesus comes back, he ever wants to see a cross? Kinda like going up to Jackie Onassis with a rifle pendant on.—Bill Hicks

Blatant Lies

Hillary Clinton was the main protégé of filth-meister Andrew Dice Clay, and her "Spank Me Till I'm Wet" routine has helped her become known as the raunchy comic on the scene today!

In the Bible, it says they asked Jesus how many times you should forgive, and he said 70 times 7. Well, I want you all to know that I'm keeping a chart.—Hillary Clinton

I tell people I'm Jewish and they don't believe me. Which is weird, because who would make that up?—Steve Hofstetter

If God dropped acid, would he see people?—author unknown

I can't get into a religion where you have to confess your sins to a man in a booth. I ain't tellin' nobody something I already got away with. "My son, what'd you do?" "What did you hear? I don't know you." "Jesus would want to know." "Jesus already know. He everywhere, right? Well, he was there when I did what I did."—D. L. Hughley

The Vatican is against surrogate mothers. Good thing they didn't have that rule when Jesus was born.— Elayne Boosler

We have to respect people who have strong religious beliefs. 'Cause if you don't, they'll kill you.—Richard Jeni

When I was a kid, I used to pray every night for a new bicycle. Then I realized that the Lord doesn't work that way. So I just stole one and asked him to forgive me.—Emo Philips

The problem with writing about religion is that you run the risk of offending sincerely religious people and then they come after you with machetes.—Dave Barry

In New Jersey, a statue of Jesus supposedly opened its eyes. Lucky for Jesus, his nose was still clogged.—Ben Schwartz

If Jesus had been killed 20 years ago, Catholic school children would be wearing little electric chairs around their necks instead of crosses.—Lenny Bruce

If you had the opportunity to be born again, why would you come back as George Bush?—Mort Sahl

The only difference between Catholics and Jews is that Jews are born with guilt and Catholics have to go learn it in school.—Elayne Boosler

The Supreme Court has ruled that they cannot have a nativity scene in Washington, D.C. This wasn't for any religious reasons. They couldn't find three wise men and a virgin.—Jay Leno

HA HA HA   **Make 'Em Laugh**

A confident joke-teller is a successful joke-teller, so to help you gain confidence, tell your joke to a friendly audience before unleashing it out in the world. "Tell it the first couple of times to a non-threatening, nonjudgmental audience," says Queen of Mean, Lisa Lampanelli. "Tell it to someone who has to love you, like your husband or close friends, someone who won't laugh at you and blow your cover if you screw it up."

Eighty percent of people in America believe that angels are around us all the time. And who's to say they're wrong? It would explain that giggling in the room when I'm jerking off with the lights on.—Richard Jeni

I spent my childhood hanging out at a place called the JCC. JCC stands for Jewish Community Center. But I always knew that JCC really stood for Jesus Can't Come-in.—Michael J. Nelson

The new *Da Vinci Code* conspiracy is that Jesus was married. I don't know if that's true, but if it is, that would explain why he didn't stop his crucifixion.—Scott Dunn

I'm a Jew. We probably killed Christ. We probably did. He might not have been an easy kid to hang out with. All day long, "my father" this, "my father" that. Try to play tag with somebody who can walk on water.—Rich Vos

I'm Catholic, and … well, I'm Catholic in the same sense that if a cow is born in a tree, then it's a bird.—Richard Jeni

Wouldn't it have been weird to go to high school with the pope? Somebody did. Somebody's sitting at home, watching TV, they see the pope and they think, "That guy's a jerk. He was so mean to me, and now he's pope? I got a swirly from the pope."—Jim Gaffigan

The Vatican was upset after a church property in Moscow was turned into a brothel. The people at the brothel said they made the change because there was so much sex happening there already, it just made sense.—Larry Getlen

The Lord giveth, the Lord taketh away. The Lord is an Indian givereth.—Craig Sharf

If Jesus had been crazy, would he have thought he was Jesus?—Craig Sharf

Joseph was Jesus' step-daddy. How you gonna tell Jesus what to do, and you ain't his real dad? "Hey Jesus, come in here and clean your room." "I don't feel like cleaning my room, and you ain't my real daddy. But I bet you don't want me to call my real daddy, do you?"—D. L. Hughley

My understanding of the crucifixion—we paid a couple of Italians to rough him up a bit and things got *way* out of hand.—Craig Sharf

Who Made the Funny?

Gilbert Gottfried had one of the most thankless jobs in comedy history. He was a member of *Saturday Night Live*'s 1980 cast, the one that had to replace the classic lineup that included Bill Murray and Gilda Radner. (John Belushi and Dan Aykroyd had left one season earlier.) The 1980 cast was eviscerated in the press, and Gottfried was fired with most of the cast at the end of the season. The only two kept on were Joe Piscopo and Eddie Murphy.

I was talking to Jesus, and I said, "Jesus, I feel like no one will ever accept me," and Jesus looked at me and said, "You know what my theory is? Accept me or go to hell."
—Gilbert Gottfried

We Catholics don't read the Bible. It's true. We pay a priest to read that for us. Man's got all week off and no wife, he can show up with a 45-minute book report once a week.
—Kathleen Madigan

I pretty much don't believe in Jesus—unless there's turbulence.—Carolyn Castiglia

Salt Lake City's NBC affiliate, which is owned by the Mormon Church, declined to air last night's *The Tonight Show* because it featured an interview with the creators of *Puppetry of the Penis*. The church was extremely offended by a segment of that show in which the two men twist their genitals in the shape of the Osmond family.—Larry Getlen

Jews don't name their kids after themselves. That's why Jesus wasn't called God Jr.—Craig Sharf

I'm not bringing my kids up Catholic. I can't bring my kids up in a religion whose authority system is based entirely on the size of hats. Priests have no hats, cardinals have these little red beanies, and the pope has a collection of big hats. God must have a huge sombrero up there in heaven.—Denis Leary

Every day people are straying away from the church and going back to God.—Lenny Bruce

Sometimes I ask myself, "What would Jesus do?" Then I do the opposite, because I don't want to be crucified for it.—Geoff Holtzman

I don't believe in reincarnation, but I think I may have in a former life.—Myq Kaplan

School and Education
'Cuz Widdout an Edukasion, Your Nuttin'

I was mischievous in school. I got a hold of all my teachers' home phone numbers and called in death threats. My English teacher, Mr. Johnson, I called him. "Hello? Johnson residence." "*Is this Mr. Johnson?*" "Yes it is." "*You're a dead man, Johnson! You're gonna die—unless you change Dave Chappelle's grades!*" I don't know how they caught me. —Dave Chappelle

A student at a Delaware school is in trouble after breaking into the school computers and changing her grades to As from Fs. The girl got in trouble, but has also been asked to go work for WorldCom.—Conan O'Brien

My kindergarten teacher hated me. She'd find any excuse to pick on me, especially during nap time. Like I'm the only guy in the world who sleeps naked.—Brian Kiley

You don't appreciate a lot of stuff in school until you get older. Little things, like being spanked every day by a middle-aged woman—stuff you pay good money for later in life.—Emo Philips

I won't say ours was a tough school, but we had our own coroner. We used to write essays like "What I'm Going to Be *If* I Grow Up."—Lenny Bruce

Hackity Hack

Hearing a singer try to hit notes out of her range is never fun, right? Well, same goes for jokes. "Don't do something you're not good at," says veteran comic D. C. Benny. "If your Uncle Shammy does a great Irish Brogue and you can't, don't tell the joke in a lousy accent and explain that it's funnier when Shammy does it in his accent. Just tell it, and if it doesn't work without the accent, then tell another one instead."

School uniforms—bad theory. Don't these schools do enough damage making all these kids think alike? Now they're gonna get 'em to look alike, too? And it's not a new idea. I first saw it in old newsreels from the 1930s, but it was hard to understand because the narration was in German.—George Carlin

When I was in high school, I was in the French club. We didn't really do anything. Once in a while, we'd surrender to the German club.—Brian Kiley

When I went to college, my parents threw a going-away party for me—according to the letter.—Emo Philips

I was a physical education major with a college psychology minor. Which means that if you ask me a question about a child's behavior, I will tell you to tell the child to take a lap.—Bill Cosby

In my high school, there were the guys who got laid and the guys who did those guys' homework. Which worked out well for me, because all that homework really got me ready for college.—Larry Getlen

Our bombs are smarter than the average high school student. At least they can find Kuwait.—A. Whitney Brown

The career adviser used to come to school, and he said, "What do you want to do? Tell me your dreams." And I said, "I want to be a space astronaut, discover things that have never been discovered." And he said, "Look, you're British. Scale it down a bit."—Eddie Izzard

Blatant Lies

Eddie Izzard defied his counselors and in 1997 became the first British comedian ever to walk on the moon.

Every time some guy with an AK-47 strolls into a school-yard and kills three or four kids, the school is overrun with counselors and psychiatrists and grief counselors and trauma therapists trying to help the children cope. When I was in school, if someone came to school and killed three or four of us, we went right on with our arithmetic. Thirty-five classmates, minus four, equals thirty-one.—George Carlin

For just about everybody, at some point in your life, there's one teacher you had a secret crush on. For me, it's my wife's aerobics teacher.—Brian Kiley

I don't think my dad wanted a lot of kids. When I gave him the permission slip for school field trips, under the line "in case of an emergency," he'd write, "DO NOT RESUSCITATE."—Moody McCarthy

As part of the New York Comedy Festival, comedians will replace teachers at five schools in the city. Now kids will finally learn "what the deal is with urinal cakes."—Ben Schwartz

My nephew is in high school. He's a member of the abstinence society, where a group of students have pledged to maintain their virginity. We had something similar at my high school—it was called the math club. Those guys are still hanging in there.—Brian Kiley

Science

Blinding You with Science—or Hydrochloric Acid. Whichever Works.

I saw somewhere that scientists think they can now clone an all-white zebra. Now, I'm no expert—but isn't that called a horse?—Jay Leno

Helmut Simon, who 13 years ago found the 5,000-year-old remains of a prehistoric man frozen in the ice of an Alpine glacier, has himself disappeared in the snow-covered Alps. Helmut, if you can hear me, don't give up. Help is on the way—in *5,000 years.*—Tina Fey

Scientists announced that they have located the gene for alcoholism. They found it at a party, talking way too loud.—Conan O'Brien

My theory on evolution? I think Darwin was adopted.
—Steven Wright

It's a scientific fact that your body will not absorb cholesterol if you take it from another person's plate.—Dave
Barry

Researchers have discovered the gene that leads to large
buttocks in sheep. Some scientists are skeptical about the
study's intent; however, because the research team was led
by Sir Mix-a-Lot.—Larry Getlen

Cloning is B.S. because the only thing they clone is sheep.
When is the last time you've seen two sheep that didn't
look alike?—Jayson Cross

Make 'Em Laugh

Can't tell jokes as well as one of your dashing, sophisticated
co-workers? So what? Tell 'em anyway. "Who says we all have
to be Mozarts?" wrote science fiction master Isaac Asimov in *Asimov
Laughs Again.* "To learn how to play piano sufficiently well to amuse
yourself and your friends is surely something; in the same way, to learn
to tell jokes that will amuse your friends, even if you don't attain a professional level, will certainly add to your enjoyment of life."

There are a lot of theories for why the dinosaurs went
extinct. Most likely the dinosaurs got bored staring at the
exhibits in natural history museums, and they died on the
spot.—Danny Hirsh

Scientists have developed a way to conduct archaeological
expeditions into human genes, making it possible for the
first time to examine how the human race has evolved over
the past 10,000 years. The most surprising finding? The
earliest humans all looked like Carrot Top.—Larry Getlen

Okay, so what's the speed of dark?—Steven Wright

I built a cheap time machine. It sends me into the present.—Craig Sharf

NASA scientists recently landed a probe on the second-largest near-Earth asteroid. The asteroid is named Eros after the Greek god of love, because, like love, it is a cold, dead, gray rock.—Jason Reich

Scientists have completed the first human genome map. It's the greatest scientific discovery in history, if you don't count silicone breast implants.—Craig Kilborn

It's a good thing we have gravity, or else when birds died they'd just stay right up there.—Steven Wright

Scientists say the only way to control killer bees is to mate them with milder bees. So if we have a mass murderer, we don't execute him? We fix him up with Marie Osmond? —David Letterman

It is impossible to travel faster than the speed of light, and certainly not desirable, as one's hat keeps blowing off.—Woody Allen

Scientists have located the gene for impulsive behavior. Not surprisingly, it was getting its nipples pierced.—Conan O'Brien

Self-Esteem and Mental Health

The Little Engine That Could—on Zoloft

I did one politically incorrect joke on television about obsessive-compulsive disorder. It wasn't bad, but you don't wanna insult those people, 'cause if they start writing letters, they don't quit. Letter, letter, letter, check the stove, letter, letter, letter ...—Ray Romano

All the commercials on TV now are for anti-depressants, for Prozac or Paxil. And they get you right away. "Are you sad? Do you get stress, do you have anxiety?" Yes, yes, I have all those things. I'm *alive*.—Ellen DeGeneres

I don't mean to sound bitter, cold, or cruel, but I am, so that's how it comes out.—Bill Hicks

I prefer to see the dark side of things. The glass is always half empty. And cracked. And I just cut my lip on it. And chipped a tooth.—Janeane Garofalo

I was in analysis. I was suicidal. As a matter of fact, I would have killed myself, but I was in analysis with a strict Freudian. And if you kill yourself, they make you pay for the sessions you miss.—Woody Allen

I view a visit to the therapist in much the same way I view a visit to the hairdresser. When I leave the office my head looks great; around an hour later it's all f*cked up and I can't get it to look that way on my own.—Dennis Miller

I have a new book coming out. It's one of those self-help deals; it's called *How to Get Along with Everyone*. I wrote it with this other a**hole.—Steve Martin

HA HA HA   Make 'Em Laugh

Do you *believe* you can tell a funny joke? If not, you're doomed to failure. "You have to believe you'll get laughs," wrote Milton Berle in *Milton Berle's Private Joke File*. "If you don't brainwash yourself into believing in your talent, you won't get the desired reaction. Your comedy starts with a pep talk to yourself."

They made Barbie change her body because they were accusing her of giving unrealistic body images to young girls. So they lessened her bust size and increased her waist size—and now Barbie is back waiting tables.—Bill Maher

I was in analysis for years because of a traumatic childhood. I was breast-fed from falsies.—Woody Allen

I had a stick of Carefree gum, but it didn't work. I felt pretty good while I was blowing that bubble, but as soon as the gum lost its flavor, I was back to pondering my mortality.—Mitch Hedberg

Last week was a rough week. My psychiatrist told me I was going crazy. I said, "If you don't mind, I'd like a second opinion." He said, "All right, you're ugly, too."—Rodney Dangerfield

Trying to kill yourself takes dedication. But don't give up. Quitters never win.—Mike Cotayo

There's really only one way to describe my mother. There's an old saying—neurotics build castles in the air and psychotics live in them. My mother cleans them.—Rita Rudner

We had a crazy guy in our neighborhood who thought he was a rooster. It was sad. The day after he died, the entire neighborhood overslept.—Gene Perret

I live life according to the Limbo philosophy: set the bar really low, and still manage to slide under.—Craig Sharf

My therapist told me the way to achieve true inner peace is to finish what I start. So far today, I have finished two bags of M&M's and a chocolate cake. I feel better already. —Dave Barry

I know there's no way I could handle combat. I sh*t in my pants playing paintball.—Paul Gilmartin

We had a depression fair in the backyard. A major game there was "Pin the Blame on the Donkey."—Richard Lewis

Most people look normal but are really crazy, and that's why you have to like a guy like Charles Manson. Say what you will about Manson, he's one of the only people with the decency to look like a dangerous maniac the first time you meet him.—Richard Jeni

All these psychopaths, they all hear voices. Everybody hears voices. I hear voices, don't you? They just say different things. Mine say things like, "Don't wear white after Labor Day." They don't say, "Kill the people next door."—Larry Amoros

My mother talks to herself, then complains she hears voices.—Phyllis Diller

I have no self-esteem. Frankly, I don't deserve it.—Bruce Cherry

My psychiatrist told me I have to learn to love myself. I'm like, "Doc, I'm up to three times a day as it is. I'm a chain stroker."—Tom Cotter

People are always telling me I'm too quiet. You know what I say to them? Nothing.—Debbie Shea

HA HA HA

Make 'Em Laugh

Penn Jillette produced *The Aristocrats*, a film about the dirtiest joke ever told. So he may be biased, but in his view, if you wanna be funny, dirty is the way to go. "Always work blue—without exception," says Jillette. "There's nothing funnier than f*ck and c***, ever. Make sure you have the word *motherf*cker* in there, make sure you have the word *a**hole*, and make sure it is offensive. You can work clean, but why bother. There's nothing funnier than f*cking a monkey. In fact, I don't think you can have a truly funny joke unless you have a talking animal engaged in a sex act."

I was going to invite my friends over, but then I remembered they told me not to call them that. Then I realized I was talking to myself.—Molly Anderson

On the one hand, I don't care what other people think of me; but on the other hand, I want to be remembered as the guy who didn't care what other people thought of him.—Dennis Miller

I read somewhere that 77 percent of all the mentally ill live in poverty. Actually, I'm more intrigued by the 23 percent who are apparently doing quite well for themselves.—Emo Philips

Identical twins have it so easy. Anytime they feel down, they can give themselves a little ego boost. They can just look at their twin and be like: "You're so pretty. You have a great body. Guys love you."—Carmen Lynch

If the Manson Family had taken Prozac instead of speed or acid, today they'd be Fleetwood Mac.—Bill Maher

My sister was a really depressed kid. When she was 8, my parents caught her sticking her head in her EZ Bake oven. I'm just glad my parents got there in time. If they'd arrived just 18 hours later, she could have been lightly burned. —Todd Levin

A friend said I was afraid of success. Which may be true, because I have a feeling that fulfilling my potential would really cut into my sittin'-around time.—Maria Bamford

Some people don't believe in ADD. They think it's a fad or something. I have it, it's a fact, and it's provable. All I need is a remote control and a girlfriend.—Mike Storck

Hackity Hack

When you tell a joke, do your hands wave ferociously, like you're signaling ships? Or maybe they're frozen, statuelike, at your side, making you look like Will Smith's nemesis in *I, Robot*. "Practice your hand gestures in front of a mirror," advises Jay Leno in *How to Be Funny*. "You'd be surprised how many times a person telling a joke looks like one of those Irish dancers with the feet moving back and forth and the arms and hands glued to the side."

I'm an NYU student. The past couple years we've had a lot of suicides, and I'm beginning to realize that even I'm subconsciously hurting myself. But I'm doing it in a smart way. I mean, why else would I be getting a liberal arts degree?—Chris Cardenas

Depression runs in my family. Actually, it meanders. It can't get up the energy to run.—Mike Cotayo

Sex and Sexuality

Oh God ... Oh God ... OH GOD!!!

I saw an ad for the Wonder Bra. Is that really a problem in this country—men not paying enough attention to women's breasts?—Jay Leno

I know I'm not sexy. In high school, I was voted "most likely to masturbate."—Rodney Dangerfield

How is it in this country that if you pore over the *Sports Illustrated* swimsuit issue, you're a pervert, but if you ogle the same babes in alphabetical order by state, you're patriotic?—Bill Maher

I feel sex is a beautiful thing between two people. Between five, it's fantastic.—Woody Allen

The other night I was making love to my wife and she said, "Deeper, deeper." So I started whispering Nietzsche quotes into her ear. "Man is a rope, stretched over the abyss." She's like, "Whoa, not that f*ckin' deep. I'm trying to get off over here."—Dennis Miller

I called one of those 900 talk-dirty numbers. I got a girl who stuttered, and it cost me $1,700.—Larry the Cable Guy

At the request of the Catholic Church, a 3-day sex orgy to be held near Rio de Janeiro was cancelled last Friday. Organizers expected 500,000 men and 8 women.—Tina Fey

Women have two types of orgasms—the actual ones, and the ones they make up on their own. I can give you the male point of view on this. We're fine with it. You do whatever the hell it is you gotta do.—Jerry Seinfeld

What's the number-one fantasy for most guys? Two women. Fellas, I think that's a bit lofty. If you can't satisfy that one woman, why do you wanna piss off another one? —Wanda Sykes

Blatant Lies

Wanda learned this lesson the hard way, after a particularly unsatisfying encounter with Woody Allen and Janeane Garofalo.

I was walking in Times Square last week and saw that all the hookers were topless. Then I realized it was Casual Friday.—Craig Sharf

Women are really not that exacting. They only desire one thing in bed— take off your socks.—Dennis Miller

I hate love scenes in the movies, because they're not real. You wanna show me a real love scene, show me a couple in bed and their dogs are watching them at the end of the bed.—Bill Engvall

A girl phoned me the other day and said, "Come on over, there's nobody home." So I went over—there was nobody home!—Rodney Dangerfield

My wife only has sex with me for a purpose. Last night she used me to time an egg.—Rodney Dangerfield

I don't think I'm good in bed. My husband never said anything, but after we made love he'd take a piece of chalk and outline my body.—Joan Rivers

The most common theory women have about men is, "Well, if he's got big feet, then you know ..." Or if he's got big hands. Or a big nose. Or big ears. Well I tell you what, he better be packin', cause that's one goofy-lookin' guy.—Jeff Foxworthy

Guys have it made. Every time you have sex, you're gonna complete the act. For guys, sex is like going to a restaurant, and no matter what you order off the menu, you walk out of there going, "Damn, that was good! My compliments to the chef!"—Wanda Sykes

The problem is that God gives men a brain and a penis, and only enough blood to run one at a time.—Robin Williams

I was with this girl the other night, and from the way she responded to my skillful caresses, you would have sworn that she was conscious—from the top of her head, to the tag on her toes.—Emo Philips

I like girls. I like their breasts. I don't even know why I like breasts; they don't even do anything. They just bounce up and down, and it makes me happy. It would make sense if they gave milk all the time. That way if you were having sex and you got thirsty, you wouldn't have to stop. You could be like, "Yeah, baby, that feels good. Which one's chocolate?"—Mitch Fatel

Sex alleviates tension. Love causes it.—Woody Allen

My wife was afraid of the dark, then she saw me naked. Now she's afraid of the light.—Rodney Dangerfield

I didn't have any sex during the blackout. How could I? My computer wasn't working.—Lewis Black

Circumcision. This is why the penis is such a troublemaker when he gets older—because he was abused as a small child.—Richard Jeni

I'd like to do some observational humor for you now—I hope you can relate. "Don't you hate when you're in bed with three women, and the least attractive one whispers, 'Save it for me!' Man, that's a drag!"—Jim Carrey

The Web brings people together, because no matter what type of twisted sexual mutant you happen to be, you've got millions of pals out there. Type in, "find people who have sex with goats that are on fire," and the computer will say, "specify type of goat."—Richard Jeni

I've never been interested in backdoor sex. It's all I can do to keep the front entrance nice for company.—Laura Kightlinger

My classmates would copulate with anything that moved, but I never saw any reason to limit myself.—Emo Philips

If it wasn't for masturbation, most men wouldn't know that anything could happen.—Jerry Seinfeld

Pitchers say the split-finger fastball is like sex. When it's good, it's terrific, and when it's bad, it's still pretty good. —George Will

I went into Victoria's Secret. They have underbritches with holes in the crotch. Can you believe that? Twenty-four dollars women are paying for under shorts with holes in the crotch. I got a whole drawer full of them at the house, for Pete's sake. I bet I'm sitting on two, three hundred dollars.—Larry the Cable Guy

I'll tell you how I feel about porn channels. They don't educate us, they don't enlighten us, and they don't come in clearly enough where I live.—Bill Maher

My love life is terrible. The last time I was inside a woman was when I visited the Statue of Liberty.—Woody Allen

Make 'Em Laugh

I've said it before—more than once, in fact—but I really can't say it enough. *Memorize your jokes!* "*Don't* start a joke when you have absolutely no idea how it ends—it won't come to you in the middle," says John Marshall, who has written for *The Chris Rock Show*, *Politically Incorrect*, and *Tough Crowd with Colin Quinn*. "You wouldn't drive your car if it only had enough gas to get you three quarters of a city block, but that's what terrible joke tellers do, *every day*."

I had a woman friend come over all upset. She said, "Jake, I don't understand. How can a man want to have sex with a plastic doll?" And I said, "Well, it's not Plan A ..."—Jake Johannsen

You know you haven't had sex in way too long when little things start to arouse you, like, sticking your key in the ignition. The other day I was sharpening a pencil and I swear to God, I said, "Take it all, you whore."—Tom Cotter

Don't you ever wish you could have sex with the first person you ever had sex with again, just to show them how good you got at it? "Hey, made it past your thigh."—Dave Attell

My father taught me about the birds and the bees. He didn't know anything about girls.—Joey Adams

Pornography cheapens sex. Fortunately, prostitution makes it expensive again.—Geoff Holtzman

I don't like strip clubs. They don't make any sense to me—
it's almost like someone just put a hot, juicy turkey in
front of you, and all you can do is yell at it. You're like,
"Whoooo! I bet you go good with gravy!" And then you
shove a dollar in its ass.—Mitch Fatel

I love lingerie, oh my God. I even have a subscription
to the Victoria's Secret catalog. Well, I don't have a
subscription—my neighbor does. She just hasn't received
it in a couple of years.— Mitch Fatel

The only advice I ever got from my dad is this: sex is like
pizza. Even when it's bad, you still gotta pay for it.—Nick
DiPaolo

A woman can say to a man, "I'm not wearing any underwear," and the man's first thought is, "All right. Might get
lucky." But if a man says to a woman, "I'm not wearing any
underwear," her first thought is, "Oh no. I'm gonna have to
wash those pants twice."—Jeff Foxworthy

For the first time in China's history, the government has
cleared the way for drug stores to start selling condoms.
Those Chinese condoms will be available in the U.S. under
the name "Thimbles."—Craig Kilborn

There's a new medical crisis. Doctors are reporting
that many men are having allergic reactions to latex
condoms. They say they cause severe swelling. So what's
the problem?—Jay Leno

Here's a strange story. In Connecticut, a man was arrested
for having sex with a cow. When the man was asked what
he was thinking at the time, he said he was thinking about a
younger, hotter cow.—Craig Kilborn

When the authorities warn you of the dangers of having sex, there is an important lesson to be learned. Do not have sex with the authorities.—Matt Groening

Last week, my girlfriend had the nerve to complain about my stamina in the old sack-er-ooni. So this is what I did. I popped six Viagra, and I drank a case of Red Bull. Her funeral's this Tuesday.—Harland Williams

When I went to Bible College, I told them I was gay, but had never acted on my feelings. So they put me in a dorm with 1,000 single men who ran around half naked. That's like putting Janis Joplin in charge of the drug lock-up. They said if I felt tempted I should get on my knees and pray until the feelings went away. Thank God it was only a 2-year program. Otherwise, I would still be on my knees.—Nick Tarr

Hackity Hack

Tony Hendra admits that he is not a fan of traditional "jokes," or, as he refers to them, "formalized, supposedly funny set-pieces that are supposed to give others the impression you have a sense of humor." But as a best-selling humorist and driving force behind the two funniest magazines of the past half-century, *National Lampoon* and *Spy*, Hendra knows funny. So listen as he shares his rules on telling jokes: "Never tell a joke that involves three types of nationalities. Never tell a joke that involves someone arriving at the pearly gates. And never tell a joke that involves a blonde, a dead baby, a person with more melanin in their skin than you have, or golf."

Last week, I made love to an inflatable girl. Now I got an inflatable guy looking for me.—Rodney Dangerfield

My girlfriend always laughs during sex—no matter what she's reading.—Emo Philips

Sex is not that important. You know what's really important? The afterward part. When you're both naked, and it's warm, and you're watching the sun come up through the windshield. You look in her good eye and help strap on her leg, and you know—you f*cked a pirate.—Dave Attell

It's very emotionally satisfying for men to deal with strippers, because you don't have to worry about what they want. They don't want to know when you're coming home, why you left, where the relationship is going—they want the one thing that every emotionally stunted idiot has — they want a dollar.—Richard Jeni

Ducking for apples—change one letter and it's the story of my life.—Dorothy Parker

To this day I can't get aroused until I see a pair of rubber dice hanging from the mirror. —Johnny Carson

Who Made the Funny? _____

Like many great stand-ups, Johnny Carson got his first big break as a comedy writer. He worked for famed comedian Red Skelton.

My girlfriend doesn't let me go to strip clubs, so I don't let her go to strip malls. We both spend a lot of time on the Internet, taking care of business.—Craig Sharf

Never yell at your girlfriend if she's 45 minutes late. If she's 45 days late, yelling is highly appropriate.—David Ridings

I opened my dresser drawer, and a box of condoms fell out of the back and landed at the bottom of the dresser. That tells you everything you need to know about my sex life. It's gotten so bad, my condoms are committing suicide. And the worst part is, they left a note. "Dear Larry. No one should ever be made to feel this useless, for this long. Yours in misery, the Trojan Variety Pack."—Larry Getlen

I've got a midget friend, an albino friend, and another friend who thinks *Lord of the Rings* is real. Together we call ourselves The Unf*ckables.—Dave Attell

I've been lonely and depressed for so long that when I masturbate, only tears come out.—Todd Levin

Some girls make you wait before they have sex with you. What's that about? I was out on a date with this girl, she was like, "I like to wait six months before I have sex with a guy," and I was like, "Wow, I really respect that ... okay, guess I'll see you in six months. Do you just e-mail me, or how does that work? Because I wanna be sure to block off the date."—Mitch Fatel

A man sleeps around, no questions asked. But if a woman makes 19, 20 mistakes, she's a tramp.—Joan Rivers

There's a TV show called *Clean Sweep* where these women invade your home and make you throw away what you don't need. Their motto is, "If you haven't used it in 6 months, throw it out." I have 3 weeks to get laid. And they said I couldn't write an interior decorating d*ck joke.—Basil White

If it wasn't for pick-pockets and frisking at airports I'd have no sex life at all.—Rodney Dangerfield

Someone told me that love is a sickness. If that's the case, that would be a good excuse to call in sick to work. "Hi. I can't come in today. I'm in love. My doctor said I should stay in bed ... with my legs elevated.—Debbie Shea

If I ever write a sex manual, I'd call it *Ow, You're on My Hair*.—Richard Lewis

I asked my friend how she realized she was a lesbian. She said that whenever she had heterosexual sex, she just never felt any emotional attachment. So now I'm starting to think *I* might be a lesbian.—Phil Mazo

There's nothing more sexy than watching a lady have an orgasm. I just hate when I slip and fall out of the tree. —Rich Vos

Hackity Hack

This advice is about listening to a joke, not telling one. If you're listening to a joke and realize you know (or think you can guess) the punch line, *do not*, under any circumstances, blurt it out. This is the height of rudeness—what writer Isaac Asimov called an "absolutely unforgivable offense"—and qualifies you for a beating. Let the teller finish his or her predictable joke. Then, when they're done, walk away and find someone more fun to talk with.

It's not the quantity of your sexual relations that counts. It's the quality. On the other hand, if the quantity drops below once every 8 months, I would definitely look into it.—Woody Allen

I used to date a girl who had one boob bigger than the other. She entered a wet T-shirt contest and took first and third place.—Larry the Cable Guy

Tittie bars are weird places. They got weird morality. The bouncer started yellin' at me, "Hey! Hey buddy! You wanna take your hat off? It's disrespectful to the ladies." Yeah, I can shove a 20 up her ass, but I better not have a hat on when I do it.—Dave Chappelle

I'm an ass man. I'm addicted to ass. It's like crack to me. —Kevin Garvey

I love to find bargains. It's so exciting. It's like having an orgasm. Well, not really, 'cause I can't fake a bargain. —Kerri Louise

The most-asked question I always get is, "Steve, do you know where you got HIV?" And I know for a fact where I got it, and you better be careful out there—I got it from a toilet seat. Of course, there was a man sitting on it at the time.—Steve Moore, HIV+ comedian

A small town in Brazil has declared May 9 "Orgasm Day"—a holiday women celebrate privately, late at night, after the men have fallen asleep.—Ben Schwartz

Sometimes girls spend too much time on our nipples. We appreciate the effort, I just don't know if you realize— they're not hooked up. They're show nipples. They're like those towels you can't use in the bathroom. They're just there 'cause they match the soap.—Mitch Fatel

Every time you open the paper, another celebrity's getting arrested for masturbation—first Pee Wee Herman, then George Michael. If masturbation's a crime, I should be on death row. I should have been executed years ago. By age 12, I was already Al Capone.—Gilbert Gottfried

I named my private part "pride." It's not much, but at least I have my pride.—Jay London

If you're in the mile-high club but got there by yourself, does that only count for half a mile?—Larry Getlen

I don't believe in premature ejaculation. If I come, it was right on time.—Dave Chappelle

I require only three things of a man. He must be handsome, ruthless, and stupid.—Dorothy Parker

I rented the movie *40 Days and 40 Nights*. It's about a guy who takes on the challenge of going 40 days without having sex. That's right—the *challenge*. You know, if I ever had sex and then had sex *within* 40 days, I'd make a movie about that. It would be called, *Holy Sh*t, I Actually Had Sex Twice in 40 Days!*—Larry Getlen

Isn't it strange? When you're single, all you see are couples. And then when you're part of a couple, all you see are hookers.—Jim Gaffigan

My girlfriend is an orphan, which is really great, because I don't have to worry about meeting her parents. But the first time we had sex I said, "Who's your daddy?" and she said, "I don't know."—Jay Gates

Have you noticed that you never seem to get laid on Thanksgiving? I think it's because all the coats are on the bed. —George Carlin

HA HA HA **Make 'Em Laugh** _____

If there's something you do while telling a joke that makes people laugh—a vocal inflection, the way you pronounce a certain word, or even a hand gesture—take note of it, and try to do it again next time. If you stumble across something funny by accident, that doesn't make it any less legitimate. After all, as comedy legend George Carlin says, "When you hear the phrase 'sense of humor,' you always hear the accent on *humor*, but to me, it's the *sense* of humor, an understanding and a feeling."

A government worker accused his manager of sex discrimination for making him wear a tie to work every day. Apparently, the man was forced to wear the tie around his genitals.—Larry Getlen

I was in an online chat room where an orgy was taking place. And I was participating, but they kept on ignoring me ... just like in real life.—Chris Cardenas

The first time I went to the gynecologist, I was so nervous and scared. The doctor lifted up my paper gown and said, "Oops, you forgot something. I need you to take your underwear off." I said, "Oh, I thought it might be nice if you took them off." 'Cause you have to make them feel uncomfortable, too.—Debbie Shea

I just found out my ex-girlfriend needs a kidney transplant, and I'm not really worried, 'cause her body hasn't rejected an organ in 25 years. That's not fair. In all fairness to her, she could probably count every guy she every slept with on one hand—if she was holding a friggin' calculator.—Tom Cotter

I blame my mother for my poor sex life. All she told me was, "The man goes on top and the woman underneath." For 3 years my husband and I slept on bunk beds.—Joan Rivers

Who Made the Funny?

As a young man, Redd Foxx, who had taken a job washing dishes, was known around town as "Chicago Red, the funniest dishwasher on earth." One reason for the nickname was to distinguish him from a good friend of his who was known as "Detroit Red." Detroit Red was later to be known by another name—Malcolm X.

The definition of *indecent*—when it's in long, and it's in hard, and it's in deep—it's in decent.—Redd Foxx

I want to know who invented edible panties. Someone, somewhere was going down on his lover and thought, *God, I could go for a fruit roll-up right about now.*—Bob Reinhard

Ever realize your dream might be someone else's nightmare,

and your nightmare might be someone else's dream? Like, my dream to f*ck Cindy Crawford—don't you think that's her nightmare?—Dave Attell

A new report says girls begin experiencing sexual harassment as early as high school. I think that's a pretty good time to start learning how our government works.—Craig Kilborn

I don't watch pornographic movies. 'Cause if you watch pornographic movies, you start to think what they're doing is normal and then you get in trouble. My girlfriend would be like, "What are you doing?" And I'd be like, "Spanking you." And she's like, "Why?" "'Cause I'm your daddy?" And then she's like, "Oh, okay." And then she started spanking me. And then she started beating the crap out of me. I'm like, "I think we have a misunderstanding." —Mitch Fatel

Women have come up with all these expressions to reassure us. "Oh honey, it's not the size of the ship, it's the motion of the ocean." Which might be true, but I know it takes a long time to get to England in a rowboat.—Jeff Foxworthy

Women can have more than one orgasm? Right. I'll believe *that* when I see it.—Garry Shandling

According to a new survey in *Glamour* magazine, 60 percent of women say they can't have an orgasm unless they use a specific position. Strangely enough, the position is the Heimlich maneuver.—Conan O'Brien

The girl I'm dating took a banana and teased it in a suggestive manner. When she finished, she said, "Did you like that? That could be you." I replied, "Well then, I should get that dark soft spot looked at."—Deric Harrington

In Hong Kong, there's seven million people on this little island. You wanna scream at people, "Stop f*cking! You have to stop f*cking!" But I don't think they can, because it's so crowded. As soon as you get home and take your pants off, you're inside another person.—Jake Johannsen

Have you ever had a girl yell another man's name out in the height of passion? Well, this girl took it the whole 9 yards. She's yelling out names of men who've never lived. She's like, "Oh, fuck me, Santa. Give it to me, Aquaman. Ram it, Blue M&M. I'm going to come, Papa Smurf." And I'm thinking, *Is she crazy, or is she just looking at my sheets?*
—Dave Attell

I was born gay, but eight months of breast-feeding wiped that right out. I'm just glad my dad wasn't walking around naked when I was teething.—Nick DiPaolo

I bang a lot of black guys. It's not by choice; I just haven't lost enough weight to get a white guy to f*ck me.—Lisa Lampanelli

I was with this girl one time. We're about to have sex, everything's cool, and she took one look at my penis and just started screaming, which is weird. All right, well, she didn't *know* we were about to have sex. But that is not my fault—she sits next to me on a bus, what am I supposed to think?—Pat Dixon

My girlfriend has a weird deformity. One of her breasts is larger than the other two.—Dwight York

I went into a sex toy store, and they had a long table filled with jars of something called "Jerk-Off Cream." But that's not even the weird part. The weirdest part is that on one of the jars, on a strip across the top, it said, "Tester." So ... I'm not allowed back in that store anymore. But I'm happy to say, the product works.—Larry Getlen

My girlfriend has crabs. I bought her fishnet stockings.
—Jay London

The Supreme Court says pornography is any act that has
no artistic merit and causes sexual thoughts. Sounds like
every commercial on television, doesn't it? When I see
those two twins on that Doublemint commercial, I'm not
thinking of gum. I am thinking of chewing. Maybe that's
the connection.—Bill Hicks

My girlfriend claims the best sex we ever had was the time
I wore a ski mask and came in through the bedroom window pretending to be a burglar. I have no idea what she's
talking about.—Dwight York

The definition of a phallic symbol is an object that is
longer than it is wide. Great. My penis isn't even a phallic
symbol.—Mike Morse

My wife insists on turning out
the lights before we make
love, which does not bother
me. It's the hiding that seems
so cruel.—Jonathan Katz

I always wanted to sleep with
twins. The closest I got was a
girl with an extra set of chro-
mosomes.—Bruce Cherry

Who Made the Funny?

Jonathan Katz attended
Goddard College in
Vermont with filmmaker David
Mamet, has appeared in three
of Mamet's films (*State and
Main*, *Things Change*, and
The Spanish Prisoner), and co-
wrote the story for Mamet's
House of Games.

You realize it only costs 70 cents a day to sponsor a starving
person, and it costs $2.99 a minute to talk dirty to some-
body. One hour of phone sex will feed 259 starving people.
If we could just get these starving people to just talk dirty
to us …. "I'm famished. Call me."—Gregg Rogell

New York officials were embarrassed when they placed an ad around the city that said, "Read Books, Get Brain," then discovered that "get brain" is street slang for oral sex. However, they still don't see the problem with the ad, "Study Hard, Mind the Balls."—Ben Schwartz

Prostitution is legal in Amsterdam. They actually display prostitutes in store windows. I think that's nice, because it makes window-shopping nice for men. "Hey, she would look really good on me!"—Debbie Shea

I once made love for an hour and five minutes. Well … it was the day you push the clocks ahead. But I don't think she saw that.—Garry Shandling

Fellas, let's say you go to a strip club, and you weren't supposed to be there. Don't get the stripper wearing the glitter. That's a tough one to get out of. "What are you doing with all that glitter on you?" "Uh, I was making you a card?"—John Heffron

I slept with a girl. In the morning I asked if she wanted breakfast in bed. She said that one pig in a blanket was enough.—Jay London

I masturbated in the car once. That's a cry for help. I wouldn't do it again, though, 'cause the cab driver got really pissed off. I'm like, "I'm sorry, sir. All I saw was a 'No Smoking' sign."—Mitch Fatel

Sex with one person is like a slinky. At first you stretch it out and see how long it can go. But after a while it just gets old and rusty, and you have to start playing with other toys.—Danny Hirsh

I'm thinking of filing sexual harassment charges at work. No one has ever even glanced my way sexually, and as a man I find that offensive.—Nick Tarr

Wouldn't it be cool to have sex on one of those memory foam beds they show on TV, then jump up real quick to see what kind of design you made?—Chris Loud

Money can't buy you love, but love can't buy you hookers.—Geoff Holtzman

My fiancée buys generic birth control. It's called "Eh, What're the Odds?"—Deric Harrington

Hackity Hack

Timing is everything in comedy—not just in *how* you tell a joke, but in *when* you tell it as well. You may not want to tell a joke "right after your dead aunt's eulogy," says comic Kerri Louise, comedically making the point that there's a right time and a wrong time for everything, and that goes double for telling jokes. You want an audience that's already in a good mood, because they're more inclined to laugh.

You know your sex life has been bad when you finally go to the gynecologist for contraceptives and he congratulates you.—Debbie Shea

Sometimes when I'm eating a sandwich, I'm thinking, *Man, this is really good.* And sometimes when I'm making love, I'm thinking, *Man, this is really expensive.*—Chris Cardenas

If we call having sex "sleeping with someone," I think we should call sleeping "having sex with someone." Just to be consistent. "I was so tired last night, I was screwing before my head hit the pillow!" "I can't stay up that late. I need my beauty sex!" "Tonight, I'm going to f*ck like a baby!" —Michael "Ziggy" Danziger

I thought I got a girl pregnant once. She called me up and she's like, "I think I'm pregnant," and I was like, "the number you have reached ..."—Mitch Fatel

My friend asked me if you eat edible condoms before or after you have sex. That's just gross. Personally, I eat them right out of the bag.—Debbie Shea

I hate most spam, but I hate my spam blocker more. Spam is anything I don't want to read, and that's subjective. What makes it think I *do* want to read the e-mail from my co-worker Jerry reminding me that Friday is Hawaiian shirt day, but that I *don't* want to read an e-mail about Horny, Barely Legal Sluts Taking It in the Face?—John Westerhaus

There have to be gay retarded people. Where's their march? "We're here! We're queer! *Apples!*"—Patton Oswalt

Gay people think everybody's gay. Ben Affleck. Gay. Matt Damon. Gay. Tom Cruise. Gay. Ever notice they only claim the attractive ones? Have you ever heard a gay guy go, Danny DeVito. Gay. Al Roker. F*cked him!—Ant

People say gay marriage will ruin the sanctity of marriage. C'mon, we've screwed that up pretty good by now. It might actually raise the bar, because it'll be rare to see a gay couple getting married *just* because one of them's pregnant.—Vic Alejandro

The state of Louisiana wants to pass a new law that requires students to refer to their teachers as "sir" or "ma'am." However, students will still be allowed to refer to certain gym teachers as "she-man."—Conan O'Brien

They don't want gays in the Boy Scouts. But who are the Boy Scouts? Young men in matching uniforms, short shorts, knee-high socks, little kerchiefs around their necks, and every time they do something good they get a patch they can sew on a sash. That's gay.—Ant

Let's make a law that gay people can have birthdays, but straight people get more cake—you know, to send the right message to kids.—Bill Maher

I was talking to my son the other day, and he said that his friend Billy has two mommies. I thought, wow. Billy's daddy is a lucky guy. My wife would never go for that. —Brian Kiley

I chased a girl for two years only to discover that her tastes were exactly like mine: we were both crazy about girls. —Groucho Marx

Here's what it is about gay marriage. Gay people don't think things all the way through. You wanna marry me? That means I gotta meet your family. I already have one family that hates me. Why do I want two?—Ant

HA HA HA   Make 'Em Laugh

For reasons that fall almost beyond explanation, some words are funnier than others. Don't try to figure out why—they just are. And one of the golden rules of word choice in jokes is that words with a K sound are funnier. As Milton Berle put it, "Cabbage is a funnier vegetable than lettuce. Broccoli is funny. Tomatoes aren't. If you have to name a character in an anecdote, call him Ken Plotnick rather than Sid Lowell."

President Bush is expected to endorse a constitutional amendment banning gay marriages. I don't think President Bush understands this whole gay marriage issue. Today he said, "I don't have anything against gay guys, I just don't want to see one marrying my daughter."—Jay Leno

My brother is gay, and my parents don't care—as long as he marries a doctor.—Elayne Boosler

Shopping
32
If You Can Find a Better Joke ...

Buying a used rental car is like going to a house of ill repute looking for a wife. Anything that's been driven that hard by that many people, you really don't wanna put your key in it.—Jeff Foxworthy

I went to a vending machine to get a candy bar, and the thing said "HH," so I pushed the "H" button twice. Potato chips came out, 'cause they had an "HH" button, for Chrissake. I mean, you need to let me know! I am not familiar with the system of "HH!" I did not learn my AA BB CCs. God God dammit dammit!—Mitch Hedberg

You know what I like to do when I'm in a video store? You know the quick drop they have in there? I like to stick my penis in there and then look at the help and go, "Have you seen this? Is this any good? Oh ... it's due back Tuesday?"—Zach Galifianakis

What I don't get are these people who, instead of buying a 4-pack or an 8-pack of toilet paper, they buy the single, individual roll. Are they trying to quit?—Brian Kiley

I wanted to buy a candle holder, but the store didn't have one. So I got a cake.—Mitch Hedberg

My favorite shelf at the big book store? The staff recommendation shelf. Oh, golly, I need help finding a book. How about 7 *Habits of Highly Effective People*, as recommended by Jimmy the stock clerk?—Todd Barry

Hackity Hack

There are many reasons Woody Allen is a success. Perhaps more than anything else, he understands that audiences love a performer who is self-deprecating. Conversely, no one is more hated than a bully. Remember this when telling jokes or stories you've personalized. "I think it often backfires, when telling comedic stories about yourself, if you demonize others," says acclaimed humorist and author Jonathan Ames. "It's an easy thing to do and perhaps will make you unsympathetic to the audience. That's why I always like to make myself the butt of my jokes—it gets the audience on my side."

American consumers have no problem with carcinogens, but they will not purchase any product—including floor wax—that has fat in it.—Dave Barry

The flap on the inside of the vending machine is a great invention. Before that, it was hard times for the vending machine owner. "Hey, which candy bar are you getting?" "That one … and every one on the bottom row!"—Mitch Hedberg

I was in a candle store and picked one up called "A Perfect Christmas." It smelled like my parents not fighting. —Veronica Mosey

Why is it that K-Mart won't take back underwear that's been opened, but they'll take back a toilet seat within 30 days?—Nick Tarr

I'm one of those people who can't stick to a wish list when getting someone a present. I always have to go above and beyond. One time I was like, "I know you wanted those new sneakers for your birthday, but instead I got you a make-your-own sneakers kit. It comes with fabric, patterns, and this small Ethiopian boy."—Bri Cowan

Ever notice that Soup for One is eight aisles away from Party Mix?—Elayne Boosler

I was at the grocery store buying eight apples, and the clerk asked me if I would like a bag, and I said, "No, man, I juggle! But I can only juggle eight. If I'm ever here buying nine apples, bag 'em up!"—Mitch Hedberg

I went to the bookstore. I spent $100 on books, and I go to the guy, "Can I have a book marker?" He goes, "We don't give 'em away. We sell 'em for a dollar." Do I look that dumb? Why don't I just take the dollar and put *that* in the book?—Rich Vos

Every pack of Marlboro has 5 Marlboro miles on it. Collect 340,000 miles, you can get a kayak. That's 68,000 packs of cigarettes. If I'm smoking 68,000 packs of cigarettes, I don't need a kayak. I need an oxygen tank.—Ant

Make 'Em Laugh

If you love telling jokes but haven't had much success getting actual laughs—don't give up. Making people laugh can be a difficult thing, but if you pay attention to what works and what doesn't, you can tweak things and improve. "It's kind of like asking: how do you talk to people?" notes former *Saturday Night Live* writer Leo Allen. "It's largely intuitive, and you have to learn what works for you. Everyone is different, and that is why people who cultivate what is unique in them and learn how to honestly share it are always more interesting than those who learn some tricks to make a crowd laugh like trained seals." So take your time, don't be afraid to fail, and learn what is unique in how *you* tell jokes.

I want to get a vending machine with fun-sized candy bars and the glass in front is a magnifying glass. You'll be mad, but it will be too late.—Mitch Hedberg

I saw a security guard at the 99-cent store. I'm thinking, do you know how much I'd have to steal to make it worth paying you?—Alonzo Bodden

Guys, have you ever woken up with an erection and then you realize you're just in the massage chair at Brookstone?—Zach Galifianakis

Every McDonald's commercial ends the same way—"prices and participation may vary." I wanna open a McDonald's and not participate in anything. Cheeseburgers? Nope. We got spaghetti. And blankets.—Mitch Hedberg

Cologne ads are pretty stupid. "It smells like a man." Who wants that? They don't even tell you which man. It could be Slappy, the bait shop guy.—Monica Piper

Sports

Buy Me Some Peanuts and Cracker Jack ...

You play baseball, with the World Series, and America's won every year. It's impressive, in a world event, for America to win so many years. Well done to you.—Eddie Izzard

If I was an Olympic athlete, I would rather come in last than win the silver medal. You win the gold, you feel good. You win the bronze, at least you got something. But the silver's like, congratulations, you almost won. Of all the losers, you came in first.—Jerry Seinfeld

My husband's from England. I watched a football game with him, and that was lots of fun, because he had never seen one before. So I could tell him anything I wanted. I told him it was over at halftime.—Rita Rudner

Blatant Lies

This began a string of little white lies that ultimately led to disaster for Rita's husband, after he mistakenly declared victory in an important tennis match at 30-Love, and when he was later barred from a Vegas casino after trying to collect blackjack winnings after being dealt an ace and a five.

I think poker should be an Olympic sport. The French guy could lead off the betting with 10,000 euros. Then the guy from Zimbabwe would say, "I see your 10,000 euros, and I raise you this baby."—Steve Hofstetter

This one time I was in a convenience store, and a guy came up and asked me, "What's the score?" and I said, "What's the game? If it's a competition between me and you, and the object is to ask the other guy questions he doesn't give a sh*t about, then you are winning, one to nothing.—Mitch Hedberg

Fishing is boring, unless you catch an actual fish—then it is disgusting.—Dave Barry

Roger Clemens has come out of retirement to play for the Astros in his hometown of Houston. He retired after the World Series and is now back out of retirement. He said he ended his retirement because he wants to spend less time with his family.—David Letterman

Pete Rose yesterday was denied membership into the Canadian Baseball Hall of Fame. Which is okay, because the only person in the Canadian Baseball Hall of Fame is Wayne Gretzky.—Conan O'Brien

Skiers view snowboarders as a menace; snowboarders view skiers as Elmer Fudd.—Dave Barry

In the U.K., a man celebrated a rugby victory by cutting off his own testicles. He cut off his own testicles! What do you do when your team *loses?*—Craig Ferguson

In Athens, a taxi driver returned an Olympic silver medal left in his cab. Unfortunately, the world will only remember the driver who came in seconds earlier, returning the gold medal.—Ben Schwartz

Hackity Hack

How dangerous to a joke is the impulse to "punch it up"? Even David Lee Roth, one of the world's most outrageous performers, advises against it. "Resist the temptation to underline your own material," says Diamond Dave. "Skip the question mark at the end of your sentence, skip the exclamation mark, skip the semi-colon, skip the dot dot dot, skip the comma. Most people cannot resist the temptation to make a face to show you what they really mean, or to wink an eye to say "we're all in on this, aren't we?" Most individuals can't resist stopping and looking to the audience. But if you can get real, real Zen, and you can drop all of that, then you're forever."

The Supreme Court ruled that disabled golfer Casey Martin has a legal right to ride in a golf cart between shots at PGA Tour events. Man, the next thing you know, they're going to have some guy carry his clubs around for him.
—Jon Stewart

The fastest-growing sport in the country is NASCAR. Cars going around in a circle. That's like seeing your clothes spinning around in the dryer and saying, "Hey, let's make a day of this."—Larry Getlen

What brought me to California was the Olympics. I tried every event for the Olympics. Pole vault? I drove that sucker right into the ground. I did a good thing though. I straightened out those uneven parallel bars. Broad jump? Killed her.—Louie Anderson

Due to poor ratings, the XFL is giving away free advertising time on broadcasts, which would explain why tonight's game was brought to us by "Happy Graduation! Love, Neil's Parents."—Jimmy Fallon

Football combines the two worst features of American life: it is violence punctuated by committee meetings.—George Will

When I play sports, I like to cheat, but in the wrong sport. Like when I play football, I dribble with two hands. Or when I figure skate, I use a cork-filled bat.—Geoff Holtzman

I love all the great rivalries in college football. But I think there's one game that's really unfair, and that's Army-Navy. I mean, every year they play it on land.—Tim Cavanagh

I saw the hottest woman ever wearing a Chicago Bears jersey. I thought that was awesome—a hot chick who likes failure.—Pete Lee

Foosball messed up my perception of soccer. I thought you had to kick the ball and then spin 'round and 'round. I can't do a back flip, much less several ... simultaneously with two other guys ... who look just like me.—Mitch Hedberg

Men in America are way too invested in sports. Guys—you are not the tenth man. You're a machine for turning beer into piss. It's so sad, when the team wins, and they go, "We won!" No—you didn't win anything. Ten black guys who would hate you if they knew you won.—Bill Maher

According to *The New York Post*, due to steroid use, some players have actually seen their heads balloon four hat sizes. Four hat sizes! How creepy is that? These guys are turning into their own bobble heads.—Jay Leno

There's always one of my uncles who watches a boxing match with me and says, "Sure. $10 million. You know, for that kind of money, I'd fight him." As if someone is going to pay $200 a ticket to see a 57-year-old carpet salesman get hit in the face once and cry.—Larry Miller

The quarterback's spending so much time behind the center that he may jeopardize his right to lead a Boy Scout troop.—Dennis Miller (on *Monday Night Football*)

You never have to keep score when you play golf with Jerry Ford. You just look back along the fairway and count the wounded.—Gene Perret (written for Bob Hope)

Karate is a form of marital arts in which people who have had years and years of training can, using only their hands and feet, make some of the worst movies in the history of the world.—Dave Barry

A computer once beat me at chess. But it was no match for me at kick-boxing.—Emo Philips

HA HA HA   Make 'Em Laugh

So you've memorized your joke, you've rehearsed it, you know it like the back of your hand—and you trip over your words or mix up a sentence anyway. Now what? "If you screw it up, acknowledge that you screwed it up," says Lisa Lampanelli, who adds that you should "maybe make a joke about yourself that you screwed it up, because people sense when you screw it up. So if I repeat a joke onstage tonight, I'm gonna have to say, 'Oops, did I say that? Sorry,' and kinda make a joke on myself a bit. You need to have a sense of humor about yourself as much as the material."

I took up speed fishing. I fish in a goldfish bowl. I'm done in one minute.—Craig Sharf

Performance-enhancing drugs are banned from the Olympics. But performance-debilitating drugs should not be banned. Smoke a joint and win the hundred meters— that's pretty damned good.—Eddie Izzard

Bullfights are hugely popular because you can sit comfortably with a hot dog and possibly watch a man die. It won't be me, but I can sit comfortably and watch it.—Albert Brooks

In a recent interview, a NASCAR driver said, "We ain't got no nuthin' standin' in our way for Sunday." That's a triple negative. He screwed up and accidentally said what he meant.—Greg Volk

The depressing thing about tennis is that no matter how good I get, I'll never be as good as a wall.—Mitch Hedberg

You know you're out too late when you come home and there's two white guys boxing on ESPN.—Jeff Foxworthy

I love Darryl Strawberry, but he's been in and out of Betty Ford more often than Jerry Ford.—Jeffrey Ross

HA HA HA **Make 'Em Laugh**

If you wanna talk about that weird thing happening in Washington or in the tabloids but don't have a joke handy— well, you may not need one. "Topical doesn't have to be as funny, because it's topical," says comedian D. C. Benny, who points out that current events seem like "something that just happened in the room, which is always funniest." So giving a snarky quip about something current can be as funny as a prepared punch line.

The luge is the only sport where you could have people competing in it against their will and it would be exactly the same.—Jerry Seinfeld

Some buddies of mine talked me into going bungee jump-
ing with them. Learned something important about myself.
Turns out I will jump off a bridge if my friends do, too.
—Dwight York

Warner had more hands in his face than an OB-GYN
delivering Vishnu's triplets!—Dennis Miller (on *Monday
Night Football*)

I'm not good at golf. I never got a hole in one, but I *did* hit
a guy once, and that's way more satisfying. I hit a guy-in-
one. What's par for hitting a guy? One. If you hit a guy in
two, you are an a**hole.—Mitch Hedberg

I was watching ESPN when poker came on, and I thought,
finally … I'm an athlete.—Deric Harrington

Members of a Uruguayan rugby team that crashed in the
Andes 30 years ago and were forced to eat human flesh to
survive, won the rugby match they were supposed to play
30 years before. The team credited their victory to aggressive play, and to the fact that every time someone on the
other team had the ball, they would yell, "Give me the ball,
or I'll eat your flesh!"—Larry Getlen

Ninety-nine-pound Sonya
Thomas ate 35 bratwursts in
10 minutes. Even more
impressive, Kirstie Alley ate
Sonya Thomas in 5 minutes.
—Ben Schwartz

Maybe it's because I'm from
the city, but I don't understand
NASCAR. These guys just go
in circles all day, and after 5 or
6 laps, I'm just like, "Come on,
buddy, you're not gonna find a
spot."—Geoff Holtzman

Hackity Hack

"Never tell people 'this
is funny' before you tell
the joke," says comedian
and Sirius radio host Steve
Hofstetter. The reason—you're
immediately setting up expectations your joke may not meet,
and asking for prejudgment of
a joke you haven't even told
yet. Just tell the joke and let the
listeners decide.

A Russian mobster was charged with fixing the Olympic figure skating events, arranging for skaters to win medals in exchange for a French visa for himself. Russian sports officials dispute the charges, calling them, "a funny fantasy that belonged in a Hollywood film script." As opposed to, say, *Men in Black II*, which would have been more entertaining as an Olympic skating scandal.—Larry Getlen

What is the point of the helmet in skydiving? Can you *kinda* make it? You jump out of the plane and the chute doesn't open, the helmet is now wearing *you* for protection.—Jerry Seinfeld

I used to be a cheerleader. I cheered for soccer and hockey. People are usually pretty impressed when I tell them that, and curious. They say, "Hockey? What did you wear?" Well, we wore a facemask, and then for the after party … knee pads.—Debbie Shea

A lot of NASCAR fans don't like Jeff Gordon because Jeff Gordon enunciates. There is not a place in NASCAR for that kind of stuff.—Jeff Foxworthy

My uncle was a major league baseball pitcher. Unfortunately, he was so afraid of intimacy, he couldn't even hold the runner on first.—Bruce Cherry

I'm not into sports. If I had athlete's foot, my first reaction would be, "That's not my f*cking foot."—Mitch Hedberg

Technology

Better Living Through Geekistry

I bought one of these laser jet printers—99 bucks. What a steal, I thought—until the little ink cartridge ran out and I had to buy a new one. $700. So I went to the pet shop, bought myself a little octopus. Every time the ink cartridge runs out I just strap it to his little ass, throw my shark costume on, sneak up on his tank, and scare the crap out of him. Get my ink for free now.—Harland Williams

I just bought a computer. Fifteen hundred bucks, with extra memory. Then I find out that for an extra $10, you can get one that holds a grudge.—Jonathan Katz

Buying the right computer and getting it to work properly is no more complicated than building a nuclear reactor from wristwatch parts in a darkened room using only your teeth.—Dave Barry

I shop at a computer store called, "Your Crap's Already Obsolete."—Jeff Cesario

If you asked me to name the three scariest threats facing the human race, I would give the same answer that most people would: nuclear war, global warming, and Windows.—Dave Barry

In the wake of all these computer viruses running around lately, remember that when you link your computer up with another computer, you're actually linking up with every computer that the computer you've linked to has ever linked with.—Dennis Miller

They've finally come up with the perfect office computer. If it makes a mistake, it blames another computer.—Milton Berle

I got an e-mail from this blind guy. I can't understand a word … it's all dots.—Kai Ajaye

Experts agree that the best type of computer for your individual needs is one that comes on the market about two days after you actually purchase some other computer. —Dave Barry

A computer is a stupid machine with the ability to do incredibly smart things, while computer programmers are smart people with the ability to do incredibly stupid things.—Bill Bryson

In the computer revolution, everything changes way too fast for the human brain to comprehend. That is why only 14 year olds really understand what is going on.—Dave Barry

I'm very upset with the phone company. They have me loaded up with all these useless options. I have caller ID and caller ID blocking. What a scam that is. You caller ID me, I caller ID block you. I caller ID you, you caller ID block me. We're paying $20 a month to neutralize each other.—Joe Bolster

Bill Gates is a very rich man today … and do you want to know why? The answer is one word: *versions*.—Dave Barry

Now we have hands-free phones so you can focus on the thing you're really supposed to be doing. Chances are, if you need both of your hands to do something, your brain should be in on it, too.—Ellen DeGeneres

By the end of this century, via virtual reality, a man will be able to simulate making love to any woman he wants through his television set. You know, the day an unemployed iron worker can lie on his Barcalounger with a Foster's in one hand and channel flicker in the other and f*ck Claudia Shiffer for $19.95, it's gonna make crack look like Sanka.—Dennis Miller

We don't know where the digitial revolution is taking us, only that when we get there we will not have enough RAM.—Dave Barry

The other day I called my computer helpline, because I needed to be made to feel ignorant by someone much younger than me.—Bill Bryson

I don't own a computer. I'm waiting for the kind where I can look at the screen and say, "Hey, I need a pizza," and one comes out and hits me in the eyebrows.—Kathleen Madigan

My father worked for the same firm for 12 years. They fired him. They replaced him with a tiny gadget *this big*. It does everything my father does, only it does it much better. The depressing thing is my mother ran out and bought one.—Woody Allen

The cell phone people say there's absolutely no danger from cell phone radiation. Boy, it didn't take those tobacco executives long to find new jobs, did it?—Jay Leno

I blame the microwave for most of our problems. Anything that gets that hot without fire—that's from the devil.—Ellen DeGeneres

I got a computer. I wrote an apology note to my VCR for ever thinking it was difficult. You find someone in this country who can print out an envelope. Maybe the fifth envelope, but you have to kill four to get to the fifth one. —Elayne Boosler

They say computers can't think, but I have one that does. It thinks it's broken.—Gene Perret

Travel

It Broadens You—Now, You're Broad with Malaria!

The only thing I know about Africa is that it's far, far away. About a 35-hour flight. The boat ride's so long, there are still slaves on their way here.—Chris Rock

My hotel doesn't have a thirteenth floor because of superstition. But c'mon, man, people on the fourteenth floor, you know what floor you're really on. "What room are you in?" "1401." "No you're not. Jump out the window, you will die earlier." —Mitch Hedberg

I went on vacation last year, I was in such a rush to get to the airport, I got there and realized I forgot my luggage. I felt so stupid—carried my clothes in a big pile. Took me hours to get all my sh*t off that belt.—Brian Kiley

I was on the airplane coming over here. It's a nonsmoking plane. Get this—no smoking, but they allow *children*. Hmmm. "Well, smoking bothers me." Well, guess what …?—Bill Hicks

I've been traveling a lot. Just got back from the Vatican. Kind of disillusioning. They have a Hard Rock.—Dennis Miller

They have an Airfone on planes. I was talking to my mother, and you know how sometimes you just wanna get off the phone? I forgot I was on the plane. I said, "Mom, I gotta go, there's someone at the door." And she knew I was on the plane, but she forgot and went, "Oh, all right, I'll let you go then." —Garry Shandling

They didn't let one guy on a plane because he had a boomerang. The most he could do is hurt himself. —Rich Vos

Hackity Hack

"Wanting your audience to like you is a sure comedy killer," says former *Saturday Night Live* writer Leo Allen, who tells the story of legendary theater actors The Lunt Family. "The Lunts were in a play," says Allen, "and one of the biggest laughs was when Mr. Lunt would ask for the tea. When they were well into the run, the audience stopped laughing. Frustrated, he said to his wife, 'Why don't they laugh when I ask for the tea anymore?' And she said, 'Because you're not asking for the tea. You're asking for the laugh.' I think that is really true about jokes." If you think, "Gee, I really hope they laugh," it'll show. Just tell the story *your* way.

At the airport they asked me if anybody I didn't know gave me anything. Even the people I know don't give me anything.—George Wallace

We have too much security, and airport security is the worst 'cause they check us for the wrong things. You can't bring tweezers on an airplane. If I'm on a plane and you try to hijack it with tweezers, I'll whip your ass.—Alonzo Bodden

I was on a plane three weeks ago, and I was dressed to kill—I had a turban, a beard, exploding sandals …—Tom Cotter

My flight almost didn't take off. We were picketed by a right-to-life group after the captain had to abort a take-off. Hey, but who among us is wise enough to know when flight really begins?—Dennis Miller

In the Atlanta airport, they built a Plexiglas box that contains all the things that are no longer allowed in your carry-on luggage, and in that box there is a leaf blower and a Coleman lantern. So if you are an international yard man that likes to work nights, you're out of luck.—Jeff Foxworthy

I spent the night in a low-class hotel. When I walked in, the first thing I saw was a mint on the pillow. It was in the mouth of a dead hooker.—Mike Morse

Recently, my reservation got messed up, and I stayed at an X-rated motel room. They offered closed-circuit TV. That's a title that scares me, closed-circuit TV. If I'm watching the movie in Room 6, how do I know I'm not the movie in Room 7?—John Fox

Here's a travel tip—never ever pack when you're high. You get there, you open your bag, nothing matches. All you have to wear is a Hawaiian shirt, an oven mitt, and a lava lamp. The rest of the bag is full of cookie dough and Hot Wheels trucks—and for some reason, an anal thermometer.—Dave Attell

You know the oxygen masks on airplanes? I don't think there's really any oxygen. I think they're just to muffle the screams.—Rita Rudner

What a lousy hotel. They stole towels from us. The bridal suite was in the basement.—Phyllis Diller

Oh, we're free to move about the cabin, are we? Well, lucky us. I hear the kegger in row 4 is off the hook.—Elie Saltzman

Who Made the Funny?

Saturday Night Live is comedy's most infamous launching pad, but there's also an impressive list of performers whose time on the show proved unproductive, yet who later went on to great success. Dave Attell spent one year as a writer on the show and never found a way to integrate the cutting-edge comedic sensibility that would prove so hysterical on Comedy Central's *Insomniac*. But at least he's in good company. Other performers who fizzled on *SNL* only to blossom in other venues include Janeane Garofalo, Ben Stiller, Sarah Silverman, and Larry David.

I got back to my hotel at 7:30 in the morning and I told the little girl behind the desk I need to leave a wake-up call for 7, and she said, "Mr. White, it's past 7." I said, "No, the next one." —Ron White

A hotel minibar is a machine that makes everything expensive. And when I take something out of the minibar, I always fathom that I'm gonna replace it before they can check me off and charge me. But they make that sh*t impossible to replace. I go to the store, "Do you have Coke in a glass harmonica? Do you have individually wrapped cashews?" —Mitch Hedberg

Flew in here on a very small airplane. Limited baggage space on the plane. The stewardess came on the P.A. and said "All baggage must fit in the a** of the person in front of you." Needless to say, I lost the bag—and gained a friend and confidant for life.—Dennis Miller

In Washington, D.C., this week, passengers were forced off a Greyhound bus when it caught fire. No one was injured. Of course, Greyhound used their usual evacuation procedure ... women and drifters first.—Jay Leno

There are only two reasons to sit in the back row of an airplane. Either you have diarrhea, or you're anxious to meet people who do.—Richard Jeni

Television

1,000 Channels of Nothing on—Now in Hi-Def!

Is it me, or do commercials have nothing to do with the products anymore? This lady comes on TV with a black eye; she's crying, like, "I smoke crack. And my husband beats me." Then a voice came on, "Got milk?"—Dave Chappelle

I wanna do a reality show based on *The Mole*, but it's really about sexually transmitted diseases. It's called *God, I Hope That's a Mole*.—Zach Galifianakis

If it weren't for Philo T. Farnsworth, inventor of television, we'd still be eating frozen radio dinners.—Johnny Carson

In California, they don't throw their garbage away—they make it into TV shows.—Woody Allen

In the latter part of last year, we were introduced to the 24-hour all-cartoon channel and the 24-hour science-fiction channel. Of course, to make room for these, we had to get rid of the literacy channel, and the "What's left of f*ckin' civilization" channel.—Dennis Miller

---

Hackity Hack

While there are many notable differences between master comedians and amateurs, one main difference is in the level of commitment to the joke. Master comics are invested in every joke—they don't waver, they aren't unsure of themselves, and they never tell it half-assed out of fear it may not be funny. If you're going to tell a joke, you need the same level of commitment. "You shouldn't tell a bad joke and then say, 'I'm not a comedian,'" says comic Eugene Mirman. "If you're going to tell a joke, commit to it."

It's always been a dream of mine to be on *Hollywood Squares*. But then again, I eat my own poop.—Triumph the Insult Comic Dog

Tomorrow night Barbara Walters is interviewing Cuban dictator Fidel Castro. They are expected to talk about what it is like staying in power for so long while all your contemporaries die off—then they are going to talk about Castro.—Conan O'Brien

The Jerry Springer Show turned 10 years old today! Or as Jerry's guests would say, the show is now legal!—Craig Kilborn

Sesame Street has a character named Oscar. They treat this guy like sh*t the entire show. "Oscar, you are so mean, isn't he kids?" "Yeah Oscar, you're a grouch." He's like, "Bitch, I live in a f*cking trash can! I'm the poorest motherf*cker on Sesame Street!" Then you wonder why kids grow up and step over homeless people. "Get it together, grouch. Get a job, grouch."—Dave Chappelle

I wanna do a reality show where it's three racist white people that live in the South Bronx—and it's called *Cracker Hunt*. There'd be scenes of the white guys goin', "I didn't call you 'boy!'"—Zach Galifianakis

I find television very educating. Every time somebody turns on the set, I go into the other room and read a book.—Groucho Marx

The other day a woman came up to me and said, "Didn't I see you on television?" I said, "I don't know. You can't see out the other way."—Emo Philips

CBS is doing a movie about the life of Jesus. Today, the Fox Network announced they're doing a TV series about the life of Jesus called *Party of 13*.—Jay Leno

Who Made the Funny?

The fascinating battle between Jay Leno and David Letterman for the job of host of *The Tonight Show* was made into an equally fascinating book and movie called *The Late Shift*, written by *New York Times* reporter Bill Carter. In the movie, which aired on HBO, Letterman was played by John Michael Higgins, who has since distinguished himself as a regular in Christopher Guest's ensemble comedies, making hilarious appearances in *Best in Show* and *A Mighty Wind*.

One of the semi-finalists on the *American Idol* show was kicked out of the competition after it was found out that she had posed for a porn website. This marks the first time that anyone was too sleazy for a Fox show.—Conan O'Brien

You can always tell when television executives are in a restaurant; they keep ordering and canceling, ordering and canceling.—Bob Hope

I like TV. I learn things. I been watching *Desperate House-wives*, and I learned something watching that show. I didn't know white women just hang around the house waiting to f*ck strangers all day. If comedy don't work out, I'm gonna become a gardener.—Alonzo Bodden

If Velveeta ever morphs into a human form, it will become a local newscaster.—Dennis Miller

My favorite channel is the Lifetime channel, because Lifetime is television for women, yet for some reason there's always a woman getting beaten on that network. "Meredith Baxter Birney gets beaten with a rod in a Lifetime original— *Rod*."—Jim Gaffigan

The local news do these teases to get you to watch later on that are so incredibly cruel. "It could be the most deadly thing in the world, and you could be having it for dinner. We'll tell you what it is, tonight at 11." Is it peas?—Ellen DeGeneres

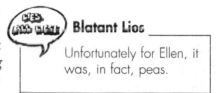

Blatant Lies

Unfortunately for Ellen, it was, in fact, peas.

My favorite part of *The Jerry Springer Show* is Jerry's "Final Thought." Like all of a sudden Jerry is going to add some perspective and sanity to tie it all together. I got news for you. Jerry only has one final thought. "Are the Siamese-Twin Hasidic Skinheads confirmed for tomorrow?"—Dennis Miller

The Fox Network has purchased the broadcasting rights to the classic movie *The Sound of Music* for the next five years. In order to boost the ratings, however, Fox will give it a new name—*When Singing Nazis Attack!*—Conan O'Brien

There's talk that Kathie Lee Gifford may get her own sit-com. The working title as of now is *Touched by a Pain in the Ass*.—Craig Kilborn

Urban Disturbances

That's No Solitary Confinement Chamber–That's My Apartment!

The funny thing about being in cabs in Manhattan is that you don't get scared, no matter how fast the guy goes. "Well, he's driving fast and recklessly, but he's a professional. He's got a cab driver's license." I don't even know what it takes to get a cab driver's license. I think all you need is a face.—Jerry Seinfeld

Garbage trucks come at 5 A.M. Why? They're picking up garbage. It's not gonna go bad *again*.—Dave Attell

Here's good news for those visiting the city and for those who live here. Crime is down 20 percent in the subways. I think it's true, too, because it's been weeks since I've had to say, "Put pressure on it while I go to find a cop."—David Letterman

There was a water main break in Chicago today that tied up traffic for several hours. The water level got pretty high in several parts of downtown. Authorities urged people to remain calm and reminded them that in an emergency, Oprah could be used as a flotation device.—Craig Kilborn

During the last couple years, one million additional people started riding New York subways. In fact, they say the subways are so crowded now, you can barely urinate without hitting someone.—Conan O'Brien

I was on the subway, sitting on a newspaper, and a guy comes over and asks, "Are you reading that?" I didn't know what to say. So I said, "Yes," stood up, turned the page, and sat down again.—David Brenner

Subway rates in New York City are going up to $2 per ticket. If the rates keep going up, this means it could eventually be cheaper to urinate in a cab.—Craig Kilborn

I like New York. This is the only city where you actually have to say things like, "Hey, that's mine! Don't pee on that!"—Louis C. K.

New York City has installed 3,000 security cameras in the subway, and it has already made a difference. The difference is 3,000 security cameras stolen.—David Letterman

I like when people valet park their SUV; that's fantastic to me. "I'm rugged, I'm outdoorsy, but I don't like to walk."—Nick Griffin

I know the Brady Bill is working. I was in New York last month, and I heard a guy say, "Give me your wallet, or I'll blow your brains out in five business days."—Jonathan Katz

New York's a funny place. I was at a coffee shop and I'm paying the cashier, and the other girl got sprayed by the espresso machine with the hot milk. Her shirt was burning her, so she just ripped it off. But she forgot she had no bra on. So she just ran to the back, and the cashier looks at me and goes, "That'll be an extra 2 bucks."—Greg Fitzsimmons

New York is an exciting town where something is happening all the time, most of it unsolved.—Johnny Carson

You know how I know New York is back to normal, like before the attacks? A woman got pushed in front of a train for the first time in, like, nine months. The city's getting back to the way it was. I got tired of people sittin' around too depressed to kill.—Patrice O'Neal

New York City can become festive at this time of the year. There's a guy, every morning when I'm coming to work, he gives me the finger. This morning, he gave me a finger puppet.—David Letterman

I love when people in New York City complain about smoking. These people are standing ankle deep in dog links, straddlin' a dead guy. Apparently, my cigarette is f*cking up the delicate balance of nature here. "Oh, this is bothering you? I'm sorry. Let me go over here to this pile of bum dung and put this out."—Bill Hicks

HA HA HA **Make 'Em Laugh**

Comedy is timing, and timing means patience. If your crowd is starting a vigorous round of who-can-top-this joke-telling, "Don't jump into it and punch yourself out," advises D. C. Benny. "Wait until the later rounds when the dust has settled and all the bad jokes have been told. Then quietly offer something attention catching like, 'My buddy Pete the contractor told me this before he got sent up to Leavenworth for that thing ....'"

I have six locks on my door, all in a row. When I go out, I lock every other one. I figure no matter how long somebody stands there picking the locks, they are always locking three.—Elayne Boosler

New York now leads the world's great cities in the number of people around whom you shouldn't make a sudden move.—David Letterman

Four in the morning my neighbor's car alarm went off. Scared me so bad I dropped my tools.—Dwight York

Vices

It's Me. Dave.

There's no smoking in bars now. And soon, no drinking and no talking.—Eddie Izzard

I knew I had a drug problem when I got a voicemail message—from myself. "This is you. Marijuana has destroyed your short-term memory, so write this down. Buy more marijuana. Save this message."—Basil White

Who Made the Funny?

Eddie Izzard holds the distinction of performing for the largest audience ever for a stand-up comic in the United Kingdom, performing for 13,632 people on December 15, 2003.

Marijuana grows everywhere. To make marijuana against the law is like saying God made a mistake.—Bill Hicks

I was so stoned in college, I thought *The Smurfs* was a documentary.—Larry Getlen

Although the IRS has begun to crack down on businessmen for the three-martini lunch, they will not bother the working man and the two-joint coffee break.—George Carlin

I can't think of anything worse after a night of drinking than waking up next to someone and not being able to remember their name, or how you met, or why they're dead.—Laura Kightlinger

Never drink and drive on toll roads. Because after a couple of six-packs, those toll baskets look just like urinals.—Mike Morse

Studies show that wine has become more popular among college students. In a related story, four frat guys were taken to the emergency room for breaking White Zinfandel bottles over their heads.—Craig Kilborn

I've been trying to quit smoking. It's the hardest thing you'll ever do in your life, and people who never smoked just don't get that. My wife goes, "I don't understand why you just don't put 'em down and quit." And I go, "All right, why don't you quit yelling? Because you can't."—Bill Engvall

HA HA HA **Make 'Em Laugh**

When asked what people should keep in mind when telling a joke, comedian Eugene Mirman advises you to "Yell very loudly!" when sharing the punch line. Of course, Eugene's kidding—that's exactly what you *shouldn't* do. The more understated the punch line, the more it'll take your listeners by surprise, thereby producing a bigger laugh.

To my delight, I find that there is a different warning on each pack of cigarettes. Mine says, *"Warning: Smoking can cause fetal damage or premature birth."* Screw it—I've found my brand! Just don't get the ones that say lung cancer, you know? Shop around.—Bill Hicks

In Texas, they have about a million drive-thru liquor stores. One on every corner. Great idea, huh? Just the thing for that drunk driver who's constantly on the go. "No time to stop at a real bar; I got things to do today—places to go, people to hit, busy, busy, busy."—Drew Carey

I know a man who gave up smoking, drinking, sex, and rich food. He was healthy right up to the day he killed himself. —Johnny Carson

I can't drink, because I don't know when to stop. Most people ease back if they puke or fall over. Not me. I don't stop drinking until I start walking toward the light.—Mike Storck

I used to do drugs. I still do—but I used to, too.—Mitch Hedberg

I've been out in L.A. a lot. L.A. is nothing but a bunch of driving. I hate all that driving, 'cause it interferes with my drinking.—Wanda Sykes

I was a very good girl, back in the day. At night, I was a whore and a coke fiend.—Joanna Parson

A drunk driver is very dangerous. So is a drunk backseat driver, if he's persuasive. "Dude, make a left." "Those are trees." "Trust me."—Demitri Martin

Hackity Hack

So you tell your joke, pour your heart and soul into it, and after the punch line you're met with blank stares? C'est la vie. Move on. Do *not* get angry, feel weird or embarrassed, or, even worse, blame your audience. Even the world's best comedians occasionally tell jokes that bomb (for proof, check out the brilliant Jerry Seinfeld documentary *Comedian*), and there could be any one of a million reasons for a joke's failure. So if your big joke falls flat, give a cute, self-deprecating shrug, and move on. Embittered, failed comics appeal to no one, but everyone appreciates grace under pressure.

They tell you that pot smoking makes you unmotivated. I think that's bullsh*t. When I'm high, I can do everything I normally do just as well—I just realize it's not worth the effort. "I'm just gonna go to that job and see that boss— f*ck it, I'm watching cartoons today."—Bill Hicks

I would never smoke crack. I would never do a drug named after a part of my own ass.—Denis Leary

My favorite alcohol is tequila, 'cos my brain cells sing the Mexican National Anthem as they die.—Basil White

Researchers are testing a new form of medical marijuana that treats pain but doesn't get the user high, prompting patients who need medical marijuana to declare, "Thank you?"—Jimmy Fallon

I'm originally from Iowa. I got kicked out when they realized I couldn't make meth.—John Vorhees

A company has come out with a brand-new breath analyzer that can tell parents if their child has been smoking pot. This is how it works: apparently, you hand your child a tube, and if he inhales and passes it to you, he's smoking pot.—Conan O'Brien

Two Wisconsin brothers, ages 74 and 80, were arrested this week after agents confiscated more than half a million dollars in pot on their property. When discovered in their home, the brothers were found laughing their asses off watching an episode of *Matlock*.—Jimmy Fallon

A friend of mine runs marathons, and he's always talking about this "runner's high." But he has to go 26 miles for it. That's why I smoke and drink. I get the same feeling from a flight of stairs.—Larry Miller

Ever pass out drunk, and leave something on all night—like a condom? You don't know till you get up to pee the next morning and there's, like, no noise. Just fills up like a water balloon. And it occurs to me, "Damn, I could have slept in another 10 minutes."—Pat Dixon

Who Made the Funny?

Redd Foxx's character on *Sanford and Son*, Fred Sanford, was the real name of Foxx's brother. Foxx's real name was John Sanford.

I feel sorry for people who don't drink or do drugs. Because someday they're going to be in a hospital bed, dying, and they won't know why.—Redd Foxx

A judge in Mobile, Alabama, has put a 90-year-old woman in jail for selling drugs. Here's my question—where are the parents?—Jay Leno

Things have good and bad sides, dangerous and beneficial at the same time. Why can't we understand that with drugs? Cars. Fire comes to mind. Only with drugs do we base the policy on what the losers do. We don't base automotive policy on how Gary Busey drives. And yet, we base drug policy on Gary Busey.—Bill Maher

New York City has a law that if you're caught drinking and driving, the police will keep your car. And they don't care who you are—they've already confiscated eight fire trucks.—Moody McCarthy

When you don't drink, people always need to know why. This never happens with anything else. "You don't use mayonnaise? Why? Are you addicted to mayonnaise? Is it okay if *I* use mayonnaise?"—Jim Gaffigan

The problem with the designated driver program— it's not a desirable job. But if you ever get sucked into doing it, have fun with it. At the end of the night, drop them off at the wrong house.—Jeff Foxworthy

It takes only one drink to get me drunk. The trouble is, I can't remember if it's the thirteenth or the fourteenth. —George Burns

Some of the best authors are alcoholics. It's odd we won't listen to a drunk talk, but we love what they write.—Jayson Cross

I had to take a drug test the other day. It came back negative. Which is good, I guess, but my dealer's got some explaining to do.—Dwight York

Drinking nonalcoholic beer is a total waste of time. It's like hiring a hooker, then going to the mall and holding her pocket book while she shops.—Mike Morse

I just recently stopped doing cocaine, and everyone asked me how I did it. It was simple. I thought about my health decline, my financial ruins, and the new black carpeting in my living room. My habit was no longer practical.—Molly Anderson

HA HA HA

Make 'Em Laugh

I said this toward the beginning of the book, but I'll say it again: *get to the punch line quickly!* "There's a certain amount of time you have before you get to the punch line before people's minds start wandering," says *Tonight Show* regular Mitch Fatel. "We're such an ADD generation and everybody has so many different things on their minds that the punch line has to come fast. So anything that has a long setup, throw it out. No matter how funny the ending is, by the time you get there, the majority of people will be zoned out and give you that fake laugh, where you know they didn't really enjoy the joke."

I had a horrible nightmare last night. I dreamt I drunk the world's largest margarita. I woke up this morning, there was salt on the toilet lid. Thank God I didn't eat the worm.—Larry the Cable Guy

Who Made the Funny?

Exactly how redneck is Larry the Cable Guy? How about this—it's been reported that when Larry (real name Daniel Lawrence Whitney) was growing up in Nebraska, he went to private school. Then, at 16, his family moved to Palm Beach, Florida—one of the richest counties in America. Pretty redneck, no? (No word on whether he's related to the Whitney's of "Whitney Museum" fame.)

Every time you read about someone famous overdosing on drugs, it's always someone really talented. Janis Joplin, Jimi Hendrix, John Belushi. The people you wanna overdose never would. Mötley Crüe would never overdose. You can put them in a room with 2 tons of crack, and they'll come out a half hour later, "*Rock on!*"—Denis Leary

Jack Daniel's has got a new magazine campaign ad: "At some point, you just know who you are." Yeah ... I think that point is when you say, "Hello, I'm Bill ... and I'm an alcoholic."—Jay Leno

Some people think that pot should be legalized. A lot of these people are involved in the Chex Mix, Frito Lay, and Cheesy Puff industry. –Danny Hirsh

I joined AA. Not because I'm an alcoholic, but because I seek anonymity.—Geoff Holtzman

Jose Cuervo is running a new promotion where on every bottle of tequila, they've attached a disposable camera. You know, if you're shooting pictures while drinking Cuervo, you're just gathering evidence for the police yourself. —Tony Deyo

Pot should be legal. You never get into bar fights, you drive 30 MPH, and you eat everything on your plate ... sometimes even the plate.—Nick Tarr

They say smoking marijuana makes you paranoid, but I found out: finding a short hair on your pizza works pretty well, too.—Deric Harrington

I was a weekend drinker. I'd start on Saturday, and end on Friday.—Bill Hicks

Who Made the Funny?

Considering how outspoken he was in talking against religion, Bill Hicks's first-ever stand-up set occurred in the unlikeliest of places—a church camp talent show!

I thank God for my inhaler, or I'd never be able to smoke.—Debbie Shea

You know what's a great way to quit smoking? Heroin. When I'm all smacked up, I don't know what the hell a cigarette is.—Greg Volk

Weather

Tonight's Forecast: Dark

It's, like, 130 degrees here in New York City. To give you an idea of how hot it is, today on my way to work my cab driver was steaming vegetables in his turban.—David Letterman

My favorite part of the weather report is the satellite photo. This is really helpful. A photograph of the earth from 10,000 miles away. Can you tell if you should take a sweater or not from that shot?—Jerry Seinfeld

The weatherman always tells you what is *almost* gonna be. "Mostly." "Chances are." You go to school, the teacher asks you how much is 3 plus 4, you can't go "Nearly 7. With a 20 percent chance of being 8."—George Wallace

Blatant Lies

Actually, this may not be a lie. This could very well be perfectly, frighteningly true. (Or not—but really, would it surprise you at all?)

It's so warm out that O. J. Simpson is planning his next murder without the glove. —Larry Getlen

It was so cold I saw a guy with a hammer trying to bust a poodle off a fire hydrant. —David Letterman

A study shows that men are hit by lightning four times as often as women—usually after saying, "I'll call you."—Jay Leno

It's so cold out, I saw someone from PETA handing out flyers saying, "Screw It, Wear the Fur."—Larry Getlen

It's so hot, Republican Congressmen are going into gay bars just for the cold stares.—Bill Maher

If it's 0 degrees out today, and it's supposed to be twice as cold tomorrow, how cold is it going to be?—Steven Wright

Snowflakes are like people: beautiful, unique, and they leave you in the springtime.
— Myq Kaplan

It was so cold today that the hookers in Times Square were handing out flannel condoms.—David Letterman

Blatant Lies

This Letterman joke is sadly true, and worse, the condoms had holes in them. Dave's son Harry holds the record for being the world's fuzziest baby.

I was struck by lightning one time—or as I call it, God's drive-by shooting. A lot of people think if you get struck by lightning you'll get magical powers, like the ability to read minds or shoot lightning. Not me. I got the ability to shake on the ground and sh*t my pants. Will I use it for good or evil? Stay tuned.—Dave Attell

It's so warm out that Hillary Clinton thawed out for summer six months early.—Larry Getlen

Thanks to modern science, we now know that lightning is nothing more than huge chunks of electricity that can come out of the sky anytime, anywhere, and kill you.
—Dave Barry

Don't you just hate it when you're shoveling snow and you uncover a Jehovah's Witness?—David Letterman

It was so warm yesterday that Winona Ryder had to return the winter clothes she stole and just shoplift a few light sundresses.—Larry Getlen

Wisdom

Early to Bed and Early to Rise Makes a Man ... My Building's Overnight Doorman!

Life is anything that dies when you stomp on it.—Dave Barry

Compared to power, crack is Fruitopia.—Dennis Miller

You can get more with a kind word and a gun than you can with a kind word alone.—Johnny Carson

There's one way to find out if a man is honest—ask him. If he says "yes," you know he's a crook.—Groucho Marx

Two heads are better than one—unless you're cleaning them.—Craig Sharf

If I've learned one thing in life, it's that I can always count on pinkeye at the most inappropriate moment.—Janeane Garofalo

I'm a very nonviolent guy, but sometimes you can't avoid confrontation. That's why I have a little trick I use to get out of fights. The first thing you want to do if you know someone wants to fight you is sh*t in your fist. If they want to fight you after that, let 'em.—Geoff Holtzman

More than any other time in history, mankind faces a cross-roads. One path leads to despair and utter hopelessness. The other, to total extinction. Let us pray we have the wisdom to choose correctly.—Woody Allen

A genius is one who can do anything except make a living.—Joey Adams

Make 'Em Laugh

Hear a joke you love but know your busy little brain won't remember it? Repeat it immediately—and not just to yourself. "If you want to remember a joke, tell it to someone as quickly as you can after hearing it," says Philip Van Munching in *How to Remember Jokes*. That way, the joke is reinforced in your mind, increasing the chance you'll remember it at that snazzy dinner party a week later.

Remember, it's lonely at the top ... when there's no one on the bottom.—Rodney Dangerfield

Blood may be thicker than water, but it is still sticky, unpleasant, and generally nauseating.—Janeane Garofalo

A word to the wise ain't necessary—it's the stupid ones who need the advice. —Bill Cosby

If life gives you lemons, make some sort of fruity juice.—Conan O'Brien

Who Made the Funny?

Sometimes, funny is just in the blood. Conan O'Brien's cousin is comedian/actor Denis Leary.

Everywhere is walking distance if you have the time.—Steven Wright

Money can't buy happiness, but it helps you look for it in more places.—Milton Berle

A word to the wise is infuriating.—Hunter S. Thompson

The quickest way to a man's heart is through his chest. —Roseanne

If you can't beat them, arrange to have them beaten. —George Carlin

Old is always 15 years from now.—Bill Cosby

You can't have everything—where would you put it? —Steven Wright

Work

The Business of America

Bill Gates is being sued by seven Microsoft employees who claim the company discriminates against minorities. Apparently, at Microsoft, a minority is any employee who has a girlfriend.—Conan O'Brien

I'd like to know who came up with "Take Your Kids to Work Day." Is this really necessary? Aren't we already surrounded by immature people who need constant supervision?—Gayle Crispin

I sold encyclopedias when I was in college. Then the librarian caught me.—Brian Kiley

I wasn't always a comic. Before I did this, I was a house-painter for five years. Five years. I didn't think I'd ever finish that house.—John Fox

I used to temp. I called a temp agency once, and they were like, "Well, do you have any phone skills?" And I was like, "I called you, didn't I?"—Zach Galifianakis

I saw a job application that wanted you to write down what grammar school you went to. Are they gonna check that far back for a reference? Wouldn't that suck if you didn't get a job because your third-grade teacher thought you didn't get your snowmobile suit off fast enough?—John Heffron

In the club, when they want you to get offstage, they turn on a red light that indicates you have five minutes left. In some clubs, they'll hold up a candle in the back. That's the worst method, because you look in the back and see a floating candle. "Aw sh*t, this place is haunted. I cannot be funny when I'm frightened."—Mitch Hedberg

Employee of the month is a good example of how somebody can be both a winner and a loser at the same time. —Demitri Martin

The first job I had was at Burger King. I didn't want to call it Burger King, so I used to call it the BK Lounge. If the girls were like, "Where do you work," I was like, "I work down at the BK Lounge. I'm a bouncer." "Can we get in? "Not without coups."—Dane Cook

I lost my job. No—I didn't really lose my job. I know where my job is. It's just, when I go there, there's this new guy doing it.—Bobcat Goldthwait

I'm suing my boss for sexual harassment, and it's real hard, and a big strain on me—because, he hasn't done anything.—Sarah Silverman

Make 'Em Laugh

Mark Katz—speech writer for corporate executives and other dignitaries and former writer for President Bill Clinton, Vice President Al Gore, Secretary of State Madeline Albright, and others—advises you to plan your escape route. "Know ahead of time what lines or paragraphs you can cut," he says. "The audience will tell you if they are digging your material or if they have heard enough, thank you. Most speeches go on too long because it is impossible to speak and edit at the same time."

According to a recent survey, 50 percent of people asked said they had a sexual encounter at their workplace. The other 50 percent said they worked in an office without a computer.—Jay Leno

I would call in sick a lot. I would say I had "female problems." My boss didn't know I meant her.—Wendy Liebman

I went to a Waffle House. I'm sitting alone, reading a book. Waitress says, "What you readin' fer?" Not, "What am I reading," but "What am I reading *for?*" I guess I read for a lot of reasons, but one of the main ones is so I don't end up being a f*cking waffle waitress.—Bill Hicks

I had a job once selling security alarms door to door. I was really good at it. If there was no one home I'd leave a brochure on the kitchen table.—Dwight York

I used to work at a temporary agency, but they went out of business.—Geoff Holtzman

We flew down to Florida to visit my dad. I made the mistake of calling in sick from the airport. Right when I was about to say why I couldn't come in, you hear, "Flight 709, now boarding. Flight 709 now boarding." So I said, "I can't come in. I'm hearing voices."—Brian Kiley

My boss says I need to sound more sunny on the phone. He wants me to smile on the phone. Because people on the other end can hear that. So now I answer the phone, "Customer service, this is Debbie. Cheese!"—Debbie Shea

I got fired from my job at the unemployment office, but they're still paying me. —Phil Mazo

You think when gym teachers are younger they're thinking, *I wanna teach, but I don't wanna read. How about kickball for 40 years?*—Jim Gaffigan

HA HA HA Make 'Em Laugh

The final word on jokes is that the joke is the final word. Be sure the punch word or phrase—the word or phrase that the laugh depends on—is the last one. After you say it, stop talking. Hopefully, the laughter will be too loud for you to get in any more words anyway.

I did security at a miniature golf course. Just standing around all day, "Hey. Hey sir. Get your putter out of the whale's ass. C'mon, this is a place of miniature business." —Dane Cook

I read the average person goes through seven jobs in a lifetime. That means I died four years ago.—Bruce Cherry

How to Tell a Joke— and How *Not* To

Throughout this book, some of the funniest people in comedy have provided you with sound advice about how to tell a joke and how *not* to tell a joke. In this appendix, I summarize that advice, giving you a quick, concise reference for when you're on your way to that big event and you've got some sweet one-liners in mind. But as soon as you think about speaking in public, flop sweat collects on your brow like a 6-year-old kid singing at her first Christmas pageant.

Of course, the advice in this book works for any type of joke—whether you've crafted some witty, urbane quips, or you're stubbornly sticking to that joke that got a great laugh at your office Christmas party in 1983—and for any occasion, large or small. Or if there's no occasion at all, and you just loved this book so much that you demand one more chapter before you have to put it down and get back to your boring, everyday existence, here it is. Or maybe you're hoping for a dramatic ending of some kind. Maybe a romantic pirate story featuring a swash-buckling Errol Flynn–type rescuing a damsel in distress from the evil, mustachioed Captain Hook—well, I've added that to this appendix as well for extra enjoyment!

So sit back, relax, get your reading shoes on, and let's tell some jokes!

(Note: all further references to pirates, damsels, and Errol Flynn were edited out at press time.)

Remembering a Joke

You're at a party. Your friend's sister's cousin from Montana tells a joke about a talking flounder, a one-armed fisherman, and a Jesuit priest from Nantucket, and you haven't laughed this hard since your Uncle Mel tried to cook Thanksgiving dinner and accidentally turned the turkey into a stew. But your memory for jokes is not the best, as you learned that time you told your co-worker, "Take my wife … ummm … tonight?"

So if you hear a joke you love and want to remember it immediately so you can tell it later on, how do you do that?

Write It Down

Excuse yourself, find a pen, and jot it on a piece of paper. If you can't find paper, use a napkin or a matchbook cover. All creative people do that, by the way. Some of the most important creative ideas of our time were scribbled furiously on whatever was lying around at the time. Most people don't know this, but Albert Einstein wrote the Theory of Relativity on a Jack-in-the-Box receipt. So why rely on a faulty memory when you don't have to? Write it down.

> **Make 'Em Laugh**
>
> If you can't find a pen, pick up your cell phone, call yourself, and tell the joke to your voicemail. That way, you can write it down or type it later. This also gives you your first shot at telling the joke.

Also, try to tell the joke to someone else in the next 24 to 48 hours, and do it more than once. If you love a joke and suddenly try to tell it several weeks later, you'll have forgotten all the important points, and you'll mess it up. Then you'll be all mad at yourself, maybe even smacking yourself in the head once or twice, subjecting your face to potential injury. Why put yourself through that? Telling the joke to someone right away helps you commit it to memory and prevents possibly scarring facial lacerations.

If you really love telling jokes, make your memory a nonissue by keeping a "joke" file on your computer. Whenever you hear a joke you like, type it up in your joke file, including the important words and phrases and, most important, the punch line. If you do this on a regular basis, you'll also have occasion to revisit your jokes on a regular basis, increasing the chance that you'll have a bunch of them memorized. Then, when you wind up at an event or with a group of friends and a joke-telling session breaks out, you'll have the advantage—which, of course, leads to you making people laugh; which then leads to them liking you more and wanting to date you, hire you, or (if single) introduce you to their single adult children who can't seem to find the right one; which could wind up being a good or bad thing. But you have to take chances in life, right?

Hackity Hack _____

If you heard a joke from a famous or even local comic—*do not* tell it as if you wrote it or just got it off the 'net. Feel free to share, but give credit where credit's due. No one likes a joke thief. If you tell a story as if it happened to you but then someone cuts in with, "Hey, I heard Garry Shandling tell that story last week! What are you trying to pull?" you'll be looked at with scorn. It's better to cut in with, "Hey, I saw this great comic last week," give his or her name, *and then* tell the joke. Credit your jokes—it's just good karma.

Cast Your Jokes

Let's say you've taken this advice, and your computer file is loaded with megabytes of jokes, puns, and one-liners. But the second you walk away from the machine, you forget every one. What else can you do to help memorize a joke?

One idea is to cast the parts in your head. If the joke is about three city guys trying to corral a herd of bison, what if you imagine your dad, your brother, and that nerdy guy Jim from your office as the three guys? I mean, Dad trying to herd bison? He can't change his oil without ruining a shirt! And Jim, the dork who once got his tie caught in the copy machine? I mean, c'mon, people! Am I right, or what?

You get the point. The more you personalize the joke in your head, the more *visual* you make it for yourself, the easier it will be to recall at a later date.

Know the Key Phrases

Visuals are great for helping you recall situations, but what about the words themselves? Jokes revolve around their words and phrases, but oftentimes, especially in jokes that are more story-oriented, only a handful of words really need to be remembered *exactly*. So if you can't remember the joke word for word, just be sure you remember the words and phrases that are essential to the joke.

Here's an example of mine from the book:

> I was so nerdy as a kid, the only thing that would have made beating me more attractive is if I'd been filled with candy.—Larry Getlen

I've been telling this joke, in different variations and paired with different other jokes, for years. When I started telling it, it was longer. Over the years, I've pared it down and altered which other jokes I've told it with and how exactly I set it up. But from day one, one phrase has remained exact:

> "… filled with candy."

In this joke, that's the key phrase—the punch phrase—and that's what gets the laugh. My job in telling that joke—or any joke, for that matter—is to keep the setup as short as possible while making sure it supports and leads up to the joke in the way that gets the best laugh possible.

Another great example is *The Aristocrats*. If you haven't seen this movie, you're missing out—as long as you have an appreciation for really crude, over-the-top, vulgar humor, that is. The point of *The Aristocrats*, from a joke-structure perspective, is that the entire joke changes depending on who tells it, with one exception—the last two words: "The Aristocrats." That's it. Everything else about that joke is up for grabs. (I'd repeat a version of the joke for you here, but then this book would have to be filed in a special "adult" section.)

Get to Know the Joke—Rehearse

So now you've got your computer file full of jokes. You've visualized so many jokes, quips, and one-liners that your mind is filled with images of your dad, your priest, and your rabbi doing shots with a talking alligator who looks like your high school principal. And you've got so many joke details and punch lines memorized that other important details, like your wife's birthday, are starting to slip out. Is there anything else you can do to ensure that you're the funniest guy or gal at your next big soiree—which, if you keep forgetting your spouse's birthday, will be your divorce party? Yes. Rehearse.

Rehearse? Isn't that just for actors? No, it's not. It's for anyone who wants to excel at a performance. And when you're telling jokes, you *are* performing. So why not rehearse? Print out your joke file, stand in front of your favorite mirror, and speak as if you're talking to a good friend. I know what you're thinking—what if the person in the mirror doesn't laugh? Well, frankly, you'll have more to worry about if he or she *does* laugh.

Repeating jokes out loud gets you used to the act of telling them, and *that's* what makes you both remember them and feel comfortable with them. Repetition is key in memorizing anything—jokes are no different—and being comfortable with your jokes is key to being funny.

In fact, not only does repeating your jokes help you memorize them, but *repeating* your jokes helps you *memorize* them. And if you repeat them—it'll really help you memorize them. (And if you don't believe me, just try getting that annoying sentence out of your head now.)

> **HA HA HA** **Make 'Em Laugh**
>
> One important tip: if you're telling the joke out loud in the mirror and you start to bore yourself, something needs to be changed, and it's probably the length of the joke. Figure out what can be cut without killing the laugh.

But not only does repeating your jokes help you memorize them—last time, I promise—but it also gives you a sense of the pace and rhythm of the joke: where to pause, where to speed up, and what parts seem like they drag on.

Keep It Short

Here's an example:

> It's so cold out, I saw this guy from PETA. He was standing outside of McDonald's with a group of his fur-hating PETA friends, and they were all shivering because of how cold it was, and they were handing out brochures to everyone who passed by saying, "Screw It, Wear the Fur."—Larry Getlen

Now, that's not the way the joke appears in the book, nor how I've ever told it onstage. I merely wrote it that way as an example. Here's the way the joke really appears, and how I tell it on stage (during wintertime only, obviously):

> It's so cold out, I saw someone from PETA handing out flyers saying, "Screw It, Wear the Fur."—Larry Getlen

See the difference? The laugh here comes from the contrast of what we know about PETA—that they hate fur—and how they act in the joke. The *surprise* of their behavior creates the laugh, and I get to it quickly. Now, look at the facts in the first version that were irrelevant to the laugh. They were at McDonald's? So what? He was with a group of his friends? Who cares? They were shivering? Well, I've already estab lished it was cold out, so no need to say that. Because there's only one quick laugh here—it is a one-liner, after all—the setup should be quick as well. If this were a longer story that had a lot of funny parts or interesting characters who were funny on their own, then it might make more sense to set a scene. But it's just a quickie. If there's only one laugh in the joke, then get in and get out.

HA HA HA   Make 'Em Laugh

One last word on memorization and preparation: if you don't have a joke sufficiently memorized so that you're *100 percent sure* you can tell the joke with confidence, hit every key piece of information, and get the punch line *exactly* right—don't tell it. Period.

How to Do It Wrong

Okay, you've followed my advice and that of my illustrious colleagues, and you've taken the time to memorize a few jokes you really like. You are 100 percent confident you can tell these jokes at a moment's notice without forgetting any of the important information—like, for example, the punch line.

So now here you are, at your nephew's confirmation, bar mitzvah, or ritual animal sacrifice—whichever applies (no judgments here, folks—we're equal opportunity jokesters). You hear laughter from another corner of the room, and as you saunter over, you realize your Uncle Jack is telling jokes to a group that includes several of his fishing buddies and some ladies he barely knows from the other side of the family. Here's your chance.

But before you wade in, let's listen in on ol' Uncle Jack:

> All right, my turn, my turn. This joke is the funniest joke you've ever heard—you're gonna die. I mean it, funniest ever. All right—so a priest, a rabbi, and an octopus are floating in a hot air balloon over the Eiffel Tower. The priest is a black guy, by the way. So the three of them are starting to sink, and they're afraid they have too much weight to land safely. So the rabbi says to the octopus .... Wait, hold on. Did I mention the octopus was Jewish? That's important. The octopus is a Jew. Yeah. Okay. And, so's the rabbi. I guess you knew that, though, right? Okay. So the priest says to the rabbi ... wait, I mean, the rabbi says to the octopus ... yeah, that's it. The rabbi says to the octopus ...

I'll stop here—this is painful enough. Before I proceed, let's examine the many mistakes dear Uncle Jack has already made—mistakes you'll want to be certain to avoid anytime you're telling a joke.

Don't Joke Drunk

It sounds like good ol' Uncle Jack has had a few—no surprise after that stunt he pulled at his daughter's wedding (although I've heard the dog is doing fine). Remember all the things I said about memorization a few paragraphs back? Well, the more alcohol you've had to drink, the smaller the chance you'll remember all the parts you need to. So if you're in a joke-telling mood, try to stay relatively coherent. *However*, if you're going to a party, and it's a given that alcohol will be part of the evening's celebratory mood, remember this—shorter is easier. The shorter the joke, the easier it is to remember it. So if you know you'll be having a few, try to have some shorter jokes at your disposal. This lessens the chance you'll screw them up.

Don't Tell Racially Sensitive Jokes in Mixed Company

There is a definite difference between jokes about or involving race, and racist jokes. However, everyone has a different barometer for this, and what may seem harmless to you may offend someone else. Society's tolerance for racial or ethnically tinged humor has changed over the years, and it is all too easy to offend someone if you don't know his or her sensibility. So unless you're *absolutely sure* you know the sensibilities of the people involved, err on the side of caution, and keep race and religion out of it.

The same goes, by the way, for sexual material and profanity. Unless you know your listeners well enough to know they're cool with it, leave it out.

Don't Start Off by Saying How Funny the Joke Is

Set low expectations and then exceed what your audience expects. In other words, just tell the joke, and let the listeners judge. Think of it this way—Jerry Seinfeld doesn't come out onstage, say hello to the audience, and say, "Ladies and gentleman, I am one of the funniest comedians in the country, and the jokes I tell you tonight will be some of the funniest jokes ever told on a stage. I'm gonna make you laugh so hard tonight your stomach's gonna hurt."

Jerry comes out onstage and starts talking. He lets the jokes speak for themselves—and that's *with* the advantage that the audience already knows he's one of the funniest comics in the world. If he knows well enough to let the jokes speak for themselves, you should, too.

In fact, don't even start off by saying, "I've got a joke for you." Just start telling it. It'll do better to help corral the crowd's attention if they wonder where you're going with your story. Surprise is everything in comedy.

Don't Double Back

Be sure you not only have the joke memorized, but have it memorized *in order*. Once you have to double back and interrupt your momentum to give the audience information you forgot to give them in the first place, the joke's pretty much dead.

Don't Misrepresent Sea Creatures

If you're gonna tell a joke about an octopus, don't put him in a hot air balloon. Everyone knows octopi are afraid of heights.

Doing It Wrong—the Sequel

So Uncle Jack gets through the horrible octopus joke, and before anyone else can get a word in edgewise, he says, "Wait—I got one more." Everyone in earshot fidgets. No one looks him in the eye. Several people glance at their watches. But before anyone can make a graceful exit, he launches into another one. And because he's such a good example of what not to do, let's stick with him for a minute.

"So there's this Frenchman, Jacques," says Uncle Jack, because he doesn't have the imagination required to name a Frenchman anything other than Jacques. And then he starts speaking in what is supposed to be a French accent but sounds more like he's gargling with glass. "Jacques tells his friend Pierre, 'Eye em in zee kitcheeeeen, waiting for deeees-ert.'" Suddenly and inexplicably, Uncle Jack sounds Southern. He has also scrunched up his face in what he thinks is a snobby French pose, but really looks like he has something in his eye.

"Now Pierre starts to leave, but ... hey! Jimbo! Over here! We're tellin' jokes!" Is that part of the joke? Nope—Uncle Jack just saw his old bowling buddy, and he's calling him over to be part of the group. Now, the heck with graceful exits. One woman takes out her cell phone as if she's getting a call—she isn't—and walks away. And within seconds, Uncle Jack is left with an audience of one—his poor bowling buddy, who's listening to the worst French accent ever attempted and regretting that he ever picked up a bowling ball.

And with that, we bid adieu to Uncle Jack, and present the final few tips we learned from him on what not to do while telling a joke:

 ◆ Don't do an accent unless you know you can do it *perfectly*—which means keeping the *exact same accent* from the beginning of the joke to the end. When telling jokes, close enough is *not* good enough. Do it right, or leave it out.

◆ Unless you graduated from mime school, leave the funny faces and voices at home. Like the accent, if they're not perfect, they'll merely call attention to how imperfect they are and detract from the joke.

◆ Do not—under any circumstances except for *maybe* a fire— interrupt your own joke in the middle. Jokes require timing, and they require momentum. If you stop your own joke in the middle, you've killed your own momentum.

Almost Ready ...

So now you know how to memorize and prepare your joke and what awful habits to avoid. Anything else to keep in mind before slaying your crowd with your blazing wit? Sure—here are a few additional pointers.

If something out of your control interrupts you in mid-joke, take a second to see what happens. The momentum is probably dead, but if your listeners return their attention to you hoping to hear the rest, pick up where you left off. Don't make a big deal about the interruption. And if they don't return their attention to you? Cut your losses and move on. Next.

Don't rush the joke. Speak at a reasonable pace—not so slow that you bore the crowd, but not so fast that important words get garbled. Pace and coherence are very important in the joke—be sure you have both.

> **Make 'Em Laugh**
>
> If you like your joke so much that you usually break into laughter mid-joke, do your best to get it under control. Your own laughter can break your momentum as much as any other interruption.

Make eye contact with the people you're telling the joke to, and distribute it evenly. This involves each person as if you're talking directly to them, but by altering your eye contact, you don't freak out any one person as if you're a staring serial killer.

If you're listening to someone else tell a joke, and realize mid-way through that you know the punch line—do *not* blurt it out. That's as rude as blurting out the surprise twist of a movie 10 seconds before it happens. Let the joke continue, and don't ruin the surprise for others who may not have heard the joke before.

Most important: commit to the joke. Believe in the joke, and believe in your ability to tell it in a funny way. If you start out by saying, "I have this joke. It's kinda funny, sometimes it gets laughs, sometimes not, but, well, I'll give it a shot," what you've actually said to your audience is "I'm not funny. My joke isn't funny. Even if it was funny, I don't have the skill or confidence to tell it in a funny way. Stop listening to my insecure babbling and just go home and watch *The Daily Show*—you'll be much better off." If you're going to tell a joke, you have to believe, as strongly as you believe anything in this world, that the joke is funny, and you have the skill and ability to tell it in a funny way.

Of course, if you've followed the advice in this book and this chapter; if you have your jokes expertly memorized and tell them in a confident and poised manner; if you leave the fake, exaggerated faces, voices, and mannerisms to the cheesy Uncle Jacks of the world and just put your own best foot forward; then you're on your way to becoming the hit of any gathering or party, or at least with the folks in the office.

One final word on telling jokes: I spoke earlier in the book about how you should never ask a comedian to tell you a joke. Well, the opposite applies as well. If you meet a comedian, do not, *under any circumstances*, try to tell *him* a joke. If you enjoyed his act, feel free to introduce yourself, compliment his jokes, buy him a drink, and save the jokes for the folks back home.

Contributors

Joey Adams was a comedian and comedy writer who wrote more than 40 books about comedy, including *The Complete Encyclopedia of Laughter* and *Here's to the Friars*. Adams spent many years as a syndicated columnist for *The New York Post* before he died in 1999.

Ahmed Ahmed (www.ahmed-ahmed.com) is an Egyptian-born Muslim comic who grew up in Riverside, California, and has been seen in *Swingers*, *Tracey Takes On*, *Roseanne*, *Tough Crowd with Colin Quinn*, and *PUNK'D*. Ahmed won the first-ever Richard Pryor Award for ethnic comedy at the Edinburgh Comedy Festival in Scotland in 2004.

Kai Ajaye (kajaye_8@hotmail.com) is a stand-up comic, writer, and actress who has appeared in the films *Just Another Girl on the IRT*, *For Love of the Game*, and *The Female Offender* and on TV shows such as *All My Children*, *New York Undercover*, and the PAX TV *Variety* show.

Vic Alejandro (www.vicalejandro.com) is a comedian and actor based in Denver, Colorado. He was a headliner at the 2005 Calgary Comedy Festival, a finalist in the 2004 Las Vegas Comedy Festival Wild Card Contest, and the winner of the 2003 Comedy Works/Comedy Central Comedy Contest in Denver.

Ted Alexandro (tedalexandro.com) has appeared on *The Late Show with David Letterman*, *Late Night with Conan O'Brien*, *The Jimmy Kimmel Show*, *The View*, and his own half-hour special, *Comedy Central Presents Ted Alexandro*. *Time Out New York* magazine named Ted one of the top comedians of 2004.

Dan Allen (www.thedanallenshow.com) is a comedian and writer based in New York City who has appeared on Comedy Central's *Premium Blend* and performs regularly at The World Famous Comic Strip in New York.

Leo Allen (leoallen.com) has performed on *Late Night with Conan O'Brien*, *Last Call with Carson Daly*, and other, more desperate things. For three seasons, he was a staff writer for *Saturday Night Live*. He's also a charter member of the comedy duo Slovin and Allen. You can track him down at leoallen.com or slovinandallen.com if they ever get made, or on MySpace, if it still exists.

Steve Allen (www.steveallen.com) might be the closest thing the comedy world has seen to a true renaissance man. In addition to a 50-year career in TV comedy, Allen published more than 50 books, including several scholarly works and poetry, and wrote more than 7,900 songs. But his most important achievement was the creation of *The Tonight Show*, on which he served as the first host and invented many of the conventions of late-night talk shows. Steve Allen died in 2000.

Tim Allen's (timallen.com) *Home Improvement* was one of America's top TV shows for eight years and the number-one show in the country during the 1993–1994 season. During the show's run, Allen won the People's Choice Award for Favorite Male TV Performer for eight consecutive years, along with many other awards, including the Golden Globe. He has also starred in films such as *The Santa Clause*, *Toy Story*, and *Galaxy Quest*, and wrote the best-selling book, *Don't Stand Too Close to a Naked Man*.

Woody Allen, in addition to being one of our greatest filmmakers, was, for a time, one of our greatest stand-up comics. While he didn't do it for long, his album *Stand-Up Comic*, a compilation of some of his funniest routines from the 1960s, is considered a classic of the genre.

Jonathan Ames (www.jonathanames.com) is the author of six books, including *Wake Up, Sir!* and *I Love You More Than You Know*. In addition to writing, Mr. Ames performs frequently as a comedic storyteller and is a recurring guest on *The Late Show with David Letterman*.

Larry Amoros, in addition to performing stand-up comedy, has written for Rosie O'Donnell, Tovah Feldshuh, and Barry Manilow.

Louie Anderson (louieanderson.com) kicked off his comedy career by winning the 1981 Midwest Comedy Competition. Still performing nationwide, he was the host of *Family Feud;* created the award-winning children's show *Life with Louie;* and has written three books, the latest being *The F Word: How to Survive Your Family*.

Molly Anderson (a-random-person@prodigy.net) has been performing stand-up comedy for four years. She appeared in the movie *My Brother* starring Vanessa Williams and was a finalist in the Las Vegas Comedy Festival.

Ant (antcomic.com) has appeared as host of VH1's *Celebrity Fit Club* and co-host of *The Ricki Lake Show*. He's been a correspondent on *The Dennis Miller Show* and a judge on WB's *Steve Harvey's Big Time* and was the only comic to appear on all three seasons of NBC's *Last Comic Standing*.

Dave Attell (daveattell.com) is one of our most wildly inventive stand-up comedians, and his love of midgets is eclipsed only by his ability to endlessly refine a joke. He's written for *SNL;* he was named by *Entertainment Weekly* as one of the 25 Funniest People in America; and his crowning achievement was Comedy Central's *Insomniac with Dave Attell*, where he got to riff with just about every American who ever graced a bar stool. See him live when you get the chance—check his website for upcoming tour dates.

Maria Bamford (www.mariabamford.com) has been one of *Variety*'s Top Ten Comics to Watch and one of the top 10 favorite comics of the viewers of Comedy Central. She's appeared on Conan O'Brien and Jay Leno, had her own half-hour special on Comedy Central, and co-starred in *The Comedians of Comedy*.

Greg Banks (gregbanks.com) afflicts the powerful. His comedy skewers all those who influence our society, but especially the media and government, and not in predictable ways. Greg's a fierce Libertarian, and he performs all over the country.

Dave Barry (davebarry.com) won the Pulitzer prize for telling fart jokes. Well, not really … more like for *writing* fart jokes. Well, that's not really true, either, but he did win the Pulitzer for writing some awfully silly (and, of course, funny) stuff. His *Miami Herald* column was syndicated to more than 500 newspapers before Barry retired it in 2004. He's written 25 books; the Harry Anderson sitcom *Dave's World* was based on him; and he plays perfectly serviceable guitar in the Rock Bottom Remainders, which also features writers Stephen King, Ridley Pearson, Mitch Albom, and Amy Tan.

Todd Barry (toddbarry.com) is a veteran stand-up comic who won the Jury Award at the 1998 U.S. Comedy Arts Festival in Aspen and was *Entertainment Weekly*'s IT Stand-Up for 2003. He's appeared on Letterman, Conan, Carson Daly, Jimmy Kimmel, and about 37 different Comedy Central shows, including *Chappelle's Show*, and his CDs *Medium Energy* and *Falling Off the Bone* are extremely funny.

Joy Behar's *The View* has received 18 Daytime Emmy Awards. As a stand-up comic, Behar starred in her own HBO special and won a CableAce Award. She has also appeared in several films, including Woody Allen's *Manhattan Murder Mystery*, and writes a column for *Good Housekeeping*.

Greg Behrendt's (www.gregbehrendt.com) stand-up can be enjoyed on his DVD *Uncool*. In addition to a successful stand-up career, Behrendt was a consultant for *Sex and the City* and co-wrote two best-selling books—*He's Just Not That Into You* and *It's Called a Break-Up Because It's Broken*.

Richard Belzer may be better known today as *Law and Order: SVU*'s Detective Munch, but he started his career as one of the most brazen stand-up comedy voices of the 1970s. He was a member of the comedy collective Channel One, which created the groundbreaking comedy sketch movie *The Groove Tube*, and was featured on the *National Lampoon Radio Hour*.

D. C. Benny (dcbenny.com) is a former male model and amateur boxer, a bizarre combination, which, when coupled with the fact that he's Jewish, could only lead to stand-up comedy. He's appeared on *Showtime at the Apollo*, *The Chris Rock Show*, and *Law and Order*; had his own half-hour special on Comedy Central; was a finalist on NBC's *Last Comic Standing*; and was the "How You Doin'" guy in a very popular commercial for Budweiser.

Milton Berle was the very first superstar of the TV era and was known as both Mr. Television and Uncle Miltie. A notorious joke thief, he also had one of the longest show business careers in history, making his first stage appearances as a performer several years before the first shots of World War I were fired—when he was just 5—and continuing on in one form or another until his death in 2002.

Sandra Bernhard (www.sandrabernhard.com) has seen success as a comic, television and film actress, author, and Broadway chanteuse. She was a cast member on the sitcom *Roseanne* for 5 years; co-starred with Robert DeNiro and Jerry Lewis in Martin Scorsese's classic *The King of Comedy;* and wrote and starred in the critically acclaimed one-woman Broadway show *I'm Still Here … Damn It!* She has also written three books and hosted her own talk show on A&E.

Billy Bingo (www.billybingo.net) retired from the New York Fire Department after 20 years, and his stand-up performance is based on being a NYC firefighter as well as what goes on in his life. Bill is married and lives with his wife, Catherine, in Suffolk County, Long Island.

Lewis Black (lewisblack.net) is one of our sharpest and most acerbic comic voices, but this Yale-educated *Daily Show* regular has spent most of his adult life as a playwright. In addition to writing more than 40 plays, Black has appeared in Woody Allen's *Hannah and Her Sisters* and was voted Viewers Choice Stand-Up Comic at the American Comedy Awards. He also tours diligently. Visit his website to see where he'll be performing next.

Mike Bobbitt (www.mikeypooh.com) delights audiences as a self proclaimed *Star Wars* and comic book geek who managed to beat the odds and find a wife, using the charm and candor of a punk kid who's just too smart for his own good.

Alonzo Bodden (www.alonzobodden.com) has appeared on Conan O'Brien, Craig Kilborn, *Friday Night Videos,* the *Apollo Comedy Hour,* and NBC's *Last Comic Standing,* which he won. He also donates much of his time to entertaining our troops through the USO and has performed for U.S. military personnel worldwide. Visit his website to see when he'll be in your country (and even your town).

Joe Bolster (www.joebolster.com) has appeared on *The Tonight Show* with both Johnny Carson and Jay Leno, written for *The Academy Awards,* had his own half-hour special on HBO, and won Showtime's New York Laff Off.

Erma Bomback was one of America's foremost humor columnists, with her syndicated column appearing in more than 800 newspapers around the country. She also wrote many books of humor, including *The Grass Is Always Greener over the Septic Tank* and *If Life Is a Bowl of Cherries, What Am I Doing in the Pits?* Erma passed away in 1996.

Elayne Boosler (www.elayneboosler.com) came of comic age in the early 1970s, and alongside a peer group that included Jay Leno, Richard Belzer, Richard Lewis, Jerry Seinfeld, and Andy Kaufman, Boosler established herself as one of the first successful female comics not to tear herself apart onstage for being female. Still touring regularly, Boosler has had seven cable television specials, made 32 appearances on *Politically Incorrect*, and performed for President Clinton at the White House Correspondents Dinner. She also formed an animal rescue charity called Tails of Joy (www.tailsofjoy.net).

Borat is a television interviewer best known for enraging the government of Kazakhstan after depicting that country as incestuous, misogynistic, and anti-Semetic. Borat's statements so angered the government that it took out a four-page ad section in *The New York Times* in response to his comments, extolling their country's virtues and proving that Kazakhstan's government, if nothing else, possesses the world's worst sense of humor. Borat's response to their ad was to praise the government and the country, stating that Kazakhstan had "some of the cleanest prostitutes in all of central Asia." Borat is, of course, a fictional character, even though the Kazakhstani government's response to him was very real. Borat is really Sasha Baron Cohen, the warped mind behind HBO's *Da Ali G Show*. *Borat: The Movie*, should be out sometime this year.

David Brenner (www.davidbrenner.net) has made an astounding 158 appearances on *The Tonight Show* as of this writing, more than any other performer in the show's history. He has also done four HBO specials and written five books.

Albert Brooks (www.albertbrooks.com) is one of the great stealth comic geniuses of our time. His early career as a stand-up comic led to more than 40 appearances on *The Tonight Show with Johnny Carson*. Turning to filmmaking, he created six short films for the first season of *Saturday Night Live* and has subsequently written, directed, and starred in the highly acclaimed films *Real Life, Modern Romance, Lost in America, Defending Your Life, Mother, The Muse*, and *Looking for Comedy in the Muslim World*.

A. Whitney Brown was a regular correspondent on *Saturday Night Live*'s "Weekend Update," delivering humorous commentary in a segment called "The Big Picture," and won an Emmy award for writing for the show. He has also written for and appeared on *The Daily Show*.

Lenny Bruce was one of the most controversial comics of our age and took the heat for a generation of comics to come. His routines in the late 1950s and early 1960s were laden with obscenities and dealt with controversial topics such as the hypocrisy of religion and government. Many communities banned him from performing, the Catholic Church helped lead the fight against him, and he faced several arrests and trials due to his incendiary routines. His career virtually ruined, Bruce died in 1966 at the age of 40 of a drug overdose. But his sacrifice cracked open a generation of comic creativity, as the First Amendment battles he fought helped cultivate acceptance of the free expression that every comedian now enjoys.

Bill Bryson (www.billbrysonbooks.com) is a much published humorist whose books cover topics from travel to science to vocabulary. The Iowa-born Bryson currently lives in the United Kingdom.

George Burns began his career in vaudeville and had a 40-year comic partnership with his wife, Gracie Allen. He continued appearing in nightclubs, on TV, and in film after her death in 1964, even winning an Academy Award for his role in *The Sunshine Boys*. He died in 1996 at the age of 100.

Red Buttons began his long showbiz career in vaudeville, and since then has mastered virtually every aspect of showbiz. An accomplished comedian, singer, songwriter, and actor, Buttons was a highlight of the old Dean Martin Roasts with his "Never Got a Dinner" routine. He has won an Emmy and an Oscar and still appears frequently on television and on the Las Vegas stage.

Charlie Callas (www.charliecallas.com) was one of the most visible comics of the 1970s and a regular on the talk-show circuit. He has appeared in more than 20 films, including some of Mel Brooks' best, like *High Anxiety* and *Silent Movie*.

Chris Cardenas (Stagemoon13@yahoo.com) is a New York University student concentrating in politics and dramatic writing. In his spare time, he performs at major clubs such as The Comedy Cellar, New York Comedy Club, and Stand Up New York.

Drew Carey's sitcom, *The Drew Carey Show*, was one of the most popular sitcoms on television for almost a decade. Carey also wrote a book called *Dirty Jokes and Beer* and has hosted two improv shows, *Whose Line Is It Anyway* and *Drew Carey's Green Screen Show*.

George Carlin (georgecarlin.com) has been one of our most successful and influential comics for more than 40 years. A mainstream comedian in the 1960s, he grew his hair and took a more radical approach in the 1970s, leading to a series of best-selling albums, well-watched HBO specials, a routine ("Filthy Words") that led to his work being debated by the Supreme Court, and the status (along with Richard Pryor) as one of the most groundbreaking comics of our time. He has also appeared in several films and written three best-selling books. Visit his website to learn more and see where he's performing next.

Jim Carrey began his performing life as an impressionist and stand-up comic before the TV show *In Living Color* put him on the map. He has since become one of our most popular actors, earning six Golden Globe nominations and winning for his work in *Man on the Moon* and *The Truman Show*.

Johnny Carson was known as America's King of Late Night. After hosting several talk and game shows in the 1950s, he took over *The Tonight Show* from Jack Paar in 1962 and quickly turned the comic monologue into an art form. His contribution to stand-up comedy is immeasurable, both for his own sly way around a joke, and for introducing America to many of the best stand-up comics of our time, including David Letterman, Jay Leno, Joan Rivers, Garry Shandling, Jerry Seinfeld, Ellen DeGeneres, Steven Wright, and Roseanne Barr, to name just a very few. Carson retired from *The Tonight Show* in 1992 and passed away in 2005.

Carolyn Castiglia (www.carolyncastiglia.com) is an Italian-by-adoption, formerly Catholic young mom on the outside and a black Jewish lesbian on the inside. She's performed in the best venues in New York, including Caroline's and the Gotham Comedy Club, and has also been featured on the Lifetime, Style, and Oxygen Networks.

J-L Cauvin (www.jlcauvin.com) is a 6'7", half-Irish and half-Haitian New York City comic with a JD from Georgetown, who looks like a cross between Adam Sandler and The Rock. His height makes the audience take notice, but his material is what they remember.

Tim Cavanagh (timcav.com) is one of America's top corporate and nightclub comics. Tim has worked with the best in the business, including Jay Leno, Jerry Seinfeld, and Drew Carey, and has appeared on ABC, Showtime, and Comedy Central. He's a regular on the syndicated *Bob and Tom Show*, and many of his parody songs have been played on the *Dr. Demento* show over the years.

Jeff Cesario (www.jeffcesario.com) has performed on *The Tonight Show*, Conan, Kilborn, Letterman, and many more. Jeff won two Emmys as writer and executive producer for *Dennis Miller Live* and also served as writer/producer on *The Larry Sanders Show* and as a writer for *Bob Costas' On The Record*. He hosts a sports movie show on ESPN Classic called *Reel Classics* and runs a sports-parody website called *Sportalicious!* (www.sportalicious.com).

Dave Chappelle (www.davechapelle.com) started performing stand-up comedy in his teens and earned his comedic chops performing both in clubs and in New York's Washington Square Park, the latter under the watchful eye of his mentor, Charlie Barnett. He co-wrote the movie *Half-Baked* with long-time writing partner Neal Brennan, and also with Brennan created *Chappelle's Show*, a massive hit for Comedy Central. The DVD of the first season of *Chappelle's Show* became the all-time best-selling DVD of a television show in late 2004, selling more than 2 million copies. Chappelle left the show in 2005 before completing season three, and currently tours around the country.

Joel Chasnoff (www.joelchasnoff.com) has performed stand-up comedy in seven countries. As one of America's premier Jewish stand-up comedians, a large part of Joel's humor focuses on what it means to be Jewish in America.

Bruce Cherry (brucecherry.com) has been a staff writer for Air America radio network, Comedy Central's *Tough Crowd with Colin Quinn*, and Court TV's *Snap Judgment*. He has been doing stand-up since 1989 and has appeared on Comedy Central and VH1. He owns brucecherry.com. Hopefully he's gotten around to putting something up on it.

Margaret Cho (www.margaretcho.com) was raised in San Francisco, started performing at 16, and starred in the sitcom *All-American Girl*, an experience so horrible that it led to severe medical problems. Her troubles with the show were chronicled in her one-woman show *I'm the*

One That I Want, which was so well received that the film version broke the record for most money grossed by a film per print in movie history. Since then, she has starred in *The Notorious C.H.O.*, *Revolution*, and *Assassin*.

Louis C. K. (www.louisck.com) developed and stars in *Lucky Louie*, the first multi-camera sitcom in HBO's history, and was the writer/director of *Pootie Tang*. He won an Emmy Award for his writing on *The Chris Rock Show* and has also written for David Letterman, Conan O'Brien, and Dana Carvey. He was named one of the "Top Ten Comics to Watch" by both *Variety* and *The Hollywood Reporter* and was named IT Comic by *Entertainment Weekly*.

John Cleese (www.thejohncleese.com) was a writer and/or performer for several influential British comedy shows in the 1960s, including *The Frost Report* and *At Last, The 1948 Show*. It was on these shows that Cleese cemented his comedic style as well as his partnerships with the men with whom he would form his next venture, *Monty Python's Flying Circus*. Python revolutionized comedy on the small screen from 1969 to 1974 and then met equal success in films with *Monty Python and the Holy Grail*, *Life of Brian*, and *The Meaning of Life*. Since then, Cleese has appeared in several films, including *A Fish Called Wanda* and *Die Another Day*; written several books on relationships; and created a business consulting company. He remains active in all these fields and is also a professor-at-large at Cornell University.

Hillary Clinton is the junior U.S. Senator from New York. She is rarely funny.

Deon Cole (www.deon-cole.com) has appeared in both *Barbershop* movies, on *Jamie Foxx's Laffapalooza*, on *Def Comedy Jam*, and on BET's *Comic View*.

Jane Condon (www.janecondon.com) has been on *The View* and Lifetime TV's *Girls Night Out* and won the 2004 Ladies of Laughter Comedy Contest. The AP calls her "an upper-crust Roseanne."

Dane Cook (www.danecook.com) broke out huge in 2005. He hosted *SNL*, sold out large venues, and his CD/DVD *Retaliation* debuted at number four on the Billboard charts, quickly becoming the best-selling comedy album in almost three decades (since Steve Martin's *Let's Get*

Small). He has been *Rolling Stone* magazine's "Hot Comic," Comedy Central's "Favorite Stand-up Comic," and *Stuff* magazine's "Coolest Comic of the Year."

Professor Irwin Corey (www.irwincorey.org) is a veteran of stages and screens large and small. Starting out on the borscht belt circuit, Corey was a regular on the talk shows of Steve Allen, Jack Paar, Johnny Carson, and Ed Sullivan; has appeared in movies such as *The Curse of the Jade Scorpion;* and appeared in theatrical productions such as *The Taming of the Shrew* and *Hamlet.*

Bill Cosby is one of America's most revered stand-up comedians and revitalized the sitcom with his 1980s mega-hit *The Cosby Show*. He also created the classic *Fat Albert and the Cosby Kids*, has written several books, and won several Grammies for his best-selling comedy albums. He was awarded the Kennedy Center Honor in 1998 and the Presidential Medal of Freedom in 2002.

Mike Cotayo (www.funnymanmike.com or mike@funnymanmike.com) is a comedian with a disability and a quick wit who makes people laugh at life's absurdities.

Tom Cotter (www.tomcotter.com) has appeared on *The Tonight Show*, had his own half hour special on Comedy Central, was voted "Best Stand-Up" at the Las Vegas Comedy Festival, and has performed at the Kennedy Center in Washington, D.C. He appeared in the film *Next Stop, Wonderland* and will star along with his wife, comedian Kerri Louise, on the WE network's *Two Funny* (www.twofunny.com). Pick up his CD, *Wise Ass*, at his website.

Bri Cowan is a comic out of the Chicago area and co-host of the *Caked On Stripes* podcast. To find out more about *Caked On Stripes*, log on to www.cakedonstripes.com.

Barry Crimmins (www.barrycrimmins.com) is a veteran political satirist, the author of *Never Shake Hands with a War Criminal*, and a writer for Air America Radio. He founded two of Boston's most esteemed comedy hot spots, The Ding Ho and Stitches, where many of America's best comedians (including Paula Poundstone, Steven Wright, and Bobcat Goldthwait) honed their craft. Barry has also written for Dennis Miller and appeared on the *HBO Young Comedians Special.*

Gayle Crispin (www.gayle.s5.com) is a writer, actress, and stand-up comic who lives, works, and sometimes sleeps in New York City. Her comedy screenplay *Blaming Eve* received honorable mention in the Epiphany Screenplay Contest, and she will be producing the script as a stage play in the fall of 2006.

David Cross (bobanddavid.com) was the creator and star, along with his partner Bob Odenkirk, of the groundbreaking *Mr. Show*, which ran for four seasons on HBO. He has appeared in many films, including *Waiting for Guffman*, *Ghost World*, and *Eternal Sunshine of the Spotless Mind*, and played the flamboyant, Blue-Man-loving Tobias Fünke on *Arrested Development*.

Jayson Cross (www.jaysoncross.com) is a comedian and model in New York City.

Mike Daisey's (mikedaisey.com) monologues, including *21 Dog Years*, *The Ugly American, Monopoly!, Wasting Your Breath*, and *I Miss the Cold War*, have been performed off Broadway and around the world. He's currently a commentator for National Public Radio's *Day to Day*, a contributor to *The New York Times Magazine*, and is writing his second book, *Happiness Is Overrated*. He lives with his wife, director, and collaborator, Jean-Michele Gregory, in Brooklyn.

Rodney Dangerfield was one of America's most-beloved comics for his self-deprecating, "no respect" routines. A late bloomer who didn't hit it big until his 40s, Dangerfield starred in *Caddyshack*, *Easy Money*, and *Back to School* and later became a strong supporter of new comics, using his HBO specials to introduce the world to Jim Carrey, Andrew Dice Clay, Tim Allen, and Sam Kinison, among many others. Rodney passed away in 2004.

Michael "Ziggy" Danziger (ziggybackride.blogspot.com or danziger@alumni.utexas.net) is a versatile comedy writer and performer who grew up in Memphis. A southern son of a rabbi, Ziggy performs his clever observations and impersonations at clubs, colleges, and for various organizations.

Ellen DeGeneres came to public attention after winning Showtime's "Funniest Person in America" contest. She starred in the hit sitcom *Ellen* and gained great acclaim for her deft handling of the hosting duties for *The Emmy Awards* shortly after 9/11. She has since become one of the country's most popular daytime talk-show hosts on *The Ellen DeGeneres Show*, which you can learn more about at ellen.warnerbros.com.

Jessica Delfino (www.jessydelfino.blogspot.com) is a quirky bird who mostly tells dirty jokes and plays silly ditties on her guitar. She was described as "a cross between Redd Foxx and Jewel" by *The Onion*. She is neither a black man nor a lousy poet but liked the attention nonetheless.

Eric Deskin (www.ericdeskin.com) is a veteran New York City–based standup comic and actor whose comedy has been described as "edgy, observant and funny ... the sort of brainy observations you wish you'd thought of ..." As an actor, he has appeared in countless indie films, theatrical productions, and TV and print ad campaigns.

Tony Deyo (www.tonydeyo.com) has opened for Brian Regan, Brett Leake, and Bob Nelson.

Mick Diflo was with the sketch comedy group Hazmat in Philadelphia for four years and has been doing standup comedy in NYC for three. He has a sick, twisted sense of humor and is tired of being a doorman. Shouldn't be long now ...

Phyllis Diller first got into comedy in her late 30s to support her five kids and became one of our most versatile entertainers. She spent decades as one of the top comedy headliners in the country and has also appeared in more than 30 films, released 5 albums, written 4 books, and in 1992 was awarded a Lifetime Achievement Award at the American Comedy Awards.

Nick DiPaolo (www.nickdipaolo.com) has been a regular guest on *The Howard Stern Show*, *Tough Crowd with Colin Quinn*, and the Comedy Central Roasts. He has also appeared on *The Tonight Show*, Letterman, and Conan; had two half-hour specials on Comedy Central; and has released two CDs: *Born This Way* and *Road Rage*.

Pat Dixon (www.comedianpatdixon.com) has appeared on Comedy Central's *Premium Blend*, hosted CMT's *Summer Games*, and has been heard many times on the widely syndicated *Bob and Tom Show*. Visit his website to see when he'll be in your town.

Bob Dole was a longtime Republican Senator from the state of Kansas and the 1996 Republican candidate for president. He has also written two books on political humor—*Great Presidential Wit: I Wish I Was in the Book* and *Great Political Wit: Laughing (Almost) All the Way to the White House*. He also gobbles Viagra like they're M&Ms. He is funnier than Hillary Clinton but not as funny as Bill.

Dominique (Dominique Whitten) has appeared on *Chappelle's Show*, *Comic Groove*, and *Def Comedy Jam*.

Roland A. Duby (www.marijuanaman.com) is a marijuana-oriented comic. The vast majority of his comedy comes from his life experiences with women and drugs. When he is not doing stand-up comedy or smoking pot, he works on computer hardware. He has a girlfriend, then he doesn't, then he does again.

Scott Dunn is a regular guest on the *Bob and Tom Show* and appears on their *Cameltoe* CD. He has also appeared on Comedy Central's *The Man Show*.

Jennifer Dziura is a New York–based comedian best known for orchestrating "The Williamsburg Spelling Bee," a cabaret-style spelling bee for adults that has been featured in *The New York Times*. She satirically reviews sex toys at www.sarcasticsex.com and writes a popular blog at www.jenisfamous.com.

Bill Engvall (www.billengvall.com) is one of the four comic stars of the insanely popular *Blue Collar Comedy Tour*. He has been the American Comedy Awards "Comedian of the Year," and his album *Here's Your Sign* was the best-selling comedy album of 1997, eventually achieving platinum status. He has since had four more number-one comedy albums. The *Blue Collar Comedy Tour* has been the number-one comedy tour in the country for several years, and the films, CDs, and DVDs of the tours have broken a multitude of sales and ratings records.

Susie Essman (www.susieessman.com) has received widespread acclaim for her portrayal of Susie Greene on the HBO hit *Curb Your Enthusiasm*. She has also displayed her biting sarcasm on *Crank Yankers*, *The Daily Show*, several Comedy Central Roasts; and appeared in films such as *Punchline*, *The Siege*, and *The Secret Lives of Dentists*.

Jimmy Fallon spent six seasons as a cast member on *Saturday Night Live*, including four as the co-anchor of "Weekend Update." He has also hosted *The MTV Movie Awards* twice; appeared in the films *Taxi*, *Almost Famous*, and *Fever Pitch*; and released an album called *The Bathroom Wall*.

Mitch Fatel (www.mitchfatel.com) has appeared numerous times on *The Late Show with David Letterman* and *Dr. Katz: Professional Therapist* and regularly does live reports from events for *The Tonight Show with Jay Leno*. *The Hollywood Reporter* declared Mitch as one of the best comic bets for future fame, and he has released two very funny CDs— *Miniskirts and Muffins* and *Super Retardo*.

Craig Ferguson was one of Britain's hottest comics when he moved to Los Angeles in 1995. The move was wise—he was quickly cast as Nigel Wick on the popular *Drew Carey Show*, where he appeared until 2003. He has also appeared in films such as *The Big Tease* and *Lemony Snicket's A Series of Unfortunate Events*, and in 2005 he replaced Craig Kilborn as host of CBS' late-night talk show, now called *The Late Late Show with Craig Ferguson*.

Michelle Ferguson-Cohen (www.mfcohen.com) is a recovering rock chick and former music industry maven who gave up baby-sitting rock bands to pursue her own rock 'n' roll dreams of comedy. Her southern accent has a sharp New York bite after many years in the Big Apple, and so does her humor.

Adam Ferrara (www.adamferrara.com) is a two-time nominee of the American Comedy Award for Best Stand-Up Comedian. He has had two Comedy Central specials and has appeared on *The Tonight Show*, Letterman, *The View*, *Politically Incorrect*, and *The Late Late Show with Craig Kilborn*. Ferrara has been a regular cast member on *Caroline in the City*, *Contest Searchlight*, and *The Job*; appeared in the films *Ash Tuesday* and *Dark Descends*; and released a CD called *Have Some*, which can be purchased through his website.

Tina Fey joined the cast of *Saturday Night Live* in 2000 as the co-anchor (with Jimmy Fallon) of "Weekend Update" and is also the show's head writer. A veteran of Chicago's Second City, Fey has been widely credited with leading the show's rejuvenation. She also wrote and appeared in the film *Mean Girls*.

Josh Filipowski (www.like2laugh.com or joshfilipowski@like2laugh.com) attended the University of Wisconsin—Madison, where he performed in the philanthropic Humorology Show each year. Pursuing his studies in humor, Josh participated in Chris Murphy's Comedy Workshop at the New York Comedy Club, jump-starting his stand-up career. He founded Like 2 Laugh Productions in March 2003 and performs all over NYC.

Christian Finnegan (christianfinnegan.com) is a regular panelist on *The Today Show*, VH1's *Best Week Ever*, and *I Love the '80s*. He had his own half-hour special on Comedy Central, was a staff writer for *Tough Crowd with Colin Quinn*, and played white housemate Chad on the hilarious *Chappelle's Show* parody of *The Real World*.

Greg Fitzsimmons (www.gregfitzsimmons.com) won two Daytime Emmy Awards in 2005 for his work as a writer and producer on *The Ellen DeGeneres Show*. He has also written for *Lucky Louie*, *Politically Incorrect*, *The Man Show*, and *The Emmy Awards* and appeared numerous times on *Best Week Ever*, Letterman, Conan, Kilborn, *The Tonight Show*, and *The Howard Stern Show*.

Jim Florentine (www.jimflorentine.com) does the voices of Special Ed and Bobby Fletcher on Comedy Central's *Crank Yankers*. He has appeared on *Tough Crowd with Colin Quinn*, *The Late Late Show with Craig Kilborn*, *Jimmy Kimmel Live*, *Last Call with Carson Daly*, *The Howard Stern Show*, and *Inside The NFL*. He has released several CDs, including *Get the Kids Out of the Room*, *Meet the Creeps*, and four CDs in his *Terrorizing Telemarketers* series.

John Fox appeared on several of Rodney Dangerfield's HBO specials and has many other TV appearances under his belt, including *Comic Strip Live*, *Make Me Laugh*, *Star Search*, and A&E's *Comedy on the Road*. He is also a regular guest on the *Bob and Tom Show*.

Jeff Foxworthy (www.jefffoxworthy.com) is the best-selling comedic recording artist of all time and a four-time Grammy nominee. The movie of his *Blue Collar Comedy Tour* (with co-stars Bill Engvall, Ron White, and Larry the Cable Guy) was broadcast on Comedy Central and became the highest-rated movie in the network's history; and the DVD and VHS of the film have sold more than 2.5 million copies, with the sequel right behind it. Jeff won a People's Choice Award for

"Favorite Male Newcomer" for his sitcom *The Jeff Foxworthy Show* and was TNN's Comedian of the Year three years in a row.

Jamie Foxx (Jamiefoxx.com) was football-tossin', music-playin' Eric Bishop when a girlfriend brought him to a comedy club in 1989 and changed his life. He started performing at open-mic nights, and when he found out that female comics got preference for stage time, took his current, more androgynous name. He was cast in *In Living Color* soon after, and that lead to his own sitcom, *The Jamie Foxx Show*, in 1996. The show ran for five years, and in addition to earning him comedic film roles in movies like *Booty Call*, brought him dramatic roles as well in the acclaimed *Any Given Sunday* and *Ali*. These led to *Ray*—and superstardom. For his roles in *Ray*, *Collateral*, and *The Tookie Williams Story*, Foxx was the first actor in history nominated for three acting awards at the Golden Globes in the same year. He was also one of only 10 actors in history (and only the second male, and the first African American) nominated for both a Supporting and Lead Actor Oscar for two different movies in the same year—the later of which, of course, he won. As if this wasn't enough, as this book goes to press, Foxx's album, *Unpredictable*, is the number-one album in the country.

Redd Foxx gained notoriety throughout the 1940s and 1950s for his vulgar, uproarious nightclub act. Increasing popularity in the 1960s led to his name becoming a household word when he starred in *Sanford and Son*, a show that featured the rarely portrayed reality of poor black life. Foxx died in 1991 on the set of his new sitcom, *The Royal Family*.

Jim Gaffigan (www.jimgaffigan.com) has appeared numerous times on *The View*, Conan O'Brien, Craig Kilborn, and David Letterman. He has appeared in more than 30 films, including *13 Going on 30, Igby Goes Down*, and *Three Kings;* was a cast member on *The Ellen Show* starring Ellen DeGeneres; and was personally selected by David Letterman to develop and star in his own sitcom, *Welcome to New York*, which was produced by Letterman's production company. Learn more or buy his DVD *Beyond the Pale* at his website.

Pat Galante is a writer, comedian, and solo artist who lives in New York City.

Zach Galifianakis (www.zachgalifianakis.com) hosted *Late World with Zach* on VH1 and co-starred in the movie and TV show *The Comedians* *of Comedy*. He has also appeared on Letterman, Conan, Kimmel, and in Fiona Apple's "Not About Love" video. His twin brother, Seth Galifianakis, has performed on *The Jimmy Kimmel Show*, even though he does not seem to actually exist.

Janeane Garofalo co-hosts "The Majority Report" with Sam Seder for Air America Radio. A veteran of stand-up with a die-hard following, Janeane is one of the comics most frequently cited in any discussion of "alternative" comedy—at least partially due to her penchant for bringing a notebook on stage with her. She has been a cast member on *Saturday Night Live*, *The Ben Stiller Show*, and *The Larry Sanders Show* and has appeared in more than 50 films, including *Wet Hot American Summer*, *Dogma*, and *The Truth About Cats and Dogs*.

Kevin Garvey (kevingarvey.net) is a stand-up comedian who performs all over Long Island and New York City. Time permitting, he plans on starring in major motion pictures and on television.

Jay Gates (www.GoldieBrown.com) has been featured on HBO's *Project Greenlight*, *Maxim Magazine Online*, and Kevin Spacey's Triggerstreet. com. He has appeared on the Discovery Channel, National Geographic, and TLC and is currently reorganizing the New Orleans Comedy Festival.

Kimmy Gatewood (kimmygatewood.com) is an acclaimed comedienne, actress, director, writer, and improviser in New York City. She is best known for her silly songs. She also likes running.

Larry Getlen (larrygetlen.com, www.myspace.com/larrygetlen, or idiotsguidetojokes.com) is a veteran journalist, author, comedian, comedy writer, and actor. He has appeared on *Chappelle's Show*, written for Comedy Central and AMC, and performed throughout the northeast. As a journalist, Larry has interviewed hundreds of the top names in comedy, including George Carlin, Dave Chappelle, Bill Maher, Lewis Black, Dane Cook, Mitch Hedberg, Ray Romano, Ellen DeGeneres, Dennis Miller, Margaret Cho, Robert Klein, and many, many others, for publications and websites including *Esquire*, *Variety*, *Salon*, and *The New York Post*. He has also written several short screenplays, one of which was produced for a film that screened at several festivals. *The Complete Idiot's Guide to Jokes* is his seventh book.

Sir John Gielgud, despite being one of the great Shakespearean actors of the twentieth century and having appeared in more than 120 films, ironically secured his only Academy Award for a comedy—the 1981 Dudley Moore hit *Arthur*. Sir John died in 2000.

Paul Gilmartin (www.paulgilmartin.com) has spent the past 10 years as the co-host of TBS's *Dinner and a Movie*. He has written for *The Emmy Awards* and Dennis Miller and has appeared on NBC's *Late Friday*, *Politically Incorrect*, *The Late Late Show with Craig Ferguson*, and his own half-hour special on Comedy Central.

Judy Gold (www.judygold.com) has twice won Emmy Awards for her work as writer/producer on *The Rosie O'Donnell Show* and has been nominated twice for the American Comedy Award for Best Female Stand-Up. Her many TV appearances include *Sex and the City*, *Law and Order*, *Comic Relief*, *Tough Crowd*, *The View*, *Politically Incorrect*, *The Tonight Show*, and her own specials on Comedy Central and HBO. Visit her website to see where she's performing next.

Bobcat Goldthwait (previously known as Bobcat) came to public atten-tion as the schreechy freak in the *Police Academy* movies. But while moviegoers were laughing at his buffoonish antics, those who endeavored to see him live discovered an intelligent, politically astute comic mind. He still tours and occasionally acts but has turned more of his attention to directing, working behind the camera at *The Man Show*, *Chappelle's Show*, and *The Jimmy Kimmel Show*.

Julia Gorin (JuliaGorin.com) served as an Election '04 AOL Comedy Correspondent and was profiled in the best-selling 2005 book *South Park Conservatives*. She is also a columnist contributing to major publications, including *The Wall Street Journal*, *New York Post*, *Washington Post*, JewishWorldReview.com, and *Christian Science Monitor*.

Gilbert Gottfried (www.gilbertgottfried.com) was introduced to the public on *Saturday Night Live* and since then has become one of comedy's more distinct personalities. He hosted *USA Up All Night* and has been a regular presence on *The Tonight Show with Jay Leno*. His version of the dirty joke "The Aristocrats" shortly after 9/11 eventually inspired the film, and he's become an in-demand voice-over artist, providing the voices of Iago the parrot in *Aladdin*, Clippy the Microsoft paperclip, a PopTarts toaster, and the AFLAC duck. Pick up his DVD, *Dirty Jokes*, at his website.

Jeremy Greenberg (www.jeremygreenberg.net) is a comedian and author.

Dick Gregory (www.dickgregory.com) was one of the first black comics to deal with race head on, coming to public attention in 1961, thanks to the support of Hugh Hefner, who booked him into the Playboy Club. He quickly segued from comedy into social activism. He has fasted for causes many times, including in Iran during the hostage crisis of the late 1970s, when he shrank to 97 pounds before returning to America. He is now a frequent public speaker and still occasionally performs comedy.

Kathy Griffin (www.kathygriffin.net) gained notoriety as Brooke Shields's wisecracking friend in *Suddenly Susan* and has carried her acerbic wit to a career as America's foremost D-list celebrity. She has appeared on *Mad About You*, *ER*, and *Seinfeld* and in Eminem's "The Real Slim Shady" video; had her own one-hour comedy specials on HBO and Bravo; hosted NBC's *Average Joe*, MTV's *Kathy's So-Called Reality*, and *The Billboard Music Awards*; and has her own reality show on Bravo called *Kathy Griffin: My Life on the D-List*.

Nick Griffin (www.nickgriffin.net) has been performing comedy since 1987. He has written for *The Keenan Ivory Wayans Show*; appeared on Comedy Central's *Premium Blend*, the David Letterman show, and *The Late Late Show with Craig Kilborn*; and is a regular on the *Bob and Tom Show*. Pick up his CD, *Shot at the Face*, at his website.

Peter Griffin is a terrible but hysterically funny father. Learn more by purchasing any of *The Family Guy* DVDs and watching the show Sunday nights on Fox or check out www.familyguy.com.

Lewis Grizzard was a popular Southern humorist who wrote for the *Atlanta Journal-Constitution* and also wrote 25 books, including *Southern by the Grace of God*, *I Haven't Understood Anything Since 1962*, and *Chili Dawgs Always Bark at Night*. Grizzard died in 1994.

Matt Groening created *The Simpsons*. For this alone, his place in heaven is assured.

Arsenio Hall (www.arseniohall.com) was one of America's top late-night talk show hosts in the early 1990s as the host of *The Arsenio Hall Show*, notable, if nothing else, for featuring presidential candidate Bill

Clinton playing "Heartbreak Hotel" on the saxophone. He also co-starred in and co-wrote the Eddie Murphy hit *Coming to America* and starred in the CBS show *Martial Law*.

Deric Harrington (www.DericHarrington.com or stripedcomic@aol.com) is the "stripes" half of the "Caked On Stripes" podcast radio show.

Mitch Hedberg (www.mitchhedberg.net) was one of America's best-loved up-and-coming comics for his way with a surreal one-liner. He was a favorite of David Letterman and Conan O'Brien and released two CDs, *Mitch All Together* and *Strategic Grill Locations*, that proved what a unique and innovative talent he was. His performances were sharp but clean, and while he appealed to hipsters and comedy fanatics, he was equally suitable for audiences of just about every stripe and sensibility. The comedy world suffered a heartbreaking loss when Mitch passed away on March 30, 2005, at the age of 37. Learn more about this brilliant comic, and pick up his CDs at his website.

John Heffron (www.johnheffron.com) was the winner of season two of NBC's *Last Comic Standing* and has also held one of the most dangerous jobs in broadcasting—serving as Danny Bonaduce's sidekick on a Detroit morning show. He has appeared on *The Tonight Show* and Craig Kilborn and also co-created a successful card game called *That Guy!* which earned him coverage in *Entertainment Weekly* and *Entrepreneur Magazine*. Learn about the game at www.thatguygame.com.

Tony Hendra is a veteran humorist and author who has had a profound impact on the history of comedy. Hendra was a driving force at *National Lampoon Magazine*, where he served in various senior editorial roles throughout the 1970s and directed the *Lemmings* stage show, which starred John Belushi, Chevy Chase, and Christopher Guest. He later served as the editor of another influential satire publication, *Spy Magazine*, and also played Ian Faith in the film *This Is Spinal Tap*. In 2004, he released the spiritual memoir *Father Joe*, which became a *New York Times* best-seller.

John Henton earned his big break when, after winning the 1991 Johnny Walker National Comedy Search, he was booked on *The Tonight Show*, where Johnny Carson sang his praises. Many TV appearances later, he was cast in the Fox sitcom *Living Single*, where he spent five years. He has also been a regular cast member on ABC's *The Hughleys* and had his own special on Showtime.

Bill Hicks (www.billhicks.com) began his career by stealing Woody Allen's jokes for a performance at a church camp talent show at the age of 14; he ended it as one of the most incendiary performers of the past 20 years. Like Lenny Bruce, Hicks made a career of decimating societal norms. He was a contempt-filled man who tore into religion, government, stupidity, and hypocrisy with a finely honed combination of vitriol and hilarity that many attempt but few can execute successfully. Hicks's radical views earned him broken bones and bird's-eye views of gun barrels, but he never wavered in his commitment to present the truth, as he saw it, through comedy. That he could express such radical opinions while never losing the funny was almost miraculous. Hicks was aggressively pro-drugs, pro-choice, and anti–Gulf War; has been saluted by bands such as Radiohead and Tool; and cemented his legend by dying way too young, at the age of 32, in 1994.

Danny Hirsh (www.danhirshon.com) first took the spotlight at Boston's Comedy Vault, and since then has competed in the Boston Comedy Festival and as a finalist in the Las Vegas Comedy Festival. Dan now performs regularly throughout New England and New York.

Steve Hofstetter (stevehofstetter.com) is a college favorite who electrified audiences with his recent CD/DVD Combo, *Cure for the Cable Guy*. A host on Sirius Satellite Radio and a columnist for *Sports Illustrated*, the NHL, and *College Humor*, Hofstetter is called "The Thinking Man's Comic" for his ability to get laughs about real issues.

Geoff Holtzman (geoffholtzman@yahoo.com) is a young comedian and writer from Philadelphia with a sly comedy wisdom and a deft way around a one-liner. He performs frequently in New York City and around the East Coast.

J. Scott Homan (www.geocities.com/jscotthoman) has appeared on Comedy Central's *Premium Blend* and Showtime's *Comedy Club Network* and has performed at the Aspen Comedy Festival. He lives in Louisville, but really lives on the road, performing throughout the country. Visit his website to see where he's performing next.

Bob Hope started dancing on vaudeville stages at the age of 18 and continued performing almost until his death at the age of 100. He appeared in more than 70 films and in several Broadway musicals, but his greatest achievements came in television and in live performances during times of war. Hope starred in specials for NBC for 60 years—an achievement the likes of which we'll probably never see again—and spent the same span entertaining U.S. troops around the world in times of both peace and conflict. One of the most honored entertainers in history, Hope received 54 honorary degrees and more than 2,000 honors and awards, including the Congressional Gold Medal from President Kennedy, the Medal of Freedom from President Johnson, an honorary knighthood by England's Queen Elizabeth II, and status as an Honorary Veteran of the U.S. military by the U.S. Congress—the first person in the nation's history to be granted that honor. Hope died in 2003.

Jeremy Hsu (www.pretentiousproductions.com) has been performing stand-up comedy since 2004 and can be seen regularly in clubs throughout New York City. He placed second in the 2005 MTV Labs Talent Show and is known for being "funny for a Chinese guy." He was born and raised in Honolulu, Hawaii.

D. L. Hughley was on his way to a hard and dangerous life as a member of the Bloods gang when he turned his life around by turning to comedy. He was the first host of BET's *Comic View*, had a hit sitcom called *The Hughleys* on ABC and UPN, and co-starred in the movie *The Original Kings of Comedy*, which captured one of the most successful tours in comedy history. D. L. has since hosted Comedy Central's *Premium Blend* and had his own show on the network, *Weekends at the D. L.*

Eddie Izzard (www.eddieizzard.com) is a British comic and actor whose surreal monologues are some of the more unique inventions in comedy today. Winner of the British Comedy Award for Top Stand-Up Comedian and two Emmys here in the States, he was one of Comedy Central's Top 100 Greatest Stand-Ups of All Time and has appeared in many films, including *The Aristocrats*, *Ocean's Twelve*, *The Cat's Meow* (as Charlie Chaplin), and *Velvet Goldmine*. He has also been nominated for a Tony and has appeared on the theatrical stage in roles as diverse as Edward II and Lenny Bruce.

Kevin James got his first big break on *Star Search* and then got another later when his good friend Ray Romano cast him as a regular on *Everybody Loves Raymond*. James has starred in the hit CBS sitcom *The King of Queens* since 1998 and has appeared in the films *50 First Dates* and *Hitched*.

Richard Jeni (www.richardjeni.com) has been a frequent guest on *The Tonight Show* under both Johnny Carson and Jay Leno. He has had several one-hour specials on both Showtime and HBO; spent two years as the host of A&E's *Caroline's Comedy Hour*; and had his own sitcom, *Platypus Man*, on UPN. The American Comedy Award for Best Male Stand-Up was presented to him on national television by George Carlin. He has also appeared in the films *Bird*, *The Mask*, and *The Aristocrats*.

Penn Jillette (pennandteller.com) is best known as the verbal half of the Penn and Teller magic act but displayed a new side to the comedy world when he conceived and produced the film *The Aristocrats*, a documentary about the world's dirtiest joke. With Teller, Penn has performed one of the world's more unique acts for 30 years. They have created many of their own television projects, including their current series, *Bullshit*, for Showtime; written three best-selling books; and even earned visiting scholar status at MIT. On his own, Penn DJs a one-hour daily talk show for CBS Radio's FREE FM and has written several books.

Jake Johannsen's (jakethis.com) one-hour HBO special, *This'll Take About an Hour*, was named one of the Ten Best Television Shows of 1992 by *People* magazine, and one of the 50 Funniest TV Moments of All Time by *TV Guide*. He has made more than 30 appearances on David Letterman's program, and many as well on Conan O'Brien, *Politically Incorrect*, and *The Tonight Show*. He has also appeared in two movies by the director Alan Rudolph—*Breakfast of Champions* and *Mrs. Parker and the Vicious Circle*. Find out where to see him live at his website.

Terry "funny plumber" Johnson (www.funnyplumber.com) is age 64, single, and lives with his mother. He's got his own room, cable TV, and HBO. Pretty soon Mom is going to die, and he'll get the whole trailer.

Jesse Joyce (www.jessejoyce.com) is a stand-up comedian and writer based in New York City. His TV appearances include *Entertainment Tonight* and the Lifetime Network, and he can be heard regularly on the nationally syndicated *Bob and Tom Show* and satellite radio. Jesse has performed at clubs and colleges all over the United States as well as in Switzerland, Canada, and Ireland.

Myq Kaplan (pronounced *Mike Kaplan*; www.myqkaplan.com) performs regularly in the Boston area and irregularly elsewhere. His comedy has been said to evoke laughter from audiences. Myq has a CD titled *Open Myq Night* and a website titled www.myqkaplan.com.

Jonathan Katz played the funniest TV therapist this side of Frasier (well, maybe even funnier) on the animated show *Dr. Katz: Professional Therapist*, which ran for six seasons on Comedy Central, won both an Emmy and a Peabody Award for Broadcasting Excellence, and featured many of today's great stand-up comics as his patients. Jonathan has also made many late-night TV appearances and had his own Comedy Central special, and he has appeared in films including *Daddy Day Care*, *State and Main*, and *The Spanish Prisoner*. He was diagnosed with multiple sclerosis in 1997 and now speaks frequently about how to cope with disease through laughter.

Laura Kightlinger was a writer and performer on *Saturday Night Live* and has written many episodes of the hit show *Will and Grace*. She has appeared in her own HBO half-hour comedy special and in many films, including *Shallow Hal*, *Daddy Day Care*, and *Anchorman*. A documentary she directed, *60 Spins Around the Sun*, won Best Documentary Film accolades at several film festivals.

Craig Kilborn was an anchor on ESPN's *SportsCenter* for four years before he was picked to fill the same role on a new comedy news show for Comedy Central—*The Daily Show*. He spent several years there, building a following for himself and his show until 1998, when David Letterman personally picked him to replace Tom Snyder as host of CBS's *Late Late Show*. Kilborn served in that capacity for five years and then surprised the entertainment world by stepping down to follow other pursuits, including acting and producing. As of this writing, he has three film appearances scheduled for 2006.

Brian Kiley has been a staff writer for *Late Night with Conan O'Brien* for more than a decade. A multiple-Emmy nominee, Kiley has also appeared numerous times on *The Tonight Show* and Conan, as well as on Letterman; *The CBS Morning Show*; *Dr. Katz: Professional Therapist*; and many, many others.

Alan King began his career in the Borscht Belt and symbolized the Catskills comic generation as the Abbott of the infamous Friar's Club.

He served as a regular guest host for Johnny Carson on *The Tonight Show* and hosted the Academy Awards in 1972. He has also appeared in 30 films, including *Night and the City*, *Casino*, and *Sunshine State*, and authored five books. Alan King passed away in 2004.

Sam Kinison served, along with Bill Hicks, as one of modern comedy's great angry men. But while Hicks's anger was institutional, Kinison's was largely personal. A former preacher, Kinison was discovered by Rodney Dangerfield and became a favorite in the 1980s with his madman rants against the insanity of the world and the women who did him wrong. He gained further recognition with his brazen performance as a crazed teacher in Dangerfield's *Back to School*. After finally getting clean following years of drug and alcohol abuse, Kinison was killed in 1992 by a drunk driver, six days after his wedding.

Robert Klein is a graduate of Chicago's Second City Improv and was one of the premiere album-based comics of the 1970s. His first release, *Child of the Fifties*, earned him a 1973 Grammy nomination, and he sold out Carnegie Hall later that year. Two years later, he became the first comic to have his own special on HBO and has had seven more since. He has also been nominated for a Tony Award; written a book called *The Amorous Busboy of Decatur Avenue*; and appeared in more than 40 films, including *Two Weeks Notice*, *Primary Colors*, and *Next Stop, Wonderland*.

Sue Kolinsky was the original host of Comedy Central's *Short Attention Span Theater* and has appeared on *The Tonight Show* and *Comic Strip Live*. She has written for *The Ellen Show* and *Sex and the City*, and served as a producer on *The Osbournes*, *Newlyweds: Nick and Jessica*, and *Nanny 911*.

Lisa Lampanelli (www.insultcomic.com), the Queen of Mean, keeps the tradition of the insult comic alive across the country and in TV and film. She has appeared on several Comedy Central roasts and numerous times on *Tough Crowd with Colin Quinn*. She has also appeared on *Weekends at the D. L.* and BET's *Comic View*, and her CD/DVD, *Take It Like a Man*, charted at number 13 on Billboard's Comedy Chart. She will be seen playing "a foul-mouthed dirty broad" in the film *Larry the Cable Guy: Health Inspector*, and she signed a sitcom deal with the Fox Network in 2005.

Larry the Cable Guy (larrythecableguy.com) has seen enormous success as one fourth of the *Blue Collar Comedy Tour* (see bios of Engvall, White, and Foxworthy for details). On his own, his 2001 debut CD, *Lord, I Apologize*, spent two years on Billboard's Comedy Charts. He has since released two more CDs, a DVD called *Git-R-Done*, and a book of the same name in 2005.

Catie Lazarus (www.lazarusrising.com) won the "Best Comedy Writer" award from the Emerging Comics of New York, and *The New York Resident* selected her as a "Top 100 New Yorker" for comedy. She has appeared on AMC and performed everywhere from the Kennedy Center to Caroline's on Broadway. Her sardonic wit appears in *The Forward*, *Time Out New York*, *Nerve*, and *Heeb Magazine*, where she is an editor.

Denis Leary came to public attention with a series of rants on MTV and an acerbic one-man show called *No Cure for Cancer*. He has appeared in more than 40 films, including *The Ref*, *Wag the Dog*, and *The Secret Lives of Dentists* and was the voice of Diego the tiger in *Ice Age* and *Ice Age 2*. He created and starred in *The Job* for ABC and *Rescue Me* for FX, the latter of which earned him his first Emmy nomination (for writing) in 2005. Leary also founded the Leary Firefighters Foundation, an organization that has raised millions of dollars to provide equipment, training, and technology to fire departments. Learn more at www.learyfirefighters.org.

Pete Lee (www.petelee.net) has appeared on Comedy Central's *Premium Blend*, on the *Bob and Tom Show*, and in *Prairie Home Companion: The Movie*. His latest CD is called *Gas Money*.

Chad Lehrman (chadlehrman@gmail.com) is a comedian/writer currently based in Tucson, Arizona.

Carol Leifer occupies an important place in comedy history. A writer and producer on *Seinfeld*, she was the inspiration for the character of Elaine. Carol has also written for *The Larry Sanders Show*, *The Ellen Show*, and *The Academy Awards*. She has appeared on *The Late Show with David Letterman* 25 times and spent 4 seasons as the host of A&E's *Caroline's Comedy Hour*. She also appeared on *The Tonight Show with Johnny Carson* and opened for Frank Sinatra at Bally's in Las Vegas.

Margot B. Leitman (www.margotleitman.com) has toured with Montreal Comedy Festival's "Dating It." Her solo show, *Just Here for the Day*, ran successfully for five months at the Upright Citizen's Brigade Theatre. Past television appearances include *Best Week Ever*, Conan O'Brian, ESPN, Style Network, AMC, Comedy Central, MTV, and E!.

Jay Leno is the host of *The Tonight Show*. He wrote a book of jokes and humorous advice for children in 2005 called *How to Be the Funniest Kid in the Whole World (or Just in Your Class)*.

David Letterman is the host of *The Late Show with David Letterman*. The fact that, in an alphabetical list of several hundred comedians, he happens to directly follow Jay Leno is just a really strange coincidence.

Todd Levin (www.tremble.com) is a writer and stand-up comedian living in New York City. He can be seen on Comedy Central's *Premium Blend*, and his writing has appeared in *Modern Humorist*, *Salon*, *Jest* magazine, *The Onion*, and, most frequently, his own website.

Richard Lewis (richardlewisonline.com) turned therapy into an art form, bringing his dark neurosis onstage so audiences can laugh along with his pain. A cast member on *Curb Your Enthusiasm*, Lewis starred for four years with Jamie Lee Curtis on the ABC hit *Anything but Love*. He has had specials on HBO and Showtime, and his book, *The Other Great Depression*, dealt in stark terms with his severe alcoholism. Comedy Central named him one of the 50 top stand-up comedians of all time, and *GQ* included him on the list of the twentieth century's most influential humorists.

Tony Liberati (getliberati@hotmail.com) is a high-energy comic who captivates audiences with his observational humor, wacky impressions, and unique views on the nostalgia of childhood. Tony has been performing at colleges and clubs up and down the East Coast since 1999 and has been featured on ABC's *America's Funniest People*.

Wendy Liebman (www.wendyliebman.com) won the 1996 American Comedy Award for Best Female Stand-Up. She has appeared numerous times on *The Tonight Show* with both Johnny Carson and Jay Leno, and on Letterman, Kilborn, Larry Sanders, and *Comic Relief*, to name just a few. Check out her website to see where she's performing next.

Jay London (jaylondonlive.com) appeared on seasons two and three of NBC's *Last Comic Standing* and became a favorite for his self-deprecating one-liners. He has also appeared on *The Tonight Show with Jay Leno* and CBS's *King of Queens*.

Shane Lou has written jokes and stories for the ABC Radio Networks and has worked in the news and data-entry industries for many years. He lives on Long Island with no wife and no pets.

Chris Loud was born and raised in Ann Arbor, Michigan, and has performed at colleges and clubs throughout the Midwest and the East Coast.

Kerri Louise (www.KerriLouise.com) made her movie debut in *The Next Karate Kid* and has appeared on NBC's *Access Hollywood, The Apprentice*, ABC's *The View*, Comedy Central, VH1, *20/20*, and *New Joke City*. She made it to the finals of NBC's *Last Comic Standing* and will star along with her husband, comedian Tom Cotter, on the WE network's *Two Funny* (www.twofunny.com).

Carmen Lynch (www.carmenlynch.com) is based in New York City and is a regular at clubs such as the *Comic Strip Live* and the *New York Improv*. She was seen on HBO's *Aspen Comedy Festival*, Comedy Central's *Premium Blend*, and as a finalist on the first season of NBC's *Last Comic Standing*. She has also appeared on several independent films and contributes to *Mad Magazine*.

Jon Macks is a staff writer for Jay Leno and has written for the Oscars, the Emmys, and HBO's *K Street*. He is also the author of *How to Be Funny*.

Kathleen Madigan (www.kathleenmadigan.com) was voted Best Female Stand-Up at the American Comedy Awards and was featured on NBC's *Last Comic Standing*. She's been seen on Conan, Letterman, and Leno; was a contributing writer for Garry Shandling on *The Emmy Awards*; and was referred to as one of America's funniest female comics by Jay Leno on *The Howard Stern Show*. Check out her CD, *Shallow Happy Thoughts for the Soul*, or her first DVD—cleverly titled *The First DVD*—at her website.

Bill Maher (www.billmaher.com) was the host of *Politically Incorrect* on Comedy Central and ABC from 1993 to 2002. The show earned 18 Emmy nominations until its cancellation following controversial statements by Maher regarding 9/11. The following year, he created *Real Time with Bill Maher* for HBO, which continued the free expression of ideas Maher initiated on *PI*, and has been nominated for three Emmys. Maher has also written four books, and continues performing stand-up comedy in theatrical venues. His one-man Broadway show *Victory Begins at Home* was nominated for a Tony Award, and the HBO broadcast of that show was his fifth comedy special for the network.

Ed Marques has been an MTV VJ and performed on *Comic Strip Live* and *Caroline's Comedy Hour*. He has also been seen on *The Weird Al Yankovic Show* and in the movie *Totally Blonde*.

John Marshall (www.knowledgeappendix.xbuild.com) has been a staff writer for *The Chris Rock Show*, *Politically Incorrect*, and *Tough Crowd with Colin Quinn* and a freelancer for *SNL*'s "Weekend Update" and *MAD Magazine*. He has performed on *Tough Crowd* and in comedy clubs on both coasts.

Demitri Martin (demetrimartin.com) is a correspondent for *The Daily Show with Jon Stewart* and was a staff writer for *Late Night with Conan O'Brien*. He's been on *Last Call with Carson Daly*, the Craig Ferguson and David Letterman shows, Conan, and had his own *Comedy Central Presents* special. His writing has appeared in *The New York Times* magazine, and he was the winner of the prestigious Perrier Award at the Edinburgh Fringe Festival for his show *If I*.

Steve Martin (stevemartin.com) is now best known for his movies, but his late 1970s success revolutionized stand-up comedy. He frequently sold out arenas—a virtually unheard-of feat for a comedian—and his 1978 album *Let's Get Small* remained the best-selling comedy album in the nation until 2004. His hosting appearances on *Saturday Night Live* were so well received that he was invited back enough times to lead many to incorrectly believe he was a cast member. He also won an Emmy as a staff writer for *The Smothers Brothers Comedy Hour* in 1969, and in 2000 was awarded a Lifetime Achievement Award at the American Comedy Awards. Now, he's a frequent contributor to *The New Yorker* and also writes novels, including *Shopgirl*, which was made into a movie he starred in with Claire Danes.

Groucho Marx was one of the finest wits of the twentieth century. While the country was suffering through the Great Depression of the 1930s, the Marx Brothers often gave America its only reason to smile, producing classic comedies such as *A Night at the Opera*, *Animal Crackers*, and *Duck Soup*. After the Brothers' fortunes in the movie business faded, Groucho reinvented himself as one of TV's most charismatic personalities, hosting the quiz show *You Bet Your Life* from 1950 to 1961. He was presented with an honorary Oscar in 1974 for the stunning life's work produced by him and his brothers. Groucho passed away in 1977.

Jackie Mason (www.jackiemason.com), a former rabbi, had already been famous for two decades when his one-man show, *The World According to Me*, began a 2½-year run on Broadway, earning Mason a Tony, an Emmy, an Outer Critics Circle Award, and a Grammy nomination. He's had five more successful Broadway shows since and an HBO special that earned him another Emmy.

Ralphie May (ralphiemay.com) was the runner-up in the first season of NBC's *Last Comic Standing*. He has been a writer and producer for ESPN's *Mohr Sports* starring Jay Mohr and has appeared on *The Tonight Show*, Craig Kilborn, *The Man Show*, and *Jimmy Kimmel Live*.

Phil Mazo (www.PhilMazo.com), best described as "seemingly innocent, but with a dark side," has appeared on Sirius Satellite Radio and at the New York City Underground Comedy Festival.

Moody McCarthy (www.moodymccarthy.com) has been a stand-up comic since the 1990s, when he started in upstate New York. Now based out of New York City, he's appeared on *Jimmy Kimmel Live* and become a club favorite everywhere north of I-64 and east of I-29. Check him out on *Last Comic Standing 4*.

Steve McGrew (www.stevemcgrew.com) has had his own half-hour special on Comedy Central, and has released two CDs—*Too Much Man for Just One Woman* and *Bootleg*.

Brian McKim is a writer and professional stand-up comic who has performed in all 50 states. He has appeared on numerous network, syndicated, and cable TV shows, including *Evening at the Improv*, *Into the Night*, and *Star Search*. Together with his wife, Traci Skene, he edits and publishes SHECKYmagazine.com, the Internet's most beloved magazine about stand-up comedy.

Dennis Miller came to prominence as the master of the arcane reference as the anchor of *Saturday Night Live*'s "Weekend Update." After leaving the show in 1992, he tried his hand at his own late-night talk show, which failed. Then he tried again, this time on HBO, and did not fail. The show ran from 1994 to 2002, won five Emmy Awards, and solidified his reputation as one of our sharpest social commentators. Since then, his two-season stint as a comedic analyst on *Monday Night Football* was a head scratcher, and his sharp turn to the right after 9/11 cost him some long-time fans and led to a CNBC show that few people watched. But Miller is too sharp and too funny to be counted out. His January 2006 HBO special, *All In*, was his seventh for the network. No word at press time on what he's up to next, but it's a safe bet that whatever it is, it won't take place in France.

Kevin Miller has performed stand-up all around New York City and has worked on several productions for NBC, Comedy Central, and MTV. He is a contributing writer to InsideJoke.tv online comedy magazine.

Larry Miller is a frequent guest on *The Tonight Show* and *The Late Show with David Letterman*. Miller started in the 1970s as part of a comedic circle that included Leno and Jerry Seinfeld. While performing in clubs, Milton Berle enjoyed his set and asked him to perform at a charity event. One of the attendees was Nancy Sinatra, and the next day Miller booked a week opening for her legendary dad in Vegas. He has had memorable roles in the films *Pretty Woman*, *The Nutty Professor*, and *Waiting for Guffman*, and on many TV shows, including *Seinfeld*, *Mad About You*, and *Law and Order*.

Eugene Mirman (eugenemirman.com) has appeared on *Late Night with Conan O'Brien*, *Comedy Central's Premium Blend*, *Third Watch*, and VH1. His CD/DVD, *The Absurd Nightclub Comedy of Eugene Mirman*, was named one of the Best Albums of 2004 by both *The Onion* and *Time Out New York*. In 2005, he released *Invite Me Up*, a CD/DVD of highlights of the weekly show he runs in Manhattan's East Village with comedian Bobby Tisdale, through Comedy Central Records. He has opened for The Shins and toured with Modest Mouse and Yo La Tengo, and The Marvelous Crooning Child on his website must be heard to be believed.

Steve Moore (stevemoorecomic.com) has worked with Roseanne, Dolly Parton, Ellen DeGeneres, Lily Tomlin, and others. He publicly revealed himself to be gay and HIV+ in the mid-1990s, and had his own one-hour special called *Drop Dead Gorgeous, a Tragicomedy—the Power of Positive HIV Thinking*, which won a CableAce Award. He currently lives in Virginia, where he teaches comedy, does occasional motivational speaking, and is working on a book titled *I Never Knew Oz Was in Color*.

Mike Morse (www.mike-morse.com) performs at clubs, colleges, and casinos around the country and has been seen on MTV, VH1, and Comedy Central.

Veronica Mosey (www.veronicamosey.com) has written for *US Weekly* and was most recently featured on *The Dr. Phil Show*. She appears regularly at the Comic Strip in New York City and has been seen at The Improv and The Comedy Store in Los Angeles. Recently, she was featured in a series of commercials seen nationwide.

Michael J. Nelson (www.michaelnelsoncomedy.com) is a comedian and television writer in Los Angeles, California.

Bob Newhart (www.bobnewhart.com) was honored in 2005 with his own *American Masters* episode on PBS titled *America Masters: Bob Newhart, Unbuttoned*, and by the TV Land Network, which awarded its Icon award to *The Bob Newhart Show*. Newhart was already famous before his show—his 1960 album *The Buttoned Down Mind of Bob Newhart* was quickly regarded as a classic for his unconventional conversational rhythms, and his way with a story instead of a joke. The highly regarded *Bob Newhart Show* ran from 1972 to 1978, and he had a rare double shot of sitcom success several years later with *Newhart*, which ran from 1982 until 1990. Bob still acts and performs, appearing recently in *Elf* and *Legally Blonde 2* and guesting on *Desperate Housewives* and *ER*.

Conan O'Brien had been a writer for *Saturday Night Live* and a writer/producer for *The Simpsons* when SNL-guru Lorne Michaels plucked him out of the writer's room to replace David Letterman on NBC's late night line-up. The world thought Michaels was crazy. They should all be so crazy. "Conan" is now as identifiable by his first name as Cher or Bono and will take over as the host of *The Tonight Show* in 2009.

Patrice O'Neal (www.patriceoneal.com) was a regular panelist on *Tough Crowd with Colin Quinn* and has had his own comedy specials on HBO, Showtime, and Comedy Central. He has appeared on *Arrested Development* and on NBC's *The Office* and in the films *The 25th Hour*, *In the Cut*, and *Head of State*.

Pat O'Shea (www.myspace.com/osheacomic or skippyoshea@hotmail.com) has been doing comedy for eight years and has appeared at festivals in New York, Boston, and New Hampshire. He hosts a bi-weekly show in Brooklyn called *Ed Sullivan on Acid* that is now in its third year. His comedy CD, *It's Probably Not My Fault*, was released in spring 2006, and he is currently working on an independent film, tentatively titled *Enjoy the Ride*.

Patton Oswalt (www.pattonoswalt.com) is one of the most bizarre and brilliant comedy minds around today. His take on subjects as seemingly obscure and unrelated as local ice-cream magnate Tom Carvel, producer Robert Evans, and TiVo bring out the equal absurdity in the strange and the mundane alike and meld to create an inspiringly unique comic sensibility. *Entertainment Weekly*'s IT comedian of 2002, Oswalt is a regular visitor to Conan O'Brien's show and a cast member on CBS's *King of Queens*. He's had his own specials on Comedy Central and HBO; was one of the former's Comedians of Comedy; and has appeared in films such as *Blade: Trinity*, *Starsky and Hutch*, *Zoolander*, and *Man in the Moon*. A comic book fanatic, he is scheduled to appear in an animated SCI FI channel adaptation of the comic *Amazing Screw-On Head* as the voice of Mr. Groin. His *Feelin' Kinda Patton* CD is available for purchase, but skip that one—get his *222* instead. It's the full 2½-hour version of the same concert—for the complete Patton experience.

Jack Paar took over *The Tonight Show* from Steve Allen in 1957, and over the next 5 years changed its format to more closely resemble the late-night chat show as we know it today. Paar supported young performers such as Carol Burnett, Liza Minnelli, and Woody Allen, and also took brave chances that got him in hot water, including interviewing Fidel Castro. Paar left *The Tonight Show* in 1962, ushering in the Johnny Carson era. Paar passed away in 2004.

Dorothy Parker was a poet, critic, screenwriter, and short story writer renowned as one of the sharpest wits of our age. Her way with a quip rivaled Groucho's, and yet her wit was just one side of her, as her poetry revealed a delicate vulnerability lurking beneath the hardened shell. Together, these traits made her one of the finest writers of the first half of the twentieth century. Parker died in 1967. Today, the Dorothy Parker Society (www.dorothyparkernyc.com) exists to keep her memory alive and her work well read.

Joanna Parson (www.joannaparson.com) is an actor and comic who has performed at the Comedy Store and the Gotham Comedy Club and hosts a bi-monthly variety show in New York called the "Happy Hour Salon." She also co-wrote the FringeNYC hit *Reddy or Not!* much to Helen Reddy's chagrin, and teaches other actors how to get off their duff and write their own material in ongoing workshops.

Dolly Parton (www.dollyon-line.com) is a veteran actress and singer whose funniest moments come when she's talking about her breasts.

Gene Perret (www.writingcomedy.com or comedywriting@sbcglobal.net) has written for *The Jim Nabors Hour* and *Laugh-In* and won three Emmys as a staff writer on *The Carol Burnett Show*. He produced *Welcome Back, Kotter*; *Three's Company*; and *The Tim Conway Show* and wrote jokes for Phyllis Diller. Perret served as staff writer for Bob Hope for almost 30 years, including 12 as Hope's head writer. He has also written more than 25 books and helps develop many aspiring comics and comedy writers.

Emo Philips (www.emophilips.com) is one of the most widely quoted comedians in the world for his way with a bizarre one-liner. Along with Steven Wright (and, to an extent, Mitch Hedberg, whose material is more likely to follow a conversational theme), Emo is the master of creating hilarious thoughts from ether. But from a persona standpoint, Wright is the negative to Philips' positive. While the former comes at his work almost as a depressive, Philips is light as air, producing a rare mingling of high-minded intelligence and childlike gamesmanship, and seeing him live is the closest thing comedy has to psychotropics. Visit his website to find out where he'll be next.

Monica Piper was hailed by *The Hollywood Reporter* as one of the country's top 10 comics and had her own CableAce nominated special on Showtime. She also wrote for the hit sitcoms *Roseanne* and *Mad About You* and provided voices for the children's show *Rugrats*.

Paula Poundstone (www.paulapoundstone.com) won the American Comedy Award for Best Female Stand-Up in 1989, and her 1990 HBO special, *Cats, Cops, and Stuff*, was highly regarded, winning the comedian a CableAce Award. She served as a special correspondent for *The Tonight Show* for the 1992 presidential campaign and has continued to tour extensively over the years. See where she'll be next at her website.

Otto Preminger was an acclaimed film director who also played Mr. Freeze on the Batman TV series. He died in 1986.

Phil Proctor (www.planetproctor.com) is a writer, actor, producer, and a member of the Firesign Theatre, which has garnered three Grammy nominations for their comic recordings. The Firesign Theatre recently taped a half-hour program at the London Comedy Store for BBC4 radio as part of a series honoring American comics who influenced English humorists in the 1960s, including Mort Sahl, Stan Freberg, and Shelly Berman.

Richard Pryor (www.richardpryor.com) is generally regarded as the greatest stand-up comic of all time. Born to a life of hardship and abuse, surrounded by pimps, prostitutes, and molesters, Pryor turned his agony into art. His stand-up was searingly real, filled with the pain of his past and his struggle to overcome it. A mainstream comic in the 1960s, he began dealing with the issues of his life at decade's end, and throughout the 1970s, broke boundaries regarding what constituted comedy. His appearance on *Saturday Night Live* during its first season helped solidify its reputation as TV's counterculture voice, and his 1979 concert film, *Richard Pryor: Live in Concert*, is considered a landmark event in comedy history. Pryor was diagnosed with MS in 1986 but did his best to stay active, sometimes performing while sitting in a chair. Pryor died of a heart attack in late 2005.

Rex Reed is a longtime film critic for *The New York Observer* newspaper.

Christopher Reeve first gained notoriety for his film portrayal of Superman and then for his bravery in the face of paralysis following a horse riding accident in 1995. Reeve died in 2004.

Brian Regan (www.brianregan.com) is considered a true comic's comic for his seamless ability to combine sharp writing and graceful physicality into hysterically funny and relatable stories. Already a road veteran when he won the K-Rock-Miller Lite Funniest Person in New York contest in 1998, the victory led to appearances on MTV's *Half-Hour Comedy Hour, The Pat Sajak Show*, Arsenio Hall, and *The Tonight Show with Johnny Carson*. He has since had his own specials on Showtime and Comedy Central and has become a regular guest of both Conan O'Brien and David Letterman. His DVD, *I Walked on the Moon*, is available at his website.

Jason Reich is an Emmy-winning writer for *The Daily Show with Jon Stewart* and also performs sketch and stand-up comedy at various venues in New York City.

Bob Reinhard is a young, upstart comedian with a wide variety of styles and topics—random at times, but always bringing up things in day-to-day life that people need to laugh at.

David Ridings (www.ridosworld.com) is a comedian and speaker from Nashville, Tennessee.

Joan Rivers (joanrivers.com) already had several decades of stand-up success under her belt when Johnny Carson chose her as his permanent guest host on *The Tonight Show* in the 1980s. Rivers was soon given her own talk show on the new Fox Network. That show failed, but Joan got another shot in 1989, and the result, *The Joan Rivers Show*, ran for four years and won her a Daytime Emmy. She has written several books and in recent years has become best known for her acid-laced red carpet coverage of award shows with her daughter, Melissa.

Chris Rock (chrisrock.com) first came to public attention as a three-season cast member on *Saturday Night Live*. After spending one year on *In Living Color*, Rock broke out with his 1996 HBO special *Bring the Pain*, a searingly brutal and candid examination of race that earned him two Emmy Awards and recognition as the hottest comic in the country. He followed this with his first book, *The New York Times* best-seller *Rock This*, and his own highly acclaimed HBO show, *The Chris Rock Show*, which ran from 1997 to 2000 and was nominated for seven Emmys, winning one. He has since had several more HBO specials; appeared in films such as *Head of State, Nurse Betty, Pootie Tang*, and *The Longest Yard*; and created *Everybody Hates Chris*, one of the best-reviewed sitcoms in recent years.

Paul Rodriguez (www.paulrodriguez.com) was discovered by TV impresario Norman Lear while serving as the warm-up comic for the show *Gloria* starring Sally Struthers. *Gloria* flopped, but Lear saw a star in Rodriguez and gave him a sitcom of his own. *a.k.a. Pablo* only ran for 1 season, but it put Rodriguez on the comedy map. He has since performed stand-up on shows such as *Comic Relief* and *Rodney Dangerfield's 75th Birthday Toast*, as well as several specials of his own; appeared in films such as *Born in East L.A.*, *Rat Race*, and *Ali*; and created and starred in *The Original Latin Kings of Comedy*.

Gregg Rogell has made many TV appearances, including on *The Tonight Show*, Conan O'Brien, and the USO Comedy Tour, and been seen in the films *Half-Baked* and *The Aristocrats*.

Ray Romano (www.rayromano.com) was a successful stand-up with appearances on shows like *MTV's Half-Hour Comedy Hour*; *Dr. Katz: Professional Therapist*; *The Tonight Show*; and *The Late Show with David Letterman* under his belt. Then, in 1995, Letterman signed him to a deal to develop a sitcom based on his life, and all hell broke loose. *Everybody Loves Raymond* became TV's top sitcom. It ran for 9 seasons, winning 15 Emmy Awards, and making Ray Romano the highest-paid performer in television history. The show now runs in syndication, and Romano just stays home all day counting his money. Of course, when not doing that, he'll appear in the occasional film, such as *Ice Age*, or write the occasional book, like the children's tome he penned with his brothers, *Raymie, Dickie, and the Bean*. See what ridiculously revenue-enhancing endeavor he has up next at his website.

Roseanne (www.roseanneworld.com) redefined what it meant to be a female television star with her depiction of the average blue-collar housewife—in other words, herself—on her hit show *Roseanne*, which ran from 1988 to 1997. Since then, she has had several short-lived talk shows, made the occasional stand-up comedy appearance, immersed herself in Kabbalah, and cursed herself for launching the career of Tom Arnold.

Jeffrey Ross (www.jeffrey-ross.com) is a modern-day master of the put-down, best known for his work on the Comedy Central Roasts and his ever-changing joke about who he wouldn't use Bea Arthur's penis to have sex with. His frequent TV appearances include *The Tonight Show*, Letterman, *Jimmy Kimmel Live*, and *Real Time with Bill Maher*, and he has also written for many shows, including *The Academy Awards*, *The MTV Music Video Awards*, and *The Man Show*. He recently directed his first film, *Patriot Act*, a documentary recounting his time entertaining our troops in Iraq.

David Lee Roth (www.davidleeroth.com) was the original singer for the band Van Halen, leading them to international stardom on the power of the smash 1984 album, *1984*. Roth has released several solo albums since then, written an autobiography, traveled the world, worked as an EMT in the Bronx, and taken over Howard Stern's slot as syndicated morning man for CBS Radio. See what Diamond Dave is up to next at his website.

Dr. Laurie E. Rozakis (members.aol.com/Rozakile) has published dozens of books, including *Shaum's Quick Guide to Writing Research Papers*, *Study Skills for the Utterly Confused*, and *The Complete Idiot's Guide to Grammar and Style*. She is a full professor of English and humanities at State University of New York at Farmingdale and has taught English and research skills for more than 15 years.

Rita Rudner (www.ritafunny.com) shunned a glamorous career as a dancer on Broadway for a life of open mics in dank, moldy basements, and to her parents' glee, it paid off in spades. Rita has appeared on *The Tonight Show* with both Johnny and Jay, and on the shows of Letterman, Conan, Dennis Miller, Martin Short, Oprah, Regis, and many others. She has had three HBO specials and written three books. *Peter's Friends*, a film she wrote with her husband, starred Kenneth Branagh and Emma Thompson and won England's Peter Sellers Award for Best Comedy Film of the Year. These days, Rita can most often be found on the Vegas stage.

Mort Sahl (www.mortsahl.com) is one of comedy's oft-neglected influences. Coming to public attention in the time of Eisenhower, his straight-forward, almost square delivery belied his intellectually challenging material, ultimately influencing the likes of Lenny Bruce, Woody Allen, and George Carlin. He was one of the first to eschew blatant punch lines in favor of more textured descriptions and stories, and his ardent political radicalism ultimately led to a creative demise of sorts, as his fervent belief in Kennedy assassination conspiracies grew tiresome to many in the general public. While out of the limelight in recent decades, Sahl still performs sporadically, earning rave reviews when he does.

Elie Saltzman (www.comedysoapbox.com/comedianstemplate. cfm?comedianID=1683) was born and raised in Chicago and has performed improv throughout the city at venues such as Comedy Sportz, Improv Olympic, and others. Only 20 years old, Elie plans to move to New York to start a stand-up career, and, hopefully, develop a shorter URL.

Drake Sather was a writer for *Saturday Night Live*, *The Dennis Miller Show*, *The Larry Sanders Show*, and *The Academy Awards*, and co-wrote the movie *Zoolander* with Ben Stiller and John Hamburg. Drake died in 2004 at the age of 44.

Schizo Bill (www.clevelandyucks.com) was a finalist in the Carnival Cruise Comedy Challenge and many other contests.

Ben Schwartz (schwartzcomedy@gmail.com) is a freelance writer for *Saturday Night Live* as well as *The Late Show with David Letterman*. He can be seen performing improv and sketch comedy at the Upright Citizen's Brigade Theater. Check out his website: rejectedjokes.com.

Jerry Seinfeld is a stand-up comic who ... oh, for heaven's sake, do you really need a *bio?* He's *Seinfeld!* You know what you need to know. See him live if you can, rent the show DVDs (especially Season 4, which includes perhaps the funniest half-hour of television in sitcom history, "The Contest"), and if you really want to understand the stand-up comedy life, rent his documentary *Comedian*. (And when you're finished watching the movie, be sure to listen to the commentary track—it's like a whole new movie.)

Garry Shandling served as a regular guest host for Johnny Carson on *The Tonight Show*, carrying on the tradition of the neurotic Jewish comic with warmth and originality. He then created two ground-breaking television comedies—*It's Garry Shandling's Show*, on which Shandling broke the fourth wall and talked to the audience as his sitcom life unfolded around him, and *The Larry Sanders Show*, which skewered the late-night talk show world so perfectly that fantasy and reality often mixed, including Shandling's being offered David Letterman's show when Letterman went to CBS. Shandling has also hosted the Grammy and Emmy Awards and showed a surprisingly strong dramatic side opposite Sean Penn and Kevin Spacey in the film *Hurlyburly*.

Craig Sharf (www.craigsharf.com) is a stand-up comedian and writer whose jokes have appeared in several books and newspapers, and he has sold material to joke services and comedians including Joan Rivers and the Weinerville Show.

Debbie Shea (debbieshea.com) is a regular at The Comic Strip and has also performed at Luna Lounge, Gotham Comedy Club, Caroline's, Stand-Up NY, and Upright Citizen's Brigade. She was first runner-up in Comedy Central's Laugh Riots Competition 2000, a semi-finalist in 2001, and has also performed at The Aspen Comedy Festival, Boston Comedy Festival, and the Howl Festival. She recently made her television debut on Comedy Central's *Premium Blend.*

Sarah Silverman (www.jesusismagicthemovie.com) became a writer and featured performer on *Saturday Night Live* at the age of 22 and found it difficult squeezing her outré sensibility into the show's long-established structures. Frequent appearances on *Mr. Show with Bob and David* proved a better fit, and over the years, she has developed a fanatical following for her fearless approach to controversial topics. She has made numerous appearances on *Late Night with Conan O'Brien* and *Jimmy Kimmel Live;* co-starred in the FOX sitcom *Greg the Bunny;* been seen in films such as *Bulworth, There's Something About Mary, The Aristocrats,* and *School of Rock;* and in 2005 released the concert film *Sarah Silverman: Jesus Is Magic,* which earned the best reviews of any comedy concert film in eons.

Sinbad got his big break as a finalist on *Star Search* and was soon a cast member on *The Redd Foxx Show* and *A Different World.* He has served as host of *Showtime at the Apollo;* appeared in films such as *Houseguest* and *Jingle All the Way;* and had several HBO specials, including 1990's *Brain Damaged,* which was one of the highest-rated comedy specials in HBO's history at the time.

Steve Skrovan was a stand-up comic and actor who hosted a talk show on MTV, a hidden-camera show on Fox, and a show about dogs on The Family Channel. A switch to writing proved wise, as he wrote an episode of *Seinfeld* in 1990, and in 1996 joined *Everybody Loves Raymond* as a writer and producer, where he remained until the show's final days. He recently co-directed *An Unreasonable Man,* a documentary about Ralph Nader, which was nominated for the Grand Jury Prize at the Sundance Film Festival.

Kelly Smith (www.kellycomedy.com) performs for corporations, clubs, and churches, bringing her brand of high-energy fun and hilarious humor.

Jon Stewart found TV success just a few years into his stand-up career, hosting Comedy Central's *Short Attention Span Theater* only three years after moving to New York to give comedy a shot. He got his own show on MTV several years later, a syndicated show soon after that, and, after several close calls at a network gig, took over for Craig Kilborn on *The Daily Show* in 1999. While ably executing his task from the get-go, Stewart excelled in satirizing the political and media machines, and the show won the prestigious Peabody Award for television excellence in 2000. After 9/11, though, Stewart and the show took a new approach. Guests from the worlds of news and politics were now as frequent as those from entertainment, the satire developed a sharper bite, and Jon slowly became the voice of a disenfranchised and disgusted generation, often presenting insight into current events considerably deeper than that of the mainstream news outlets. He's led *The Daily Show* to numerous Emmys and another Peabody; turned the show into an *SNL*-type talent incubator that has so far ignited the careers of Steve Carell and Stephen Colbert; was widely credited for the demise of CNN's *Crossfire* after exposing its flaws during a tirade while on that show; and, with his staff, created *America, The Book*, one of the best-selling books of 2004.

Jeff Stilson has served as a writer and producer for *The Daily Show*, *The Chris Rock Show*, *The Osbournes*, and *Da Ali G Show*. He has also written for *Politically Incorrect*, *The Late Show with David Letterman*, and *The Academy Awards*. He has been nominated for 11 Emmy Awards and has won 2.

Ian Stone is a British comedian who's found great success in Britain and around the world, performing at the Edinburgh Fringe Festival three times and in countries as diverse as Dubai, Abu Dhabi, Kuwait, Bosnia, and South Africa. He was also the first British comedian to ever perform in Moscow.

Mike Storck (www.mikestorck.com) was voted the Funniest Comedian in Baltimore and winner of the Carnival Comedy Challenge, as well as the Washington D.C. Comedy Competition. Storck also performed at the 2002 Boston Comedy Festival and has been featured on *Entertainment Tonight* and The Lifetime Network.

Linda Sweig (www.lindasweig.com) is now focusing her talent and energy squarely on the world of stand-up comedy after many years of acting and clowning. Linda has appeared at numerous Chicago-area comedy venues, opened for several Midwest headliners, and is now working rooms in Indiana, Wisconsin, and Florida as well.

Wanda Sykes (www.wandasykes.com) was called one of the 25 Funniest People in America by *Entertainment Weekly* and has been spreading that funny across TV, books, and film. She has starred in Fox's *Wanda at Large* and Comedy Central's *Wanda Does It*, and has written and performed for *The Chris Rock Show*, where she won her first Emmy Award. She won her second Emmy for her work on *Inside the NFL*, and in 2001 also won the American Comedy Award for Outstanding Female Stand-Up. Other TV appearances include *Curb Your Enthusiasm*, *Crank Yankers*, and her own one-hour special on Comedy Central, and she's been seen on the big screen in *Pootie Tang*, *The Nutty Professor*, and *Down to Earth*. She also published her first book, the essay collection *Yeah, I Said It*, in 2004.

Nick Tarr (www.nicktarr.com) has been entertaining full-time since 1987, traveling the nation doing stand-up comedy and motivational speaking with a humor base, and performing at both mainstream and gay-themed shows.

Judy Tenuta (www.judytenuta.com) was the first comedian to win Best Female Stand-Up at the American Comedy Awards and has since had her own comedy specials on HBO, Showtime, and Lifetime. This self-proclaimed "Aphrodite of the Accordion" has been nominated for two Grammy Awards for her CDs *Attention Butt-Pirates and Lesbetarians* and *In Goddess We Trust*. She also wrote a book, *The Power of Judyism*, for HarperCollins.

Hunter S. Thompson was known for his gonzo style of journalism, pouring his heart and soul into his work while fueled by copious amounts of drugs and madness. His books *Fear and Loathing in Las Vegas* and *Fear and Loathing on the Campaign Trail 1972* were landmark events in writing. Thompson died in 2005, and as per requests made while he was alive, his ashes were later shot out of a cannon.

Rosie Tran (www.rosietran.com) has performed at clubs, colleges, comedy festivals, competitions, parties, private events, bars, and coffee shops all over the United States and Canada.

Triumph the Insult Comic Dog (www.triumphtheinsultcomicdog.com) has had a long and distinguished comedy career, including joke writing for Mr. Ed, and, according to his official bio, hanging with "a modern-day Rat Pack that included himself, Robert Goulet, Merv Griffin, and the Chuck Wagon dog." When not bringing laughter to the world and pooping on things, Triumph spends time with writer/performer Robert Smigel. Smigel has been writing for *Saturday Night Live* for the past 20 years, including the "Saturday's TV Funhouse" segments and Phil Hartman's infamous Sinatra Group sketch. He has also written for *Late Night with Conan O'Brien* since the show's inception in 1993.

Sheryl Underwood (www.sherylunderwoodandfriends.com) is the host of BET's *Comic View*. She has appeared on *Tough Crowd with Colin Quinn*, *Weekends at the D. L.*, and *Def Comedy Jam* and in the films *Bulworth* and *Beauty Shop*. She released her first CD, *Too Much Information*, in 2005.

Philip Van Munching is the author of several books, including *Boys Will Put You on a Pedestal (So They Can Look up Your Skirt): A Dad's Advice for Daughters*, *Beer Blast: The Inside Story of the Brewing Industry*, and *How to Remember Jokes*.

Gore Vidal has been one of America's foremost historical novelists, essayists, playwrights, and screenwriters since the mid-twentieth century. He won the prestigious National Book Award in 1993.

Greg Volk (gregmvolk@yahoo.com) is a freelance comedy writer and performer living in New York City.

John Vorhees (www.loserwhiteguy.com) started performing comedy in 1996 at the Funny Bone in Davenport, Iowa. Since then, he has been entertaining audiences in comedy clubs, casinos, colleges, and bars around the country. He has been on *Radio-Uncensored* and was a finalist at the Peoria, Illinois, Jukebox Comedy Club's "Funny Man" contest in both 2002 and 2003.

Rich Vos (richvos.com) was featured on the first season of NBC's *Last Comic Standing* and was the first white performer to appear on HBO's *Def Comedy Jam*. He was a regular panelist on *Tough Crowd with Colin Quinn;* had his own half-hour special on Comedy Central; and has also been seen on *The View*, *The Rosie O'Donnell Show*, and *Chappelle's Show*. In 1999, he was *Back Stage Magazine*'s New York Comic of the Year.

George Wallace (www.georgewallace.net) went from vice president of a transit advertising firm to writer for *The Redd Foxx Show* in a relatively short amount of time. From there, he became a top club headliner, racking up many appearances on *The Tonight Show*, *The Late Show with David Letterman*, and *Oprah*, and won the American Comedy Award for Best Stand-Up after four consecutive nominations. Now a regular in the hottest rooms in Las Vegas, he has appeared in films such as *A Rage in Harlem* and *Mr. Deeds*, and opposite Tom Hanks in the Coen Brothers' *The Ladykillers*.

John Westerhaus (www.myspace.com/johnwesterhaus or John. westerhaus@yahoo.com) is an aspiring comedian originally from Overland Park, Kansas. He currently resides in Topeka, Kansas, and attends Washburn University. His influences include the late Bill Hicks, Mitch Hedberg, and Rodney Dangerfield, as well as Dave Attell, Robert Schimmel, Lewis Black, Chris Rock, and Doug Stanhope.

Basil White (www.basilwhite.com) is a weird, scary man-child.

Ron "Tater Salad" White (www.tatersalad.com) is one fourth of the *Blue Collar Comedy Tour* Crew. In addition to their astounding success, White's *Drunk in Public* CD sold more than 450,000 copies—an insane number for a comedy album—and spent almost two years in the Top 10 of Billboard's Comedy Charts. The corresponding *Drunk in Public* tour made Pollstar's Top 50 tours of the year, and his first hour-long Comedy Central special, *They Call Me Tater Salad*, helped give the network the highest-rated Sunday in its history.

George Will is a widely syndicated columnist who won the Pulitzer prize for editorial journalism in 1977, served as the editor of the *National Review* for three years, and loves baseball.

Harland Williams's (www.harlandwilliams.com) distinctive comic drawl has landed him on *The Tonight Show*, Letterman, Conan, Jimmy Kimmel, and a gig hosting a season of Comedy Central's *Premium Blend*. But in addition to his talents as a comedian and actor—you've seen him in *Half-Baked*, *Wag the Dog*, *There's Something About Mary*, and *Dumb and Dumber*, and heard his voice in *Robots*—he's also an accomplished musician and artist. He occasionally tours in a duo called The Cousins with his real-life cousin, Barenaked Ladies' Kevin Hearn, and has written and illustrated several children's books. Pick up his CD, *Har-Larious*, and see what else this man can do at his website.

Robin Williams trained as an actor at Julliard, and, before becoming an Oscar-winning actor, was one of the most absurd comic voices of the late 1970s. His *A Night at the Met* and *Reality, What a Concept* albums reveal a unique comedic sensibility at the height of its invention and discipline. Hearing his early work, it's clear that the step to *Good Morning, Vietnam* and movie stardom was virtually assured.

Dennis Wolfberg's punchy, googly eyed delivery made him one of the more playful comics of the 1980s, with a truly unique presentation that was hard not to laugh along with. The 1990 winner of the American Comedy Award for Best Stand-Up, he conquered TV with appearances on *The Tonight Show*, Letterman, and *Comic Strip Live* and had a recurring role on NBC's *Quantum Leap*. Dennis died after a two-year battle with cancer in 1994, working up until his death.

Tony Woods has been seen on *Def Comedy Jam, Showtime at the Apollo*, BET's *Comic View*, A&E's *Caroline's Comedy Hour,* and P. Diddy's *Bad Boys of Comedy*.

Steven Wright (www.stevenwright.com) turned a monotone mumble into one of the most easily identifiable and desirable sounds in comedy. His flat-lined vocal cadence gave his surreal one-liners a Zen power and highlighted the uniqueness of his writerly gift. An in-demand comic headliner who's been a regular on the late-night circuit for two decades, Wright has also made several short films—including *The Appointments of Dennis Jennings*, which won him an Oscar—and appeared in films such as *Reservoir Dogs, So I Married an Axe Murderer,* and *Natural Born Killers*.

Dwight York (DwightYork.com), a 15-year comedy-writing veteran and the author of *The Vile File: Jokes Too Sick for the Stage*, performs at many of the nation's top comedy clubs. He can be heard regularly on the nationally syndicated *Bob and Tom Show* and is featured on their CD *You Guys Rock. The St. Paul Pioneer Press* called Dwight's material "the best one-liners this side of Stephen Wright."

Henny Youngman was the original master of the one-liner, a man who felled the audience in brief sets that contained enough rapid-fire jokes to rob the crowd of breath. While he appeared in several films and was a regular guest on TV shows such as *The Ed Sullivan Show* and *Rowan and Martin's Laugh-In*, live performance was his love and his gift. Henny Youngman passed away in 1998.

Index

G

I

J

X-Y-Z